Whitson Pub.
Troy N.Y

1/28/74
standing order

#11.24

Abortion Bibliography
For 1972

Abortion Bibliography

For 1972

compiled by

Mary K. Floyd

The Whitston Publishing Company
Troy, New York
1973

Library of Congress Catalog Card Number 72-78877

ISBN 0-87875-044-4

Printed in the United States of America

PREFACE

Abortion Bibliography for 1972 is the third annual list of books and articles surrounding the subject of abortion in the preceeding year. It appears serially each fall as a contribution toward documenting in one place as comprehensively as possible the literature of one of our central social issues. It is an attempt at a comprehensive world bibliography.

Searches in compiling this material have covered the following sources: *Art Index; Applied Science and Technology Index; Bibliographic Index; Biological Abstracts; Books in Print; British Books in Print; British Humanities Index; Business Periodicals Index; Canadian Periodical Index; Cumulative Book Index; Current Index to Journals in Education; Current Literature of Venereal Disease; Education Index; Hospital Literature Index; Index to Catholic Periodicals and Literature; Index to Legal Periodicals; Index Medicus; Index to Nursing Literature; Index to Periodical Articles Related to Law; Index to Religious Periodical Literature; International Nursing Index; Law Review Digest; Library of Congress Catalog: Books: Subjects; Philosophers Index; Public Affairs Information Service; Readers Guide to Periodical Literature; Social Sciences and Humanities Index.*

The bibliography is divided into two sections: a title section in alphabetical order; and a subject section. Thus, if the researcher does not wish to observe the subject heads of the compiler, he can use the title section exclusively. The 124 subject heads have been allowed to issue from the nature of the material indexed rather than being imposed from Library of Congress subject heads or other standard lists.

Countries are listed alphabetically under subjects: "Abortion: Africa," etc.; drugs are listed under the specific drug involved; and "Students," and "Youth" are given separate subject heads in this bibliography.

LIST OF ABBREVIATIONS

ABBREVIATIONS	TITLE
AORN J	AORN Journal (Engelwood, Colorado)
Acta Endocrinol	Acta Endocrinologica (Copenhagen)
Acta Obstet Ginecol Hisp Lusit	Acta Obstetrica y Ginecologica Hispano-Lusitana (Barcelona)
Acta Obstet Gynecol Scand	Acta Obstetricia et Gynecologica Scandinavica (Lund)
Acta Physiol Scand	Acta Physiologica Scandinavica (Stockholm)
Acta Urol Belg	Acta Urologica Belgica (Brussels)
Actual Pharmacol	Actualites Pharmacologiques (Paris)
Adv Age	Advertising Age (Chicago)
Akush Ginekol	Akusherstvo i Ginekologiya (Moscow)
Akush Ginekol	Akusherstvo i Ginekologia (Sofiia)
Albany L Rev	Albany Law Review (Albany)
Am Biol Teach	American Biology Teacher (Washington)
Am Economist	American Economist (New York)
Am J Hum Genet	American Journal of Human Genetics (Chicago)
Am J Nurs or Amer J Nursing	American Journal of Nursing (New York)
Am J Obstet Gynecol	American Journal of Obstetrics and Gynecology (St. Louis)
Am J Orthopsychiatry	American Journal of Orthopsychiatry (New York)
Am J Psychiatry	American Journal of Psychiatry (Hanover, New Hampshire)
Am J Public Health	American Journal of Public Health and the Nation's Health (New York)
Am J Vet Res	American Journal of Veterinary Research (Chicago)
Amer Med News	American Medical Association News (Chicago)
America	America (San Francisco)
Anat Anz	Anatomischer Anzeiger (Jena, E. Germany)
Anat Rec	Anatomical Record (Philadelphia)
Anesth Analg	Anesthesia and Analgesia (Cleveland)

Anesthesiology	Anesthesiology (Philadelphia)
Ann Chir Gynaecol Fenn	Annales Chirurgiae et Gynaecologiae Fenniae (Helsinki)
Ann Clin Res	Annals of Clinical Research (Helsinki)
Ann Genet	Annales de Genetique (Paris)
Ann Inst Pasteur	Annales de l'Institut Pasteur (Paris)
Antibiotiki	Antibiotiki (Moscow)
Arch Dermatol	Archives of Dermatology (Rochester, Minnesota)
Arch Gen Psychiatry	Archives of General Psychiatry (Chicago)
Arch Kriminol	Archiv fuer Kriminologie (Luebeck, W. Germany)
Arch Ostet Ginecol	Archivio di Ostetricia e Ginecologia (Naples)
Arch Toxikol	Archiv fur Toxikologie; Fuehner-Wielands Sammlung von Vergiftungs-faellen (Berlin)
Ariz Med	Arizona Medicine (Phoenix)
Arkh Patol	Arkhiv Patologii (Moscow)
Aust NZ J Obstet Gynaecol	Australian and New Zealand Journal of Obstetrics and Gynaecology (Melbourne)
Aust Vet J	Australian Veterinary Journal (Sydney)
Australas Nurses J	Australian Nurses' Journal (Sydney)
Beitr Gerichtl Med	Geitraege zur Gerichtlichen Medizin (Vienna)
Berl Munch Tieraerztl Wochenschr	Berliner und Muenchener Tieraerztliche Wochenschrift/Berlin and Munich Veterinarian's Weekly (Berlin)
Bibl Anat	Bibliotheca Anatomica (Basel)
Birth Defects	Birth Defects (New York)
Bol of Sanit Panam	Boletin de la Oficina Sanitaria Pan-americana (Washington)
Bord Med	Bordeaux Medical (Bordeaux)
Br J Anaesth	British Journal of Anaesthesia (Cheshire)
Br J Clin Pract	British Journal of Clinical Practice (Sussex)
Br J Psychiatry	British Journal of Psychiatry (London)
Br Med J	British Medical Journal (London)
Bull Am Coll Nurse Midwives	Bulletin of the American College of Nurse-Midwives (Thorofare, New Jersey)

Bull Fed Soc Gynecol Obstet Lang Fr	Bulletin de la Federation des Societes de Gynecologie et d'Obstetrique de Langue Francaise (Paris)
Bull Soc Int Chir	Bulletin de la Societe Internationale de Chirurgie (Bruxelles)
Bull Soc Pathol Exot	Bulletin de la Societe de Pathologie Exotique et de ses Filiales (Paris)
Bulletin of the Atomic Scientists	Bulletin of the Atomic Scientists (Chicago)
Bus Week	Business Week (New York)
C Dgst	Catholic Digest (St. Paul)
C Mind	Catholic Mind (New York)
CLW	Catholic Library World (Haverford, Pennsylvania)
C R Soc Biol	Comptes Rendus des Seances de la Societe de Biologie et de ses Foliales (Paris)
Calif Med	California Medicine (San Francisco)
Can Doctor	Canadian Doctor (Gardenvale, Quebec)
Can Hosp	Canadian Hospital (Toronto)
Can J Comp Med	Canadian Journal of Comparative Medicine (Ontario)
Can J Public Health	Canadian Journal of Public Health (Toronto)
Can Med Assoc J	Canadian Medical Association Journal (Toronto)
Can Month	Canada Month (Montreal)
Can Nurse	Canadian Nurse (Ottawa)
Can Psychiatr Assoc J	Canadian Psychiatric Association Journal (Ottawa)
Can Wel	Canadian Welfare (Ottawa)
Cas Lek Cesk	Casopis Lekaru Ceskych (Prague)
Case W Res L Rev	Case Western Reserve Law Review (Cleveland)
Cath Hosp	Catholic Hospital (Ottawa)
Cathol Nurse	Catholic Nurse (Bristol, England)
Cesk Gynekol	Ceskoslovenska Gynekologie (Prague)
Chi-Kent L Rev	Chicago-Kent Law Review (Chicago)
Christian Century	Christian Century (Chicago)
Chr Today	Christianity Today (Washington)
Christ Nurse	Christian Nurse (Nagpur, India)
Christian Scholar's	Christian Scholar's Review (Wenham,

Review	Massachusetts)
Civilta Cattolica	Civilta Cattolica (Rome)
Clin Obstet Gynecol	Clinical Obstetrics and Gynecology (New York)
Commonweal	Commonweal (New York)
Conn Med	Connecticut Medicine (New Haven)
Consultant	Consultant (Philadelphia)
Consumer Rep	Consumer Reports (Mount Vernon, New York)
Cornell Vet	Cornell Veterinarian (Ithaca, New York)
Curr Psychiatr Ther	Current Psychiatric Therapies (New York)
DCB J	District of Columbia Bar Journal (Washington)
Del Med J	Delaware Medical Journal (Wilmington)
Demography	Demography (Washington)
Dermatol Monatsschr	Dermatologische Monatsschrift (Leipzig, E. Germany)
Diakonia	Diakonia (Austria)
Dist Nurs	District Nurse (London)
Doc Cath	Documentation Catholique (Paris)
Dtsch Gesundheitsw	Deutsche Gesundheitswesen (Berlin)
Dtsch Krankenpflegez	Deutsche Krankenflege-Zeitschrift (Stuttgart)
Dtsch Med Wochenschr	Deutsch Medizinische Wochenschrift (Stuttgart)
Duodecim	Duodecim (Helsinki)
Economist	Economist (London)
Ed & Pub	Editor and Publisher-the Fourth Estate (New York)
Emergency Med	Emergency Medicine (New York)
Endocrinology	Endocrinology (Philadelphia)
Entschluss	Entschluss (Austria)
Esprit et vie	Esprit et vie (France)
Ethics	Ethics (Chicago)
European Demographic Info Bul	European Demographic Information Bulletin (The Hague, Netherlands)
Experientia	Experientia (Basel)
Fam Dgst	Family Digest (Huntington, Indiana)
Fam Plann Perspect	Family Planning Perspectives (New York)
Fertil Steril	Fertility and Sterility (New York)
Fordham L Rev	Fordham Law Review (New York)

Freeman	Freeman (Irvington-on-Hudson, New York)
Gallup Opinion Index	Gallup Opinion Index (Princeton, New Jersey)
Geburtshilfe Frauenheilkd	Geburtshilfe und Frauenheilkunde (Stuttgart)
Gig Sanit	Gigiyena i Sanitariya (Moscow)
Gig Tr Prof Zabol	Gigiyena Truda i Professional'nyye Zabolevaniya (Moscow)
Ginecol Obstet Mex	Ginecologia y Obstetricia de Mexico (Mexico City)
Ginekol Pol	Ginekologia Polaska (Warsaw)
Good H	Good Housekeeping (New York)
Group Adv Psychiatry	Group for the Advancement of Psychiatry (Topeka, Kansas)
Guardian	Guardian (New York)
Gynecol Prat	Gynecologie Pratique (Paris)
Harefuah	Harefuah (Tel Aviv)
Harv Civil Right L Rev	Harvard Civil Rights-Civil Liberties Law Review (Cambridge)
Hawaii Med J	Hawaii Medical Journal (Honolulu)
Health Bull	Health Bulletin (Melbourne)
Health Serv Rep	Health Service Reports (Rockville, Maryland)
Health Visit	Health Visitor (London)
Herder Korrespondenz	Herder-Korrespondenz (Briesgaw, W. Germany)
Hosp Admin Can	Hospital Administration in Canada (Ontario)
Hosp Pract	Hospital Practice (New York)
Hosp Progress	Hospital Progress (St. Louis)
Hosp Top	Hospital Topics (Chicago)
Hosp World	Hospital World (London)
Hospitals	Hospitals (Chicago)
Hum Hered	Human Heredity (Basel)
Humangenetik	Humangenetik (Berlin)
Ind Legal F	Indiana Legal Forum (Indianapolis)
Infirm Can	Infirmiere Canadienne (Ottawa)
Infirmiere	Infirmiere (Brussels)
Int Hosp Rev	International Hospital Review (The Hague, Netherlands)
Int Philos Q	International Philosophical Quarterly/ IPQ (Bronx, New York)

Int Surg	International Surgery Bulletin (Chicago)
Isr J Med Sci	Israel Journal of Medical Sciences (Jerusalem)
JAMA	Journal of the American Medical Association (Chicago)
JOGN Nurs	JOGN Nursing
J R Coll Gen Pract	Journal of the Royal College of General Practitioners (Darmouth, England)
J Am Acad Child Psychiatry	Journal of the American Academy of Child Psychiatry (New York)
J Am Med Wom Assoc	Journal of the American Medical Women's Association (New York)
J Am Osteopath Assoc	Journal of the American Osteopathic Association (Chicago)
J Am Vet Med Assoc	Journal of the American Veterinary Medical Association (Chicago)
J Amer Med Ass	Journal of the American Medical Association (Chicago)
J Biosoc Sci	Journal of Biosocial Science (London)
J Clin Endocrinol Metab	Journal of Clinical Endocrinology and Metabolism (Philadelphia)
J Florida Med Ass	Journal of the Florida Medical Association (Jacksonville)
J Gynecol Obstet Biol Reprod	Journal de Gynecologie, Obstetrique et Biologie de la Reproduction (Paris)
J Hered	Journal of Heredity (Baltimore, Maryland)
J Indian Med Assoc	Journal of the Indian Medical Association (Calcutta)
J Jap Obstet Gynecol Soc	Journal of the Japanese Obstetrical and Gynecological Society (Tokyo) In Japanese: Nippon Sanka-Fujinka Gakkai Zasshi
J Kans Med Soc	Journal of the Kansas Medical Society (Topeka)
J Ky Med Assoc	Journal of the Kentucky Medical Association (Louisville)
J Med Genet	Journal of Medical Genetics (London)
J Med Liban	Journal Medical Libanais: Lebanese Medical Journal (Beirut)
J Med Lyon	Journal de Medecine de Lyon (Lyon)

J Miss State Med Ass	Journal of the Mississippi State Medical Association (Jackson)
J Natl Med Assoc	Journal of the National Medical Association (New York)
J Obstet Gynaecol Br Commonw	Journal of Obstetrics and Gynaecology of the British Commonwealth (London)
J Okla State Med Ass	Journal of the Oklahoma State Medical Association (Oklahoma City)
J Reprod Fertil	Journal of Reproduction and Fertility (Oxford)
J Reprod Med	Journal of Reproductive Medicine (Chicago)
J Sci Med Lille	Journal des Sciences Medicales de Lille (Lille)
J Tokyo Med Coll	Journal of the Tokyo Medical College (Tokyo)
J Urol Nephrol	Journal of Urology (Baltimore)
Jap J Hum Genet	Japanese Journal of Human Genetics (Tokyo)
Jap J Public Health Nurse	Japanese Journal of Public Health Nurse (Tokyo)
Journal of Religion and Health	Journal of Religion and Health (New York)
Katilolehti	Katilolehti (Helsinki)
Krankenpflege	Krankenpflege (Berlin)
L & Soc Order	Law and the Social Order; Arizona State Law Journal. (Tempe)
Lab Anim Sci	Laboratory Animal Science (Argonne, Illinois)
Lakartidningen	Lakartidningen (Stockholm)
Lancet	Lancet (London)
Laval Med	Laval Medical (Quebec)
Life	Life (New York)
Liguorian	Liguorian (Liguori, Missouri)
Linacre Q	Linacre Quarterly (Milwaukee)
Loyola U L J	Loyola University of Chicago Law Journal (Chicago)
MD	MD Medical News Magazine (New York)
M U L R	Melbourne University Law Review (Melbourne)
Md State Med J	Maryland State Medical Journal (Baltimore)
Marq L Rev	Marquette Law Review (Milwaukee)

Marriage	Marriage (Meinrad, Indiana)
Matern Infanc	Maternidade e Infancia (Sao Paulo)
Med Ann Dist Columbia	Medical Annals of the District of Columbia (Washington)
Med Arh	Medicinski Arhiv (Sarajevo)
Med Insight	Medical Insight (New York)
Med J Aust	Medical Journal of Australia (Sydney)
Med J Malaya	Medical Journal of Malaya (Singapore)
Med Klin	Medizinische Klinik (Munich)
Med Leg Domm Corpor	Medecine Legale et Dommage Corporel (Paris)
Med Monatsschr	Medizinische Monatsschrift (Stuttgart)
Med Pregl	Medicinski Pregled (Novi Sad)
Med Sci Law	Medicine, Science and the Law (London)
Med Trial Tech Q	Medical Trial Technique Quarterly (Chicago)
Med Welt	Mediznische Welt (Stuttgart)
Med World News	Medical World News (New York)
Mich Med	Michigan Medicine (East Lansing)
Midwife Health Visit	Midwife and Health Visitor (London)
Midwives Chron	Midwives Chronicle (London)
Minerva Ginecol	Minerva Ginecologia (Turin)
Minerva Med	Minerva Medica (Turin)
Minn Med	Minnesota Medicine (St. Paul)
Miss L J	Mississippi Law Journal (University, Mississippi)
Mod Hosp	Modern Hospital (Chicago)
Monatsh Vet Med	Monatshefte fuer Veterinaermedizin (Jena)
Mt Sinai J Med NY	Mount Sinai Hospital. Journal (New York)
Munca Sanit	Munca Sanitara (Bucharest)
Munch Med Wochenschr	Muenchener Medizinische Wochenschrift (Munich)
N Engl J Med	New England Journal of Medicine (Boston)
NC Med J	North Carolina Medical Journal (Raleigh)
NY Med	New York Medicine (New York)
NY State J Med	New York State Journal of Medicine (New York)
NY Times Mag	New York Times Magazine (New York)
NZ Med J	New Zealand Medical Journal (Wellington)

Nat Cath Rep	National Catholic Reporter (Kansas City)
Nat R	National Review (New York)
Nation	Nation (New York)
Nations Health	Nation's Health (Chicago)
Natl Inst Anim Health Q	National Institute of Animal Health Quarterly (Tokyo)
Nature	Nature (London)
Ned Tijdschr Geneeskd	Nederlands Tijdschrift voor Geneeskunde (Amsterdam)
Nervenarzt	Nervenarzt (Berlin)
New Blckfrs	New Blackfriars (London)
New England L Rev	New England Law Review (Concord, New Hampshire)
New Humanist	New Humanist (Chicago)
New Statesm	New Statesman (London)
New York Law Journal	New York Law Journal (Middletown, Connecticut)
Newsletter (Amer Soc Attorneys)	Newsletter (Society of Hospital Attorneys, Chicago)
Newsweek	Newsweek (New York)
Nouv Presse Med	Nouvelle Presse Medicale (Paris)
Nurs J India	Nursing Journal of India (New Delhi)
Nurs Res	Nursing Research (New York)
Nurs Times	Nursing Times (London)
Nursing Mirror	Nursing Mirror and Midwives' Journal (London)
OR	OR Nursing (Chicago)
OSV	Our Sunday Visitor
Observer	Observer (London)
Obstet Gynecol	Obstetrics and Gynecology (New York)
Orv Hetil	Orvosi Hetilap (Budapest)
Osterr Schwesternztg	Oesterreichische Schwesternztg (Vienna)
PTA Mag	PTA Magazine (National Congress of Parents and Teachers) (Chicago)
Pa Med	Pennsylvania Medicine (Lemoyne)
Paraplegia	Paraplegia (London)
Past Psych	Pastoral Psychology (Manhasset, New York)
Pediatr Akush Ginekol	Pediatriia Akusherstov i Ginekologiia (Kiev)
Pediatr Clin North Am	Pediatric Clinics of North America (Philadelphia)

Pediatrics	Pediatrics (Springfield, Illinois)
Penn BA Q	Pennsylvania Bar Association Quarterly (Philadelphia)
Pol Tyg Lek	Polski Tygodnik Lekarski (Warsaw)
Population Studies	Population Studies (London)
Postgrad Med	Postgraduate Medicine (Minneapolis)
Practitioner	Practitioner (London)
Presenza Pastorale	Presenza Pastorale (Rome)
Proc R Soc Med	Proceedings of the Royal Society of Medicine (London)
Progressive	Progressive (Madison, Wisconsin)
Psychiat News	Psychiatric News (Washington)
Public Welfare	Public Welfare (Chicago)
RANF Rev	RANF Review (Queensland)
RN	RN; National Magazine for Nurses (Oradell, New Jersey)
R Radical Pol Econ	Review of Radicol Political Economics (Ann Arbor)
R Soc Health J	Royal Society of Health Journal (London)
Radiol Diagn	Radiologia Diagnostica (Berlin)
Rass Int Clin Ter	Rassenga Internazionale di Clinica e Terapia (Naples)
Razon y fe	Razon y fe (Madrid)
Ref	Refermation (Utica, New York)
Regno	Regno (Bologna)
Relations	Relations (Montreal)
Res Vet Sci	Research in Veterinary Science (Oxford)
Rev Chil Obstet Ginecol	Revista Chilena de Obstetricia y Ginecologia (Santiago)
Rev Fr Gynecol Obstet	Revue Francaise de Gynecologie et d'Obstetrique (Paris)
Rev Inst Med Trop Sao Paulo	Revista do Instituto de Medicina Tropical de Sao Paulo (Sao Paulo)
Rev Med Suisse Romande	Revue Medicale de la Suisse Romande (Lausanne)
Rivista del clero italiano	Rivista del clero italiano (Milan)
Rocky Mt Med J	Rocky Mountain Medical Journal (Denver)
Rutgers L Rev	Rutgers Law Review (Newark, New Jersey)
S Afr Med J	South African Medical Journal (Capetown)

S Tomas Nurs J	Santo Tomas Nursing Journal
SC L Rev	South Carolina Law Review (Columbia)
Sanfujinka Jissai	Sanfujinka no Jissai (Tokyo)
Schweiz Arch Tierheilkd	Schweizer Archiv fuer Tierheilkunde (Zurich)
Sci Am	Scientific American (New York)
Sci News	Science News (Washington)
Science	Science (Washington)
Scott Med J	Scottish Medical Journal (Glasgow)
Seventeen	Seventeen (New York)
Sisters	Sisters Today (Collegeville, Minnesota)
Soc Act	Social Action (New Delhi)
Soc Biol	Social Biology (Chicago)
Soc Casework	Social Casework (New York)
Soc Just	Social Justice Review (St. Louis)
Soc Work	Social Worker (Ontario)
Spectator	Spectator (London)
Srp Arh Celok Lek	Srpski Arhiv za Celokupno Lekarstvo (Beograd)
St Anth	St. Anthony Messenger (Cincinnati)
St Louis U L J	St. Louis University Law Journal (St. Louis University)
Stimm Zeit	Stimmen der Zeit (Freiburg)
Studies in Family Planning	Studies in Family Planning (New York)
Sud Med Ekspert	Sudebnomedicinckaya Expertiza (Moscow)
Suffolk U L Rev	Suffolk University of Law Review (Boston)
Sunday Times	Sunday Times (Philadelphia)
Supervisor Nurse	Supervisor Nurse (Chicago)
Tablet	Tablet (London)
Tenn Med Ass	Tennessee Medical Association. Journal (Nashville)
Teratology	Teratoloty; Journal of Abnormal Development (Philadelphia)
Tex Med	Texas Medicine (Austin)
Th St	Theological Studies
Theologie und Glaube	Theologie und Glaube (Paderborn)
Ther GWW	Therapie der Gegenwart (Berlin)
Tidskr Sver Sjukskot	Tidskrift for Sveriges Sjukskoterskor (Stockholm)
Tijdschr Ziekenverpl	Tijdschrift voor Ziekenverpleging (Leidschendam)

Time	Time (Chicago)
Today's Health	Today's Health (Chicago)
Trans-Action	Trans-Action - Social Science and Modern Society (Brunswick, New Jersey)
Triumph	Triumph (Washington)
Tunis Med	Tunisie Medicale (Tunis)
Turk Hij Tecr Biyol Derg	Turk Hijiyen ve Tecrubi Biyoloji Dergisi (Ankara)
UCLA-Alaska L Rev	UCLA-Alaska law Review (Los Angeles)
U Chi L Rev	University of Chicago Law Review (Chicago)
U Cin L Rev	University of Cincinnati Law Review (Cincinnati)
U Fla L Rev	University of Florida Law Review (Gainesville)
U Ill L F	University of Illinois Law Forum (Champaign)
US Cath	U.S. Catholic and Jubilee (Chiacgo)
US Med	U.S. Medicine (Washington)
US News or US News World Rep	U.S. News and World Report (Washington)
Ugeskr Laeger	Ugeskrift for Laeger (Copenhagen)
Va Med Mon	Virginia Medical Monthly (Richmond)
Valparaiso Univ Law R	Valparaiso University Law Review (Valparaiso, Indiana)
Vestn Akad Med Nauk SSSR	Vestnik Akademii Nauk SSSR (Moscow)
Vet Med	Veterinarni Medicina (Prague)
Vet Med Small Anim Clin	Veterinary Medicine/Small Animal Clinician (Bonner Springs, Kansas)
Vet Rec	Veterinary Record (London)
Veterinariia	Veterinariia (Moscow)
Vie Med Can Fr	Vie Medicale au Canada Francais (Quebec)
Virology	Virology (New York)
Vopr Okhr Materin Det	Voprosy Okhrany Materinstva i Detstva (Moscow)
Vopr Virusol	Voprosy Virusologii (Moscow)
WHO Chron	WHO Chronical (Geneva)
Wake Forest L Rev	Wake Forest Intramural Law Review (Winston-Salem, North Carolina)

Wall St J	Wall Street Journal (New York)
Washington Mo	Washington Monthly (Washington)
Wiad Lek	Wiadomosci Lekarskie (Warsaw)
Wiad Parazytol	Wiadomosci Parazytologiczne (Warsaw)
Wien Med Wochenschr	Wiener Medizinische Wochenschrift (Vienna)
Wis Med J	Wisconsin Medical Journal (Madison)
Woman Physician	Woman Physician (New York)
World Med J	World Medical Instrumentation (Oxford)
Z Aerztl Fortbild	Zeitschrift fur Aerztliche Fortbildung (Jena)
Z Allgemeinmed	Zeitschrift fur Allgemeinmedizin; der Landarzt (Stuttgart)
Z Ev Ethik	Zeitschrift fur Evangelische Ethik (Guetersloh, W. Germany)
Z Geburtshilfe Perinatol	Zeitschrift fur Geburtshilfe und Perinatologie (Stuttgart)
Z Krankenpfl	Zeitschrift fuer Krankenpflege/Revue Suisse des Infirmieres (Solothurn, Switzerland)
Z Rechtsmed	Zeitschrift fuer Rechtsmedizin (Berlin)
Z Versuchstierkd	Zeitschrift fuer Versuchstierkunde (Jena)
Zentralbl Gynaekol	Zentralblatt fuer Gynaekologie (Leipzig)
Zentralbl Veterinaermed	Zentralblatt fuer Veterinaermedizinl. Journal of Veterinary Medicine (Berlin)

SUBJECT HEADINGS USED IN THIS BIBLIOGRAPHY

Abnormalties
Abortion (General)
Abortion Act
Abortion: Bulgaria
Abortion: Canada
Abortion: China
Abortion: Europe
Abortion: Finland
Abortion: France
Abortion: Germany
Abortion: Great Britain
Abortion: Japan
Abortion: Latin America
Abortion: Netherlands
Abortion: New Zealand
Abortion: Norway
Abortion: Romania
Abortion: Spain
Abortion: Sweden
Abortion: USSR
Abortion: United States
Alylestenol
Aminoglutethimide Phosphate
Anesthesia
Behavior
Bibliography
Birth Control
Bishydroxycoumarin
Blood
Blood Types and Abortion
Cervical Incompetence and Insufficiency
Cesarean Section
Choriogonin
Clinical Aspects
Complications
Contraception
Cyproheptadine
Demography
Diagnosis
Dilatol
Drug Therapy
Duvadilan
EDTA
Education and Abortion
Epilespy
Family Planning
Fees and Public Assistance
Fetus
Furosemide
Genetics
Gynaecology
Habitual Abortion
Hemorrhage
History
Hormones
Hospitals and Abortion
Immunity and Abortion
Induced Abortion
Infection
Isoxsuprine Hydrochloride
IUCD
Ketamine
Law Enforcement
Laws and Legislation
Legal Counselling and Abortion
Male Attitudes
Marriage Counselling and Abortion
Menstruation
Microbiology
Miscarriages
Morbidity
Mortality
Multiple Sclerosis
Myasthenia
NAACOG
NACPA
Nurses and Abortion
Obstetrics
Outpatient Abortion

TABLE OF CONTENTS

BOOKS

ABORT OG MENNESKEVERD. Oslo: St. Olav, 1970.

ABORTUS, (g)een lijdensweg. Uit bestaand materiaal samengesteld door een VCSB-werkgroep. Rotterdam: Universitaire Pers Rotterdam, 1971.

ABTREIBUNG IN DER DISKUSSION; medizinische, psychologische, juristische, ethische und politische Aspekte der Reform des Art. 218. Munster: Verlag Regensberg, 1972.

AVORTEMENT ET CONTRACEPTION. Brussels: Edit. de l'Universite de Bruxelles, 1972.

AVORTEMENT ET RESPECT DE LA VIE HUMAINE: Colloque du Centre catholique des medecins francais. Paris: Seuil, 1972.

Baumann, Jurgen. DAS ABTREIBUNGSVERBOT DES ART. 218 StGB; eine Vorschrift, die mehr schadet als nutzt. Neuwied: Luchterhand, 1971.

BIRTH CONTROL AND ABORTION. New York: MSS Information Corp., 1972.

Bouma, H., M. G. van der Graaf and A. N. Hendriks. GEZINSVORMING. Rotterdam: Gereformeerd Sociaal en Economisch Verband, 1970.

California conference on abortion, 1969. ABORTION AND THE UNWANTED CHILD. New York: Springer Publishing Company, 1969.

California. Legislature. Assembly. Interim Committee on Judiciary. TRANSCRIPT OF HEARING ON LEGAL ASPECTS OF STERILIZATION, abortion and family planning. October 22, 1970,

San Francisco. Sacramento: The Committee, 1970.

Commissie Zedelijkheidswetgeving. ABORTUS PROVOCATUS; rapport. Den Haag: Commissie Zedelijkheidswetgeving, 1971.

Cooper, Boyd. SEX WITHOUT TEARS. Los Angeles: Charles Publishing Corp., 1972.

DAN NYE ABORTLOV. Ved Tage Mortensen. Kobenhavn: Idag, 1970.

Dedek, John F. HUMAN LIFE: some moral issues. New York: Sheed & Ward, 1972.

Draijer, J. W., and A. Geelhoed. ABORTUS PROVOCATUS. Groningen: De Vuurbaak, 1972.

Ebon, Martin. EVERY WOMAN'S GUIDE TO ABORTION. New York: Universe Books, 1971.

EN QUETE SUR LA CONCEPTION, La Naissance, et L'Avortement. New York: International Scholastic Book Services, 1972.

Enden, Hugo van den. ABORTUS PRO/CONTRA. Baarn: Het Wereldvenster, 1971.

Ferris. ABORTION IN BRITAIN TODAY: "The Nameless." Harmondsworth: Penguin, 1972.

Floyd, M. K., compiler. ABORTION BIBLIOGRAPHY FOR 1970. Troy, New York: Whitston Publishing Company, 1972.

Foletti, Lara. PER IL DIRITTO DI ABORTO. Con un'appendice sulle tecniche contraccettive. Roma: La nuova sinistra, 1972.

Gall, Norman. BIRTHS, ABORTIONS, AND THE PROGRESS OF CHILE. Hanover, New Hampshire: American Universities Field Staff, 1972.

Gardner, R. F. R. ABORTION: the personal dilemma. Grand Rapids: Eerdmans, 1972.

Girardet-Sbaffi, Maria, compiler. L'ABORTO NEL MONDO. Milano: A. Mondadori, 1970.

Gobry, Ivan et Hubert Saget. UN CRIME: l'avortement. Paris: Nouvelles editions latines, 1972.

Granfield, D. THE ABORTION DECISION. New York: Image Books, 1971.

Granger, Bruce and Sharon Robins. HAVING A WONDERFUL ABORTION. New York: Exposition Press, 1971.

Grisez, G. G. ABORTION. New York: Corpus, 1970.

Grundel, Johannes. ABTREIBUNG, PRO UND CONTRA. Wurzburg: Echter, 1971.

Guy, Francois and Michele Guy. L'AVORTEMENT; documents pour une information et une reflexion sur un probleme d'actualite. Paris: Les Editions du Cerf, 1971.

Harris, Maureen, editor. EARLY DIAGNOSIS OF HUMAN GENETIC DEFECTS; scientific and ethical considerations. Washington: GPO, 1971.

Hickey, Owen. LAW AND LAXITY. London: Times Newspapers, 1970.

Hindell, Keith and Madeleine Simms. ABORTION LAW REFORMED (GREAT BRITAIN); with a forward by David Steel. London: Peter Owen, 1971.

Horden, Anthony. LEGAL ABORTION: the English experience. With a forward by Michael Brundenell. Oxford, New York: Pergamon Press, 1971.

Huntemann, Georg Hermann. ART. 218 i. e. PARAGRAPH ZWEIHUNDERTACHTZEHN. Um Leben oder Tod d. Ungeborenen. Kassel-Harleshausen: Weisses Kreuz, 1971.

Jochimsen, Lukrezia. ART. 218 PARAGRAPH ZWEIHUNDERTACHTZEHN: Dokumentation e. 100jahrigen Elends. Hamburg: Konkret-Buchverlag, 1971.

Karkal, Malini. A BIBLIOGRAPHY OF ABORTION STUDIES IN INDIA. Bombay: International Institute for Population Studies, 1970.

Kentucky. House. Special judiciary subcommittee. LEGISLATIVE HEARING: abortion; hearings on Section 276 of House bill 197, Regular session 1972, February 14, 15, 21, and 22, 1972. Frankfort: Legislative Research Commission, 1972.

Kolstad, P. THERAPEUTIC ABORTION. Boston: Universitet forlaget, 1957.

Lagroua Weill-Halle, Marie Andree. L'AVORTEMENT DE PAPA; essai critique pour une vraie reforme. Paris: Fayard, 1971.

LE PERMIS LEGAL DE TUER OU L'AVORTEMENT DEVANT LE PARLEMENT, par une commission de juristes, de medecins, d'elus locaux et d'universitaires. Versailles: S.I.D.E.F., 1970.

Lindeboom, Gerit Arie. VRIJERE VRUCHTAFDRIJVING: Kritische beschouwing van een theologisch-ethisch pleidooi voor abortus-op-verzoek, tevens inleiding tot het vraagstuk van de liberalisering der zwangerschap-afbreking in Nederland. Amsterdam: Buyten & Schipperheijn, 1970.

Mace, David Robert. ABORTION: the agonizing decision. Nashville: Abingdon Press, 1972.

Marx, Paul, O.S.B. THE DEATH PEDDLERS: War on the Unborn. Collegeville: St. John's University, 1972.

Milanesi, Maria Lucila. O ABORTO PROVOCADO; estudo retro-spectivo em mulheres nao-solteiras, de 15 a 49 anos, residentes no distriro de Sao Paulo, em 1965. Sao Paulo: Pioneira, 1970.

Nardi, Enzo. PROCURATO ABORTO NEL MONDO GRECO ROMANO. Milano: A. Giuffre, 1971.

Nederlands Instituut voor Sociaal Sexuologisch Onderzoek. ABORTUS PROVOCATUS IN DE ONDERZOEKSLITERATUUR NA 1958. Zeist, 1970.

Nederlandse Federatie van Instellingne voor de Ongehuwde Moeder en haar Kind. DRAAGLAST--draagkracht; de abortus provocatus in het kader van de hulprerlening aan de ongehuwd zwangere vrouw. Den Haag: Nederlandse Federatie, 1970.

Neubardt, Selig and Harold Schulman. TECHNIQUES OF ABORTION. Boston: Little Brown, 1972.

Newman, Sidney H., Mildred B. Beck and Sarah Lewit, editors. ABORTION, OBTAINED AND DENIED; research approaches. New York: Population Council, 1971.

Osofsky, Howard J. and Joy Osofsky. THE ABORTION EXPERIENCE: Psychological and Medical Impact. New York: Harper & Row, 1972.

Pawlowski, Harald. KRIEG GEGEN DIE KINDER? Fur und wider die Abtreibung. Mit einer Dokumentation. Limburg: Lahn-Verlag, 1971.

Pross, Helge. ABTREIBUNG; Motive und Bedenken. Stuttgart: W. Kohlhammer, 1971.

Ransil, Bernard J. ABORTION. New York: Paulist-Neuman Press, 1969.

Schroeder, Friedrich-Christian. ABTREIBUNG; Reform des Art. 218. Berlin, New York: de Gruyter, 1972.

Schwarzer, Alice. FRAUEN GEGEN DEN ART. 218. Frankfurt a. M.: Suhrkamp, 1971.

Siebel, Wigand. SOZIOLOGIE DER ABTREIBUNG; empirische Forschung und theoretische Analyse. Stuttgart: F. Enke, 1971.

Siegrist, Harald Olav. DER ILLEGALE SCHWANGERSCHAFTS-ABRUCH, aus kriminologischer Sicht. Hamburg: Kriminalistik Verlag, 1971.

Sloane, R. Bruce and Diana F. Horvitz. A GENERAL GUIDE TO ABORTION. Chicago: Nelson-Hall, 1972.

Stucki-Lanzrein, Antoinette. DIE LEGALE SCHWANGERSCHAFT-SUNTERBRECHUNG; eine rechtsvergleichende Darstellung von Art. 120 StGB und den entspreschenden Bestimmungen der Vereinigten Staaten von Nordamerika, unter besonderer Berucksichtigung des Model Penal Code. Bern: G. Lang, 1971.

Sweden. Abortkommittee, 1965 ars. RATTEN TIL ABORT. Stockholm: Allmanna forlaget, 1971.

Thunberg, Anne Marie. DEN OLOSTA KONFLIKTEN. En etisk analys av abortutredningen. Stockholm: Gummesson, 1971.

Tietze, Christopher, et al. BIRTH CONTROL AND ABORTION. New York: MSS Information Corp., 1972.

Trussell, J. and R. A. Hatcher. WOMEN IN NEED. New York: Macmillan, 1972.

Van Vleck, David B. HOW AND WHY NOT TO HAVE THAT BABY. New York: Eriksson, 1971.

Volcher, Robert, et al. L'AVORTEMENT. Paris: Editions universitaires, 1971.

Whitehead, K. D. RESPECTABLE KILLING. New Rochelle, New York: Catholics United for the Faith, Inc., 1972.

Wieczorek, Veronika. CHROMOSOMENANOMALIEN ALS URSACHE VON FEHLGEBURTEN. Munchen: W. Goldmann, 1971.

Willke, J. C. and Mrs. J. C. Willke. HANDBOOK ON ABORTION. Cincinnati: Hiltz Publishing Company, 1971.

PERIODICAL LITERATURE

TITLE INDEX

"Abdominal aspiration hysterotomy," by D. T. Liu. LANCET 2:654, September 23, 1972.

"Abnormalities of intrauterine development in non-human primates," by J. G. Wilson. ACTA ENDOCRINOL 166:Suppl:261-292, 1972.

"ABO blood groups and abortion," BR MED J 4:314-315, November 11, 1972.

"ABO incompatibility as a cause of spontaneous abortion: evidence from abortuses," by K. Takano, et al. J MED GENET 9:144-150, June, 1972.

"Aborting a fetus: the legal right, the personal choice," by S. Lessard. WASHINGTON MO 4:29-37, August, 1972.

"Abortion," CLW 44:177-179, October, 1972.

"Abortion," by A. L. Ferguson. S AFR MED J 46:1194, August 26, 1972.

"Abortion," by J. M. Malone. AM J OBSTET GYNECOL 114:280, September 15, 1972.

"Abortion," by S. A. Nigro, et al. JAMA 219:1068-1069, February 21, 1972.

"Abortion. The fetal indications. Several reflexions," by E. Hervet. NOUV PRESSE MED 1:375-377, February 5, 1972.

"Abortion act," by C. B. Goodhart. BR MED J 2:714, June 17, 1972.

"The Abortion Act--Scotland 1968," HEALTH BULL 27:60-74, July, 1969.

"Abortion and Christian compassion," by T. Glenister. TABLET 226:518, June 3, 1972.

"Abortion and Contraception in Scripture," by C. E. Cerling, Jr. CHRISTIAN SCHOLAR'S REVIEW 42-58, Fall, 1971.

"Abortion and contraception in Sweden 1870-1970," by H. Sjovall. Z RECHTSMED 70:197-209, 1972.

"Abortion and the general practitioner," MED J AUST 2:513-514, August 26, 1972.

"Abortion and Islam," by H. Hathout. J MED LIBAN 25:237-239, 1972.

"Abortion and legislation," by A. M. Dourlen-Rollier. REV INFIRM 22: 133-137, February, 1972.

"Abortion and life's intrinsic value (emphasis on practice of abortion in New York city under liberalized statutes)," by D. C. Anderson. WALL ST J 179:8, April 7, 1972.

"Abortion and miscarriage," by R. F. Gardner. BR MED J 3:51, July 1, 1972.

"Abortion and morality," by P. R. Ehrlich, et al. CAN NURSE 68:37, June, 1972.

"Abortion and the religious liberty clauses," by J. S. Oteri, et al. HARV CIVIL RIGHT L REV 7:559, May, 1972.

"Abortion and slavery arguments same, ad says," NAT CATH REP 8:4, March 31, 1972.

"Abortion and sterilization. Comment on the outline of a fifth law for the reform of the criminal law 5th StRG from 14 February 1972 (BR-print. 58-72) prepared by the Commission on Questions of Rights," by H. Ehrhardt. NERVENARZT 43:338-340, June, 1972.

"Abortion and the value of life," by T. Cooke. OR 6(202)7, February 10, 1972.

"Abortion and women's lib," by M. K. Williams. HOSP PROGRESS 53: 17-18, February, 1972.

"Abortion: assault on human life," by P. Gastonguay. LIGUORIAN 60: 27-30, December, 1972.

"Abortion by aspiration technic," by T. B. Cheikh, et al. TUNIS MED 2:119-120, March-April, 1971.

"Abortion: changing attitudes of psychiatrists," by J. C. Little. LANCET 1:97, January 8, 1972.

"Abortion clinics: hospital hot spots," by J. Battaglia. HOSP WORLD 1:12 plus, January, 1972.

"Abortion, coercion and anti-Catholicism," AMERICA 126:502, May 13, 1972.

"Abortion consent rule struck down in District of Columbia: husband's consent not required," AMER MED NEWS 15:18, July 10, 1972.

"Abortion controversy. Remarks by L. B. Cummings; Statement by J. L. Nellis; Remarks by A. L. Scanlan; Remarks by J. V. Gartian, Jr.," DCB J 39:17, January-April, 1972.

"Abortion controversy: the law's response," CHI-KENT L REV 48:191, Fall-Winter, 1971.

"Abortion counseling," by J. D. Asher. AM J PUBLIC HEALTH 62: 686-688, May, 1972.

"Abortion counseling and behavioral change," by B. Dauber, et al. FAM PLANN PERSPECT 4:23-27, April, 1972.

"Abortion data for North Carolina," TEX MED 68:21, August, 1972.

"Abortion deaths," BR MED J 4:176-177, October 21, 1972.

"Abortion deaths," BR MED J 4:295, November 4, 1972.

"Abortion deaths," by G. E. Godber. BR MED J 4:424, November 18, 1972.

"Abortion deaths," by H. C. McLaren. BR MED J 3:826, September 30, 1972.

"Abortion debate is revealing our values," by G. L. Chamberlain. NEW CATH WORLD 215:206-208, September, 1972.

"Abortion: defining G Ps' attitudes," NEW HUMANIST 88:74-76, June, 1972.

"Abortion; do attitudes of nursing personnel affect the patient's perception of care?" by M. W. Harper, et al. NURS RES 21:327-331, July-August, 1972.

"Abortion during the 1st trimester by means of polyclinical vacuum aspiration without anesthesia," NED TIJDSCHR GENEESKD 116: 165, January 22, 1972.

"Abortion experiment in the polyclinic," by E. Vartiainen. SAIRAANH VUOSIK 48:341-343, April 25, 1972.

"The abortion explosion," by J. F. Hulka. NC MED J 33:957-959, November, 1972.

"Abortion, fetal indications. Various considerations," by E. Hervet. J SCI MED LILLE 90:176-178, April, 1972.

"Abortion: financial impact on the patient," by C. Muller. CLIN OBSTET GYNECOL 14:1302-1312, December, 1971.

"Abortion...human aspects," by D. Goyette. INFIRM CAN 14:30-34, June, 1972.

"Abortion in Canada," by J. Kettle. CAN DOCTOR 38:55-56, July, 1972.

"Abortion in a general practice. The fourth baby syndrome," by E. J. Hopkins, et al. PRACTITIONER 208:528-533, April, 1972.

"Abortion in mouse," by H. Heinecke, et al. Z VERSUCHSTIERKD 13: 320-326, 1971.

"Abortion in psychological perspective," by H. P. David. AM J ORTHO-PSYCHIATRY 42:61-68, January, 1972.

"Abortion: inalienable right," by N. Shainess. NY STATE J MED 72: 1772-1775, July 1, 1972.

"Abortion: influences on health professionals' attitudes," by J. P. Bourne. HOSPITALS 46:80-83, July 16, 1972.

"Abortion is not the answer," by M. J. Bulfin. J FLORIDA MED ASS 59:40-42, October, 1972.

"The abortion issue," by B. J. Ficarra. NY STATE J MED 72:2460-2463, October 1, 1972.

"Abortion issue; move to repeal New York state's liberalized law," TIME 99:23, May 22, 1972.

"Abortion law," by H. P. Dunn. NZ MED J 75:229-230, April, 1972.

"Abortion law," by J. Newlinds. MED J AUST 2:627, September 9, 1972.

"Abortion law," by J. Woolnough. MED J AUST 2:338-339, August 5, 1972.

"Abortion law in East Germany," J AMER MED ASS 221:516, July 31, 1972.

"Abortion law in South Carolina," SC L REV 24:425, 1972.

"The abortion--law mill. Parts 1-6," by B. J. George, Jr. NEW YORK LAW JOURNAL 167:1 plus, May 10-July 26, 1972.

"Abortion law reform and repeal: legislative and judicial developments," by R. Roemer. CLIN OBSTET GYNECOL 14:1165-1180, December, 1971.

"Abortion law reform: the English experience," by H. L. A. Hart. M U L R 8:388, May, 1972.

"Abortion laws in the federal courts--the Supreme Court as supreme platonic guardian," by H. Sigworth. IND LEGAL F 5:130, Fall, 1971.

"Abortion laws in other countries," by E. Strutz. GEBURTSHILFE FRAUENHEILKD 32:407-414, May, 1972.

"Abortion laws still in ferment," by R. J. Trotter. SCI NEWS 101:75, January 29, 1972.

"Abortion...legal aspects," by N. Isaac. INFIRM CAN 14:27-29, June, 1972.

"Abortion: a legal cop out," NEW ENGLAND L REV 7:311, Spring, 1972.

"Abortion: legal dilemma," J KANS MED SOC 73:19, June, 1972.

"Abortion: legal morass of American jurisprudence," J MISS STATE MED ASS 13:59-61, February, 1972.

"Abortion, Ltd.," ECONOMIST 243:55, May 20, 1972.

"Abortion...medical aspects," by G. Pepin. INFIRM CAN 14:24-26, June, 1972.

"Abortion: a metaphysical approach," by T. L. Johnson. FREEMAN 22:498-505, August, 1972.

"Abortion: Missouri HB 1470," by W. Brennan. SOC JUST 65:129-132, July-August, 1972.

"Abortion: new laws bring new approaches," by S. Loos, et al. HOSPITALS 46:76-79, July 16, 1972.

"Abortion? No!," by E. F. Diamond. MED INSIGHT 4:36-41, February, 1972.

"Abortion (occurrence of abortion in a catchment area," by H. Krabisch. ZENTRALBL GYNAEKOL 94:1127-1133, August 26, 1972.

"Abortion on demand," by E. B. Grogone. LANCET 1:45-46, January 1, 1972.

"Abortion on demand in East Germany," CAN DOCTOR 38:18, August, 1972.

"Abortion on request: the physician's view," by A. F. Guttmacher. AM BIOL TEACH 34:514-517, December, 1972.

"Abortion: on whose demand?" AMERICA 126:335, April 1, 1972.

"Abortion operations--the right to opt out," AUSTRALAS NURSES J 1:17, April, 1972.

"Abortion: opinion aside, you should know all the facts," BUS WEEK 2238:65-66, July 22, 1972.

"Abortion or contraception?" by P. J. Huntingford. R SOC HEALTH J 91:292-294, November-December, 1971.

"Abortion or contraception," by C. Verdoux. REV INFORM 22:117-121, February, 1972; also in Z KRANKENPFL 65:279-281 passim, July, 1972.

"Abortion: parameters for decision. A review," by R. J. Gerber. INT PHILOS Q 11:561-584, December, 1971; also in ETHICS 82:137-154, January, 1972.

"Abortion, the patient, the physician and the law. The first year's experience," by E. S. Gendel. J KANS MED SOC 73:18-19, January, 1972.

"Abortion pay limits upheal in New York," AMER MED NEWS 15:15, February 28, 1972.

"Abortion, psychiatry, and the quality of life," by Z. M. Lebensohn. AM J PSYCHIATRY 128:946-951, February, 1972.

"Abortion questionnaire and RCOG," by B. Corkill. NZ MED J 74:410-411, December, 1971.

"Abortion rate up in Canada," HOSP ADMIN CAN 14:17, July, 1972.

"Abortion recidivism. A problem in preventive medicine," by J. J. Rovinsky. OBSTET GYNECOL 39:649-659, May, 1972.

"Abortion referral agencies," by N. L. Bosworth, et al. J KY MED ASSOC 70:795-796, October, 1972.

"Abortion referral in a large college health service," by M. W. Bridwell, et al. J AM MED WOM ASSOC 27:420-421, August, 1972.

"Abortion reform," by R. G. Bubeck. J AM OSTEOPATH ASSOC 71: 842-845, June, 1972.

"Abortion reform," by M. Fishbein. MED WORLD NEWS 13:68, June 2, 1972.

"Abortion--the role of private foundations," by D. H. Minkler. CLIN OBSTET GYNECOL 14:1181-1189, December, 1971.

"Abortion rulings reported," NEWSLETTER (AMER SOC ATTORNEYS) 5:3-5, June, 1972.

"Abortion: a special demand," JAMA 221:400, July 24, 1972.

"Abortion study finds risks lower for patients not getting public aid," US MED 8:6-7, March 15, 1972.

"Abortion teaser," by J. R. Wilson. SPECTATOR 755, May 13, 1972.

"Abortion today," by G. Papola. OR 12(208)9-10, March 23, 1972.

"Abortion touts," by D. Gould. NEW STATESM 83:165-166, February 11, 1972.

"Abortion under the law," SCI AM 227:51, July, 1972.

"Abortion--United Kingdom style," by R. J. Brigden. SUPERVISOR NURSE 3:78-79, April, 1972.

"Abortion: the uptake argument," by D. Gerber. ETHICS 83:80-83, October, 1972.

"Abortion: use of prostaglandins and epidural analgesia," by I. Craft. LANCET 2:41, July 1, 1972.

"Abortion: what are the psychiatric indications?" by H. G. DeCherney. DEL MED J 44:230-231, August, 1972.

"Abortion: where it's at, where it's going?" by B. Tierney. J CAN BA 3:26, April, 1972.

"Abortion: who should certify the need?" edited by J. B. McClements. DEL MED J 44:231-232, August, 1972.

"Abortion with extra-amniotic prostaglandins," by J. E. Bruce. LANCET 2:380, August 19, 1972.

"Abortion with extra-amniotic prostaglandins," by M. P. Embrey, et al. LANCET 2:654-655, September 23, 1972.

"Abortion with prostaglandins," by B. Alderman. LANCET 2:279, August 5, 1972.

"Abortion with prostaglandins," by R. C. Strickler. LANCET 2:539, September 9, 1972.

"Abortion; work of Clergy counseling service for problem pregnancies, Los Angeles and Birthright of Chicago," by C. Remsberg, et al. SEVENTEEN 31:140-141 plus, September, 1972.

"Abortion yes or no; nurses organize both ways: New York," AMER J NURSING 72:416 plus, March, 1972.

"Abortions and acute identity crisis in nurses," by W. F. Char, et al. AM J PSYCHIATRY 128:952-957, February, 1972.

"Abortions among women on public assistance in Hawaii: implications for practice," by K. T. Kumabe. AM J PUBLIC HEALTH 62:1538-1543, November, 1972.

"Abortions in all hospitals by 1975," CAN HOSP 49:9, March, 1972.

"Abortions regaining objectivity or rationalization?" by E. F. Kal, et al. AM J PSYCHIATRY 129:484-485, October, 1972.

"Abortive politics," ECONOMIST 243:62, May 13, 1972.

"Aborto procurato e legislazione statuale," by L. Salvatore, S. J., CIVILTA CATTOLICA 328-342, February 19, 1972.

"Abortus provocatus legislation," by S. W. Schuurmans. NED TIJDSCHR GENEESKD 116:203-205, January 29, 1972.

"The absence of sweat: abortion on demand," by W. Bausch. US CATH

37:39-40, April, 1972.

"Abtreibung - ja oder nein; ein synoptischer Beitrag zur Diskussion der Reformvorschlage im Strafrecht," by K. W. Wrage. Z EVETHIK 15:239-251, July, 1971.

"Abtreibung: Moraltheologisch gesehen," by G. Ermecke. THEOLOGIE UND GLAUBE 23-33, 1972.

"An abuse of prenatal diagnosis," by M. A. Stenchever. JAMA 221: 408, July 24, 1972.

"Action of a natural progesterone associated with a synthetic progestogen and vitamin E in the treatment of threatened abortion and premature labor," by S. Panariello. ARCH OSTET GINECOL 75: 492-506, December, 1970.

"The action of PGF 2 prostaglandin on the pregnant uterus," by F. Szontagh, et al. ORV HETIL 113:919-922, April 16, 1972.

"Action of a serotonin antagonist, methysergide, on the abortive or lethal effect of bacterial endotoxins in mice," by F. Darrieulat, et al. ANN INST PASTEUR 121:665-673, November, 1971.

"Acute fatal poisoning with silver nitrate following an abortion attempt," by G. Reinhardt, et al. ARCH KRIMINOL 148:69-78, September-October, 1971.

"Acute identity crisis' hits hospital abortion staff--morality the issue: North Carolina Memorial Hospital, Chapel Hill," US MED 8:8-9, May 15, 1972.

"Administrative guidelines for an abortion service," by G. Felton, et al. AM J NURS 72:108-109, January, 1972.

"Adrenocorticotropic function of the hypophisis in postabortive sepsis," by A. D. Makatsariia, et al. VOPR OKHR MATERIN DET 17:94, May, 1972.

"Advances in obstetrics and gynaecology," by V. R. Tindall. PRACTITIONER 209:437-443, October, 1972.

"Advising about pregnancy termination," by J. D. Bottomley. BR

MED J 1:54, January 1, 1972.

"The aetiology of abortion in a rural community," by P. R. Grob. J R COLL GEN PRACT 22:499-507, August, 1972.

"After the Act," by H. L. A. Hart, et al. GUARDIAN 9, May 3, 1972.

"After we got out, will there be a bloodbath in South Vietnam?" by J. S. Carroll, et al. N Y TIMES MAG 38-40 plus, October 15, 1972.

"Against the tide of abortion laws," MED WORLD NEWS 13:7-8, February 18, 1972.

"Agonizing dilemma: abortion and birth control and the Catholic hospital," CATH HOSP 3:1-2, September, 1972.

"Air embolism and maternal death from therapeutic abortion," by R. A. Munsick. OBSTET GYNECOL 39:688-690, May, 1972.

"Alberta nurses discuss abortion care," CAN HOSP 49:12, March, 1972.

"Allegations, actions, and ad interim," by D. S. Wert. PA MED 74:59-62, May, 1971.

"Alternatives to abortion for the unwed mother," by J. S. Morris, Jr. VA MED MON 99:844-847, August, 1972.

"Alylestenol (Gestanone) in the treatment of threatened abortion," by D. Vasilev. AKUSH GINEKOL (Sofiia) 10:413-419, 1971.

"Ambulatory abortion: experience with 26,000 cases (July 1, 1970, to August 1, 1971)," by B. N. Nathanson. N ENGL J MED 286:403-407, February 24, 1972.

"American Academy of Pediatrics. Committee on Youth. Teen-age pregnancy and the problem of abortion," PEDIATRICS 49:303-304, February, 1972.

"Anaerobic sepsis following abortion," by I. R. Zak. AKUSH GINEKOL 47:11-13, November, 1971.

"Analysis of prostaglandin F 2 and metabolites in blood during constant intravenous infusion of prostaglandin F 2 in the human female," by F. Beguin, et al. ACTA PHYSIOL SCAND 86:430-432, November, 1972.

"Anecdotal contribution to the study of in-utero retention of the dead fetus in the 1st trimester of pregnancy," by G. Guiran. BULL FED SOC GYNECOL OBSTET LANG FR 23:473-475, September-October, 1971.

"Anaesthesia, pregnancy and pollution," BR J ANAESTH 44:541, June, 1972.

"Anaesthetic practice and pregnancy. Controlled survey of women anaesthetists in the United Kingdom," by R. P. Knill-Jones, et al. LANCET 1:1326-1328, June 17, 1872.

"Anesthesia for early artificial interruption of pregnancy," by R. S. Mikhaleva. AKUSH GINEKOL 47:61, December, 1971.

"Anesthesia in minor gynecologic surgery with trichloroethylene," by V. S. Lesiuk. AKUSH GINEKOL 48:70-71, April, 1972.

"Anesthesiology grand rounds Yale-New Haven Hospital. Placental abruption with coagulopathy," CONN MED 36:238-241, April, 1972.

"Anesthetic-induced abortion?" by D. H. Carr. ANESTHESIOLOGY 35:335, October, 1971.

"Anesthetics as a cause of abortion," by T. H. Corbett. FERTIL STERIL 23:866-869, November, 1972.

"Anti-abortion law upheld by Indiana Supreme Court," AMER MED NEWS 15:17, August 14, 1972.

"Anticipatory guidance for abortion," by L. W. Tinnin, et al. MD STATE MED J 21:73, May, 1972.

"Antinuclear factor in a patient with recurrent abortions," by C. Abrahams, et al. S AFR MED J 46:844, June 17, 1972.

"Antinuclear factor in 2 patients with recurrent abortions," by C. Abrahams, et al. LANCET 1:498-499, February 26, 1972.

"Appeals court blocks suit to ban abortions in New York City," HOSPITALS 46:164, February 1, 1972.

"Arias-Stella phenomenon in spontaneous and therapeutic abortion," by S. G. Silverberg. AM J OBSTET GYNECOL 112:777-780, March 15, 1972.

"Article 218 of the Legal Code," by I. von Troschke. DTSCH KRANKENPFLEGEZ 25:127-129, March, 1972.

"Artificial interruption of pregnancy and extrauterine pregnancy," by A. Cernoch. ZENTRALBL GYNAEKOL 93:1784-1791, December 25, 1971.

"Arztliche Uberlegungen zur reform des 218," by H. Hepp. STIMM ZEIT 189:375-392, June, 1972.

"Attempted abortion by the use of bishydroxycoumarin," by N. S. De Jager, et al. CAN MED ASSOC J 107:50 passim, July 8, 1972.

"Attitude of the woman to artificial interruption of pregnancy and the gynecologist's tasks," by J. Kveton, et al. CESK GYNEKOL 37:533-534, September, 1972.

"Attitudes toward abortion among young black (based on a study of 300 young Negro women in Baltimore, Md.)," by F. F. Furstenburg, Jr. STUDIES IN FAMILY PLANNING 3:66-69, April, 1972.

"Attitudes toward abortion law reform at the University of Michigan Medical Center," by D. Hickok, et al. MICH MED 71:327-329, April, 1972.

"Attitudes toward abortion of married women in metropolitan Toronto," by T. R. Balakrishnan, et al. SOC BIOL 19:35-42, March, 1972.

"Attitudes toward abortion: a survey of Milwaukee obstetricians and gynecologists," by P. Halverson, et al. WIS MED J 71:134-139, April, 1972.

"Back abortion reform," NAT CATH REP 8:4, April 7, 1972.

"Backlash on abortion; move to repeal New York state's liberal law," NEWSWEEK 79:32, May 22, 1972.

"Bacterial endocarditis with 'associated bacteria'," by E. Bergogne-Berezin, et al. NOUV PRESSE MED 1:271-272, January 22, 1972.

"Bacteriological, biochemical and virulence studies on Salmonella dublin from abortion and enteric disease in cattle and sheep," by J. R. Walton. VET REC 90:236-240, February 26, 1972.

"Baltimore hospital abortion patient given $90,000 in damages," HOSPITALS 46:133, November 1, 1972.

"Ban upheld on abortions for psychiatric reasons," AMER MED NEWS 15:10, December 25, 1972.

"The battle of women. Discussion of Paragraph 218," by M. I. Kischke. KRANKENPFLEGE 26:54-55, February, 1972.

"The beginning: the end," by J. A. Fitzgerald. NY STATE J MED 72: 2458-2459, October 1, 1972.

"Birth control among the unmarried in Massachusetts: the Supreme Court speaks in varied tongues," by W. J. Curran. NEW ENGL J MED 286:1198-1199, June 1, 1972.

"Birth control appears successful in China despite its low esteem in Marxist theory," SCI NEWS 102:51-52, July 22, 1972.

"Birth control; the establishment chimes in," ECONOMIST 243:24 plus, April 8, 1972.

"Birth control for teen-agers--is it legal?" by C. A. Gravenor, Jr. CAN DOCTOR 38:103-104, October, 1972.

"Birth control in the USA," INT HOSP REV 9:32, November 4, 1971.

"Birth-control plan for Britain," LANCET 1:675, March 25, 1972.

"Birth control usage among abortion patients," by J. G. Hill. J KANS MED SOC 73:295-301 passim, June, 1972.

"Birth: organic selection or technologic design?" by O. C. Schroeder, Jr. POSTGRAD MED 51:53-55, June, 1972.

"Birthright moves ahead," OR 30(226)5, July 27, 1972.

"Birthright New York: continued from the Lamp, October, 1971," C DGST 36:100-103, February, 1972.

"The bishops' strange love," by W. Marshner. TRIUMPH 7:11-14, June, 1972.

"Bitter abortion battle; Pennsylvania," TIME 100:32, December 11, 1972.

"Black physicians' experience with abortion requests and opinion about abortion law change in Michigan," by E. L. Hill, et al. J NATL MED ASSOC 64:52-58, January, 1972.

"Blockage of pregnancy in mice by the odor of male litter mates," by S. Bloch, et al. EXPERIENTIA 28:703, June 15, 1972.

"Blood loss and changes in total blood volume during induced abortion," by R. Raicheva. AKUSH GINEKOL (Sofiia) 10:284-286, 1971.

"Bovine abortion associated with Aeromonas hydrophila," by K. Wohlgemuth, et al. J AM VET MED ASSOC 160:1001-1002, April 1, 1972.

"Bovine abortion associated with Nocardia asteroides," by K. Wohlgemuth, et al. J AM VET MED ASSOC 161:273-274, August 1, 1972.

"Bovine abortion associated with Torulopsis glabrata," by C. A. Kirkbride, et al. J AM VET MED ASSOC 161:390-392, August 15, 1972.

"Britain and Spain; abortion, ltd.," ECONOMIST 243:55, May 20, 1972.

"British Columbia hospital receives abortion study grant," CAN HOSP 49:11, March, 1972.

"Bronchospasm complicating intravenous prostaglandin F 2a for therapeutic abortion," by J. I. Fishburne, Jr., et al. OBSTET GYNECOL 39:892-896, June, 1972.

"Burger ruling delays court abortion decision," NAT CATH REP 8:3, July 21, 1972.

"Business as usual," by M. Lawrence. TRIUMPH 7:15, June, 1972.

"California abortion statistics for 1971," by W. M. Ballard. CALIF MED 116:55, April, 1972.

"Canadian Nurses' Association position on family planning and related health care," CAN NURSE 68:11, August, 1972.

"Care and treatment of therapeutic abortion patients in Canadian hospitals: January 1 to September 30, 1971," HOSP ADMIN CAN 14:25-31, March, 1972.

"Case for abortion on demand," by L. G. Forer. PENN BA Q 43:203, January, 1972.

"A case of fecundity disorders: chromosomal discussion," by H. Dar, et al. REV FR GYNECOL OBSTET 67:193-194, February-March, 1972.

"A case of osseus tissue from the fetus residue remaining for 19 years in the uterine wall," by O. I. Stupko, et al. PEDIATR AKUSH GINEKOL 31:62, 1969.

"Catholic left torn on abortion," by J. Castelli. NAT CATH REP 8:6, July 21, 1972.

"Causes of infertility," by R. Gergova, et al. CESK GYNEKOL 37: 529-530, September, 1972.

"Cervical fistula: a complication of midtrimester abortion," by R. Goodlin, et al. OBSTET GYNECOL 40:82-84, July, 1972.

"Cervical mucus, vaginal cytology and steroid excretion in recurrent abortion," by R. R. MacDonald, et al. OBSTET GYNECOL 40:394-402, September, 1972.

"Cervicovaginal fistula as a result of saline abortion," by R. T. Gordon. AM J OBSTET GYNECOL 112:578-579, February 15, 1972.

"A challenge to abortionists: the Liverpool rally," by N. St. John-Stevas. TABLET 226:394, April 29, 1972.

"Changes in chorionic gonadotropins time as a test for the prognosis of threatened abortion in the 1st trimester," by P. De Patre. MINERVA MED 63:549-553, February 7, 1972.

"Changes in the concentration of copper and ceruloplasmin, and cholinesterase activity in the blood in threatened abortion," by L. I. Priakhina. AKUSH GINEKOL 47:61-63, April, 1971.

"Changes in serum and urinary electrolytes," by T. C. Wong, et al. NY STATE J MED 72:564-577, March 1, 1972.

"Characteristics of nonspecific immunity during pregnancy, after abortions and labor," by F. D. Aniskova, et al. VOPR OKHR MATERIN DET 16:60-63, May, 1971.

"Characteristics of uterine contractile activity in isthmico-cervical insufficiency," by G. M. Lisovskaia, et al. AKUSH GINEKOL 48: 63, January, 1972.

"Characterization of 100 women psychiatrically evaluated for therapeutic abortion," by K. H. Talan, et al. ARCH GEN PSYCHIATRY 26:571-577, June, 1972.

"Chromosome aberrations and spontaneous abortions," by A. M. Kuliev. AKUSH GINEKOL 47:38-40, April, 1971.

"Chromosome aberrations in oogenesis and embryogenesis of mammals and man," by G. Rohrborn. ARCH TOXIKOL 28:115-119, 1971.

"Chromosome studies in selected spontaneous abortions. IV. Unusual cytogenetic disorders," by D. H. Carr, et al. TERATOLOGY 5:49-56, February, 1972.

"Chromosome studies on spontaneous and threatened abortions," by T. Ikeuchi, et al. JAP J HUM GENET 16:191-197, March, 1972.

"Civil conflicts," LANCET 2:335, August 12, 1972.

"Clarification of the so-called clouded figures on abortion," by H. J. Prill. MED KLIN 67:619-622, April 28, 1972.

"A clinical and pathologic survey of 91 cases of spontaneous abortion," by J. Brotherton, et al. FERTIL STERIL 23:289-294, April, 1972.

"Clinical aspects, pathogenesis and prevention of animal toxoplasmosis (with special reference to toxoplasmosis abortion in sheep)," by J. K. Beverley. MONATSH VET MED 26:893-900, December 1, 1971.

"Clinical experiences in induced abortion using vacuum extraction and the metranoikter," by J. Hoffman, et al. ZENTRALBL GYNAEKOL 94:913-917, July 22, 1972.

"The clinical problems of fibrinolysis between the utero-placental and the feto-placental units in relation to the abortion," by K. Oyanagi. J TOKYO MED COLL 28:757-776, September, 1970.

"A clinical study on prognosticating threatened abortions by vaginal cytogram in the first trimester of pregnancy," by J. Aoki. ACTUAL PHARMACOL 23:257-266, 1970.

"Coagulation changes after hypertonic saline infusion for late abortions," by F. D. Brown, et al. OBSTET GYNECOL 38:538-543, April, 1972.

"Coexistence of abortion in tubal pregnancy with incipient prolapse of uterine myoma," by A. Cieplak. POL TYG LEK 27:1403-1404, September 4, 1971.

"Colorado parish survey reveals laity's opinions," NAT CATH REP 8:7, May 12, 1972.

"Colpocytogram and some indices of hormone levels in women with threatened abortion," by O. S. Badiva. PEDIATR AKUSH GINEKOL 4:38-41, July-August, 1971.

"Comment and controversy...should abortions be performed in doctors' offices," by S. Neubardt, et al. FAMILY PLANN PERSPECT 4:4-7, July, 1972.

"Commission backs abortion," NAT CATH REP 8:5, March 24, 1972.

"Comparative studies on effects of previous pregnancy interruption, spontaneous abortion and term labor on the incidence of immature and premature labors," by S. Rozewicki, et al. WIAD LEK 25:31-38, January 1, 1972.

"A comparison between the contribution of increasing and decreasing liveweight to ovulation and embryonic survival in the Border Leicester Merino ewe," by I. A. Cumming. J REPROD FERTIL 28:148, January, 1972.

"A comparison between unmarried women seeking therapeutic abortion and unmarried mothers," by J. Naiman. LAVAL MED 42:1086-1088, December, 1971.

"Comparison of methods for diagnosing equine rhinopneumonitis virus abortion," by A. L. Trapp, et al. VET MED SMALL ANIM CLIN 67: 895 passim, August, 1972.

"Complications of cervical suture," by A. Adoni, et al. HAREFUAH 83:146-147, August 15, 1972.

"Concealed accidental haemorrhage," by M. N. Malathy. NURS J INDIA 63:75 plus, March, 1972.

"Congenital malformations and refused termination," by T. J. David, et al. LANCET 1:1123, May 20, 1972.

"Connecticut abortion laws ruled unconstitutional," CHR CENT 89:539, May 10, 1972.

"Conscience and responsible parenthood," by F. M. Pinon. S TOMAS NURS J 11:24-33, April-May, 1972.

"Conscientious objection to abortion," by R. L. Walley. BR MED J 4:234, October 28, 1972.

"Constitutional law-abortion-lack of compelling state interests--California's American law institute-type therapeutic abortion statute substantially voided because interests in the woman's health and in the fetus dictate that abortions prior to twenty weeks of pregnancy may be restricted only for medical reasons," U CLIN L REV 41:235, 1972.

"Constitutional law-abortion statute as invasion of a woman's right of privacy," ST LOUIS U L J 15:642, Summer, 1971.

"Constitutional law-denial of medicaid reimbursement for elective abortions--City of New York v. Wyman," ALBANY L REV 36:794, 1972.

"Constitutional law-expanding the grounds for abortion," WAKE FOREST L REV 7:651, October, 1971.

"Constitutional law--'liberalized' abortion statute held constitutional," FORDHAM L REV 41:439, December, 1972.

"Constitutional right to life from the moment of conception," SOC JUST 64:408-418, March, 1972.

"Consumptive coagulopathy associated with intra-amniotic infusion of hypertonic salt," by F. K. Beller, et al. AM J OBSTET GYNECOL 112:534-543, February 15, 1972.

"Consumptive coagulopathy with generalized hemorrhage after hypertonic saline-induced abortion. A case report," by D. R. Halbert, et al. OBSTET GYNECOL 39:41-44, January, 1972.

"Contemporary psychiatric consultation: evaluation or rehabilitation?" by R. O. Pasnau. CLIN OBSTET GYNECOL 14:1258-1262, December, 1971.

"Continuing thoughts on abortion and population control," by W. M. Dabney. J MISS STATE MED ASS 13:211, May, 1972.

"Contraception, abortion, demography," by H. de Saint-Blanquat. REV INFIRM 22:107-115, February, 1972.

"Contraception, abortion, prostaglandins and sterilization," by J. H. Ravina. NOUV PRESSE MED 1:1989-1990, August 26, 1972.

"Contraception or abortion?" DIST NURS 14:262, March, 1972.

"Contraception or abortion?" NURS TIMES 69:249-250, February 24, 1972.

"Contraception or abortion? (a). Usage of contraception and abortion," by G. Chamberlain. R SOC HEALTH J 92:191-194, August, 1972.

"Contraception or abortion? (b). Is abortion a form of contraception?" by H. Gordon. R SOC HEALTH J 92:194-197, August, 1972.

"Contraception or abortion? (e). Termination of pregnancy," by H. R. Arthur. R SOC HEALTH J 92:204-207, August, 1972.

"Contraceptive antecedents to early and late therapeutic abortions," by W. Oppel, et al. AM J PUBLIC HEALTH 62:824-827, June, 1972.

"Correlates of repeat induced abortions," by M. B. Bracken, et al. OBSTET GYNECOL 40:816-825, December, 1972.

"Counseling the abortion patient is more than talk," by C, Keller, et al. AM J NURS 72:102-106, January, 1972.

"Counseling for women who seek abortion," by E. M. Smith. SOC WORK 17:62-68, March, 1972.

"Course and late effects of acute renal insufficiencies post partum and post abortum," by P. Zech, et al. J MED LYON 51:251 passim, January 20, 1970.

"The course and outcome of pregnancy for women treated for infertility," by M. S. Biriukova, et al. PEDIATR AKUSH GINEKOL 71:46-48, September-October, 1971.

"The course of pregnancy and labor in women with previous abortions," by A. Atanasov, et al. AKUSH GINEKOL (Sofiia) 10:456-459, 1971.

"Court bars fetal death notices identifying aborting patients: New York," HOSP WORLD 1:11, October, 1972.

"Court-ordered steriliaztion performed at St. Vincent's Hospital, Billings," by L. Cory. HOSP PROG 53:22 plus, December, 1972.

"Criminal abortion as dominant etiological factor in ectopic pregnancy," by V. Masic. MED ARH 26:41-44, January-February, 1972.

"Crushing the life of a child in the womb," by H. McCabe. NEW BLCKFRS 53:146-147, April, 1972.

"Current opinion on abortion," by P. Worden. PTA MAG 66:12-14, May, 1972.

"Cyanosis due to intravenous prostaglandin F," by G. Roberts, et al. LANCET 2:425-426, August 26, 1972.

"Cytogenetic aspects of induced and spontaneous abortions," by D. H. Carr. CLIN OBSTET GYNECOL 15:203-219, March, 1972.

"Cytogenetic effect of DDB," by B. Ia. Ekshtat, et al. GIG SANIT 36:26-29, December, 1971.

"Danger of Rh-isoimmunization in induced abortion and its prevention using anti-Rh (D) immunoglobulin," by G. Bajtai, et al. ZENTRALBL GYNAEKOL 94:922-925, July 22, 1972.

"Death by abortion absolutely unacceptable," by P. O'Boyle. SOC JUST 65:234-237, November, 1972.

"The death peddlers. N. Y. appeals court rules against fetus," by P. Marx. NAT CATH REP 8:21, March 10, 1972.

"Declaration of Oslo: statement on therapeutic abortion--World Medical Assembly," WORLD MED J 19:30, March-April, 1972.

"Defibrination in saline abortion," by R. Schwartz, et al. OBSTET GYNECOL 40:728-737, November, 1972.

"Defibrination syndrome after intra-amniotic infusion of hypertonic saline," by A. E. Weiss, et al. AM J OBSTET GYNECOL 113:868-874, August 1, 1972.

"Defibrinogenation after intra-amniotic injection of hypertonic saline," by J. L. Spivak, et al. N ENGL J MED 287:321-323, August 17, 1972.

"Deformed infants' suits for failure to recommend abortions," J KANS MED SOC 73:80 passim, February, 1972.

"Delayed after effects of medically induced abortion," by H. Warnes. CAN PSYCHIATR ASSOC J 16:537-541, December, 1971.

"The demand for abortion," by G. Deshaies. REV INFIRM 22:130-132, February, 1972.

"The demographic effects of legal abortion in eastern Europe," by B. Kapotsy. EUROPEAN DEMOGRAPHIC INFO BUL 3:193-207, November 4, 1972.

"Dermatoglyphics associated with fetal wastage," by L. I. Rose, et al. N ENGL J MED 287:451-452, August 31, 1972.

"Design complements patients' needs," HOSPITALS 46:42-43 passim, September 16, 1972.

"Developing applications of prostaglandins in obstetrics and gynecology," by J. W. Hinman. AM J OBSTET GYNECOL 113:130-138, May 1, 1972.

"Developing professional parameters: nursing and social work roles in the care of the induced abortion patient," by L. M. Tanner. CLIN OBSTET GYNECOL 14:1271-1272, December, 1971.

"Development of the population growth question and the abortion law," by L. Gronsky. CESK GYNEKOL 37:584, October, 1972.

"Diagnosis of bovine abortion," by E. A. Woelffer. J AM VET MED ASSOC 161:1284-1287, December 1, 1972.

"Discussion about Article 218 of the Penal Code. Position of the Federal Ministry of Justice," by A. Bayerl. DTSCH KRANKENPFLEGEZ 25:241-242, May, 1972.

"Divergence of opinion on placental damage due to hypertonic saline-induced abortion," by Y. Manabe, et al. AM J OBSTET GYNECOL 114:1107-1108, December 15, 1972.

"Do Rh-negative women with an early spontaneous abortion need Rh immune prophylaxis?" by R. D. Visscher, et al. AM J OBSTET GYNECOL 113:158-165, May 15, 1972.

"Doctor, what does the aborted baby feel while it's dying?" TRIUMPH 7:20-23 plus, March, 1972.

"Domiciliary midwives and birth control advice 1970-1971," by M. Waite. NURSING TIMES 68:193-195, December 7, 1972.

"Dr. Andre Hellegers: in the year 2000 abortion will be considered backward," by R. Simanski. NAT CATH REP 8:5-6, October 5, 1972.

"Drop in maternal deaths follows liberal abortion law enactment," US MED 8:4 plus, December 15, 1972.

"Early abortion and clinical findings in women having an abortion," by P. Drac. ZENTRALBL GYNAEKOL 94:918-921, July 22, 1972.

"Early abortion and Mycoplasma infection," by E. Caspi, et al. ISR J MED SCI 8:122-127, February, 1972.

"Early abortion without cervical dilation: pump or syringe aspiration," by A. J. Margolis, et al. J REPROD MED 9:237-240, November, 1972.

"Early abortions. Surgical technics and patient care," LAKARTIDNINGEN 69:4490-4495, September 27, 1972.

"Early complications of pregnancy interruptions according to our records," by B. Jakubovska, et al. ÇESK GYNEKOL 37:532-533, September, 1972.

"Early somatic complications in abortion," by P. Atterfelt, et al. LAKARTIDNINGEN 69:241-246, January 12, 1972.

"Easy abortion loses in two states," NAT CATH REP 9:4, November 24, 1972.

"Effect of aminocentesis, selective abortion, and reproductive compensation on the incidence of autosomal recessive diseases," by G. W. Hagy, et al. J HERED 63:185-188, July-August, 1972.

"Effect of intraamniotic sodium concentration on saline induced abortion," by R. R. Weiss, et al. OBSTET GYNECOL 40:243-246, August, 1972.

"The effect of legislation for interruption of pregnancy on the level of birth rate," by G. Stoimenov, et al. AKUSH GINEKOL (Sofiia) 11:1-7, 1972.

"Effect of levorin on the course of pregnancy and on the fetus of rabbits," by N. N. Sionitskaia, et al. ANTIBIOTIKI 17:742-745, August, 1972.

"Effect of the method of induced abortion (curettage, v. aspiration) on feto-maternal isoimmunisation," by M. Asztalos, et al. ZENTRALBL GYNAEKOL 94:926-930, July 22, 1972.

"Effects of administration of Furosemide in acute postabortum renal insufficiency," by T. Burghele, et al. ACTA UROL BELG 39:315-321, July, 1971.

"Effects of exchange transfusion on hemostatic disorders during septic shock after abortion," by C. Gibert, et al. REV MED SUISSE ROMANDE 91:689-696, October, 1971.

"Effects of haemodialysis on dynamics of some antibiotics in blood of patients with kidney insufficiency complicated by purulent infection," by M. I. Kuzin, et al. BULL SOC INT CHIR 31:298-303, July-August, 1972.

"The effects of high altitude on the reproductive cycle and pregnancy in the hamster," by R. H. Printz. ANAT REC 173:157-171, June, 1972.

"Effects of legal abortion on gynaecology," by A. H. John, et al. BR MED J 3:99-102, July 8, 1972.

"Effects of a liberalized abortion law in New York City," by J. Pakter, et al. MT SINAI J MED NY 39:535-543, November-December, 1972.

"Effects of termination of pregnancy and general anesthesia on acid-base equilibrium in blood," by J. Denk, et al. WIAD LEK 25:500-503, March 15, 1972.

"8 cases of therapeutic abortion in advanced pregnancy by injections of hypertonic saline serum," by T. B. Cheihk, et al. TUNIS MED 2:117-118, March-April, 1971.

"18 month experience in New York City with a liberalized abortion law," by J. Pakter. N Y MED 28:333 plus, September, 1972.

"18th century medical dissertations on anatomy at the Rostock University. 2. Inaugural address of Wilhelm Friedrich Zander on abortion (1748)," by H. G. Wishhusen, et al. ANAT ANZ 130:277-284, 1972.

"Elective abortion. Woman in crisis," by N. Leiter. NY STATE J MED 72:2908-2910, December 1, 1972.

"Electromyographic method of examining neuromuscular excitability in threatened abortion," by D. Dylewska, et al. POL TYG LEK 27: 1036-1039, July 3, 1972.

"The embattled minority: out of sight, out of mind," by L. J. Hogan. MARYLAND LAW FORUM 2:50-54, Winter, 1972.

"Emergency care in injuries of the uterus during abortion," by N. A. Zakhar'eva. VOPR OKHR MATERIN DET 16:77-79, May, 1971.

"The emotional conflicts behind an abortion," by R. E. Hall. MED INSIGHT 4:22-25 plus, July, 1972.

"Epidemiologic investigation of an outbreak of fatal enteritis and abortion associated with dietary change and Salmonella typhimurium infection in a dairy herd. A case report," by R. F. Kahrs, et al. CORNELL VET 62:175-191, April, 1972.

"Epidemiological and clinical factors in premature detachment of the normally inserted placenta," by A. Barone, et al. MINERVA GINECOL 23:623-625, August, 1971.

"Equine abortion (herpes) virus: purification and concentration of enveloped and deenveloped virus and envelope material by density gradient centrifugation in colloidal silica," by B. Klingeborn, et al. VIROLOGY 48:618-623, May, 1972.

"Erythocyte diameter in mothers of premature infants," by C. Hadnagy, et al. THER GGW 110:1511-1512 passim, October, 1971.

"Ethics and population limitation," by D. Callahan. SCIENCE 175: 487-494, February 4, 1972.

"The ethics of abortion," by J. Fletcher. CLIN OBSTET GYNECOL 14:1124-1129, December, 1971.

"The ethics of abortion," by J. Monagle. SOC JUST 65:112-119, July-August, 1972.

"Evacuation of the uterine cavity by vacuum aspiration," by L. V. Castro. REV CHIL OBSTET GINECOL 34:23-32, 1969.

"Evaluation of the immunologic method of determining chorionic gonadotropin in the diagnosis of threatened abortion in its early stages," by V. M. Savitskii, et al. PEDIATR AKUSH GINEKOL 71: 38-40, September-October, 1971.

"Excellent effect of sodium-citrate-EDTA-combination therapy in severe lead poisoning during pregnancy," by K. Abendroth. DTSCH GESUNDHEITSW 26:2130-2131, November 4, 1971.

"Experience in the treatment of septic shock in obstetric practice," by R. Schwarz, et al. AKUSH GINEKOL 47:8-11, November, 1971.

"The experience of two county hospitals in implementation of therapeutic abortion," by J. R. Bragonier, et al. CLIN OBSTET GYNECOL 14:1237-1242, December, 1971.

"Experience with therapeutic abortion clinic. Methods and complications," by R. Egdell. DEL MED J 44:207-212, August, 1972.

"Experience with the use of promedol in anesthesia for artifical abortion," by Z. P. Drozdovskaia, et al. AKUSH GINEKOL 47:61-62, December, 1971.

"Experiences in the therapy of spontaneous and habitual abortions with the oral administration of Gestanon A," by B. Beric, et al. MED PREGL 24:505-507, 1971.

"Experiences with cerclage," by G. Ruzicska, et al. ORV HETIL 112:1628-1631, July 11, 1971.

"Experiences with the insertion of intrauterine contraception pessaries of DANA type immediately after artificial abortion," by K. Poradovsky, et al. CESK GYNEKOL 37:497-499, September, 1972.

"Experiences with the insertion of IUD after artificial abortion," by M. Tichy, et al. CESK GYNEKOL 37:502-503, September, 1972.

"Experimental Brucella ovis infection in ewes. 1. Breeding performance of infected ewes," by K. L. Hughes. AUST VET J 48:12-17, January, 1972.

"Experimental vibrio infections in sheep," by M. A. Luchko, et al. VETERINARIIA 48:72-73, June, 1972.

"Experiments and the unborn child," by N. St. John-Stevas. TABLET 226:514, June 3, 1972.

"Eugenic abortion," by C. P. Kindregan. SUFFOLK U L REV 6:405, Spring, 1972.

"Factors affecting gestational age at therapeutic abortion," by I. Chalmers, et al. LANCET 1:1324-1326, June 17, 1972.

"Factors associated with delay in seeking induced abortions," by M. B. Bracken, et al. AM J OBSTET GYNECOL 113:301-309, June 1, 1972.

"Factors associated with instillation-abortion time during saline-instillation abortion," by M. B. Bracken, et al. AM J OBSTET GYNECOL 114:10-12, September 1, 1972.

"Factors responsible for delay in obtaining interruption of pregnancy," by G. B. Mallory, Jr., et al. OBSTET GYNECOL 40:556-562, October, 1972.

"Failure of dietary supplementation to prevent the abortions and congenital malformations of lathyrism and locoism in sheep," by R. F. Keeler, et al. CAN J COMP MED 35:342-345, October, 1971.

"Family planning and abortion," LANCET 2:748-749, October 7, 1972.

"Family planning and abortion," by D. Munday. LANCET 2:1308, December 16, 1972.

"Family planning and abortion," by M. Simms. LANCET 2:1085, November 18, 1972.

"Family planning in health services," WHO (World Health Organ) CHRON 26:73-79, February, 1972.

"Fatal embolism following abortion and surgery," by E. S. Redfield, et al. JAMA 220:1745-1746, June 26, 1972.

"Fecundity and high risk pregnancy," by D. S. F. Garnot. REV FR GYNECOL OBSTET 67:235-238, April, 1972.

"Federal court in New York invalidates order banning abortions for indigents under Medicaid," HOSPITALS 46:25, September 16, 1972.

"Federal judges rule abortion ads mailable," ED & PUB 105:12, October 7, 1972.

"Fee charged for the artificial interruption of pregnancy," by K. Jiratko. CESK GYNEKOL 37:586, October, 1972.

"Fee charged for the interruption of pregnancy," by V. Kelensky. CESK GYNEKOL 37:585-586, October, 1972.

"Fertility control through abortion: an assessment of the period 1950-

1980," by C. Dierass. BULLETIN OF THE ATOMIC SCIENTISTS 28,1:9-14, 41-45, January, 1972.

"Fertility effects of the abolition of legal abortion in Romania," by M. S. Teitelbaum. POPULATION STUDIES 26:405-417, November, 1972.

"The fertility response to abortion reform in eastern Europe: demographic and economic implications," by R. J. McIntyre. AM ECONOMIST 16:45-65, Fall, 1972.

"Fetal blood typing after induced abortion," by S. Shah, et al. OBSTET GYNECOL 40:724-727, November, 1972.

"Fetal indiactions for therapeutic abortion," by A. C. Christakos. NC MED J 33:115-119, February, 1972.

"Fetal wastage and maternal mosaicism," by L. Y. Hsu, et al. OBSTET GYNECOL 40:98-103, July, 1972.

"Fetus exitus," MD 16:261 plus, April, 1972.

"Fever and bacteremia associated with hypertonic saline abortion," by C. R. Steinberg, et al. OBSTET GYNECOL 39:673-678, May, 1972.

"Fever as a cause of abortion," by F. Dietzel, et al. MED KLIN 67: 387-390, March 17, 1972.

"Fight for life: Missouri, March 8, 1972, Missouri House Bill 1470; statements to the Committee on Civil and Criminal Procedures," by J. Doyle, et al. SOC JUST 65:89-94, June, 1972.

"Figures and fetuses; findings of New York TV surveys," by R. J. Neuhaus. COMMONWEAL 97:175-178, November 24, 1972.

"Figlu test in habitual abortion and missed abortion," by O. Sacco, et al. ARCH OSTET GINECOL 75:484-491, December, 1970.

"Findings of the Committee on Legal Abortion," by L. Pekhlivanov. AKUSH GINEKOL (Sofiia) 10:279-283, 1971.

"Florida abortion law--reform or regression in 1972," U FLA L REV

24:346, Winter, 1972.

"Florida's century-old antiabortion law declared unconstitutional," HOSPITALS 46:43, March 1, 1972.

"The fluorescent antibody technique in the diagnosis of equine rhinopneumonitis virus abortion," by I. M. Smith, et al. CAN J COMP MED 36:303-308, July, 1972.

"Folic acid deficiency and abruptio placentae," by M. H. Hall. J OBSTET GYNAECOL BR COMMONW 79:222-225, March, 1972.

"Follow-up of patients recommended for therapeutic abortion," by N. A. Todd. BR J PSYCHIATRY 120:645-646, June, 1972.

"For defence of life in the mother's womb," OR 8(204)9-10, February 24, 1972.

"Forane increases bleeding in therapeutic suction abortion," by W. M. Dolan, et al. ANESTHESIOLOGY 36:96-97, January, 1972.

"Four years' experience with mid-trimester abortion by amnioinfusion," by C. A. Ballard, et al. AM J OBSTET GYNECOL 114:575-581, November 1, 1972.

"Fractionated analysis of human chorionic gonadotropins and ultrasonic studies. Supplementary methods for the diagnosis and differential diagnosis of abortions," by H. Wallner, et al. Z ALLGEMEINMED 48:75-79, January 20, 1972.

"France; the power to start and end a life," ECONOMIST 245:45, December 2, 1972.

"Free abortions for all? Report of Commission on Population Growth and the American Future," TIME 99:71, March 27, 1972.

"The freedom and the responsibility," by D. E. Gray. J KANS MED SOC 73:32-34, January, 1972.

"Freedom of choice concerning abortion (pronouncement, United Church of Christ, 8th General Synod," SOC ACT 38:9-12, September, 1971.

"Freeing the prisoners: campaign for legal abortion goes on," TIME 99:89-90, March 20, 1972.

"Freestanding abortion clinics," by C. Tietze. N ENGL J MED 286: 432, February 24, 1972.

"The future of the abortion act," by M. Simms. MIDWIVES CHRON 85:6-10, January, 1972.

"The future of therapeutic abortions in the United States," by R. E. Hall. CLIN OBSTET GYNECOL 14:1149-1153, December, 1971.

"Geburtenregelung und Abtreibung," by H. Modesto-Niederhuber. ENTSCHLUSS 168-173, January, 1972.

"The general practitioner and the Abortion Act," J R COLL GEN PRACT 22:543-546, August, 1972.

"Georgia board rules Medicaid will cover abortion fees," RN 35:19, March, 1972.

"Governor signs Connecticut's new abortion law," HOSPITALS 46: 25, June 16, 1972.

"Greatness of the unborn child," by M. Gervais. CATH HOSP 2:7, September, 1971.

"Gynaecological aftermaths of the 1967 Abortion Act," by M. Brudenell. PROC R SOC MED 65:155-158, February, 1972.

"Gynecologist: abortion--a decision between the woman and her physician," by N. G. Holmberg. LAKARTIDNINGEN 68:5845-5848, December 8, 1971.

"The gynecologist and the problem of therapeutic abortion," by J. P. Pundel. GYNECOL PRAT 23:9-16, 1972.

"Habitual abortion and toxoplasmosis. Is there a relationship?" by P. M. Southern, Jr. OBSTET GYNECOL 39:45-47, January, 1972.

"Half favor easier abortion, poll says," NAT CATH REP 8:24, March 17, 1972.

"Harmfulness of the interruption of pregnancy in primigravidae," by K. Balak. CESK GYNEKOL 37:585, October, 1972.

"Has legal abortion contributed to U.S. 'birth dearth'?" FAM PLANN PERSPECT 4:7-8, April, 1972.

"Has life ceased to be precious," by E. Job. RANF REV 3:4-5, January, 1972.

"Hazard of saline abortion," by N. R. Kaplan. JAMA 221:89, July 3, 1972.

"Health visitors and birth control advice 1970/1971," by M. Waite. NURSING TIMES 68:157-159, October 12, 1972; 161-164, October 19, 1972.

"Hemotherapeutic safeguarding of induced abortion in inborn proconvertin insufficiency (hemagglutination factor VII) using exchange plasmapheresis," by S. Valnicek, et al. ZENTRALBL GYNAEKOL 94:931-935, July 22, 1972.

"High court hears cases on abortion," NAT CATH REP 8:18, October 20, 1972.

"High-dose intravenous administration of prostaglandin E 2 and F 2 for the termination of midtrimester pregnancies," by K. Hillier, et al. J OBSTET GYNAECOL BR COMMONW 79:14-22, January, 1972.

"Histamine reactivity of the skin in women with habitual abortion," by B. Kiutukchiev, et al. AKUSH GINEKOL (Sofiia) 11:31-36, 1972.

"A histological study of the effect on the placenta of intra-amniotically and extra-amniotically injected hypertonic saline in therapeutic abortion," by B. Gustavii, et al. ACTA OBSTET GYNECOL SCAND 51: 121-125, 1972.

"Histopathology of abortion. Study of 256 cases," by E. A. Ceron GYNECOL OBSTET MEX 31:617-623, June, 1972.

"Hormone levels during prostaglandin F 2 infusions for therapeutic abortion," by L. Speroff, et al. J CLIN ENDOCRINOL METAB 34: 531-536, March, 1972.

"Hormone therapy of threatened abortion," by S. Stojanov. ZENTRALBL GYNAEKOL 94:1323-1326, October 7, 1972.

"Hospital opposing abortions returns Hill-Burton money: Mercy Hospital in New Orleans," HOSPITALS 46:147, June 1, 1972.

"How safe is abortion?" by J. S. Metters, et al. LANCET 1:197-198, January 22, 1972.

"How safe is abortion?" by A. S. Moolgaoker. LANCET 1:264, January 29, 1972.

"How safe is abortion?" by S. V. Sood. LANCET 1:380, February 12, 1972.

"How safe is abortion?" by C. Tietze, et al. LANCET 1:198, January 22, 1972.

"Hysterectomy for therapeutic abortion with sterilization," by C. Grumbrecht, et al. GEBURTSHILFE FRAUENHEILKD 32:205-208, March, 1972.

"The identification of Mortierella wolfii isolated from cases of abortion and pneumonia in cattle and a search for its infection source," by M. E. Di Menna, et al. RES VET SCI 13:439-442, September, 1972.

"Il diritto a nascere," REGNO 128-129, March 1, 1972.

"Il diritto a nascere," by D. Tettamanzi. PRESENZA PASTORALE 207-241, 1972.

"I.M.A. and A.I.M.L.A.," by S. Raichaudhury. J INDIAN MED ASSOC 57:467, December 16, 1971.

"Immediate morbidity on large abortion service. The first year's experience," by L. A. Walton. NY STATE J MED 72:919-921, April 15, 1972.

"Immediate postabortal intrauterine contraceptive device insertion: a double-blind study," by A. Goldsmith, et al. AM J OBSTET GYNECOL 112:957-962, April 1, 1972.

"Immunologic indices and serum protein fractions in patients with peritonitis and sepsis following non-hospital abortions," by N. N. Kulikova, et al. AKUSH GINEKOL 47:14-18, November, 1971.

"The impact of the Abortion Act: a psychiatrist's observations," by R. G. Priest. BR J PSYCHIATRY 121:293-299, September, 1972.

"The impact of abortion on maternal and perinatal mortality rates," by J. R. Evrard. AM J OBSTET GYNECOL 113:415-418, June 1, 1972.

"Impact of legalized abortion laws on private practice," by W. O. Duck. J FLORIDA MED ASS 59:41-43, November, 1972.

"The impact of recent changes in therapeutic abortion laws," by J. B. Kahn, et al. CLIN OBSTET GYNECOL 14:1130-1148, December, 1971.

"Implementation of the abortion Act: report on a year's working of abortion clinics and operating sessions," by A. E. Buckle, et al. BR MED J 3:381-384, August 12, 1972.

"Implementation of legal abortion: a national problem. Epilogue," by J. R. Marshall. CLIN OBSTET GYNECOL 14:1336-1338, December, 1971.

"Implementation of therapeutic abortion in the Kaiser Hospital-Southern California Permanente medical group," by A. Saltz. CLIN OBSTET GYNECOL 14:1230-1236, December, 1971.

"In center of latest dispute on abortion: Nixon, Rockefellers," U S NEWS 72:50, May 22, 1972.

"Incidence of abortion in a group of young patients with rheumatic cardiopathy," by R. M. Del Bosque, et al. GINECOL OBSTET MEX 32:167-171, August, 1972.

"Incidence of chromosome abnormalities in spontaneous abortion and study of the risk in subsequent pregnancies," by J. G. Boue. REV FR GYNECOL OBSTET 67:183-187, February-March, 1972.

"Incidence of congenital transmission of Chagas' disease in abortion," by A. L. Bittencourt, et al. REV INST MED TROP SAO PAULO 14: 257-259, July-August, 1972.

"Inconsistency or misunderstanding?" by H. S. Morris. CAN MED ASSOC J 106:857-858, April 22, 1972.

"Increasing consumer participation in professional goal setting: contraception and therapeutic abortion," by R. W. Tichauer, et al. J AM MED WOMENS ASSOC 27:365 passim, July, 1972.

"Indiana Supreme Court upholds state abortion law," by M. McKernan, Jr. SOC JUST 65:197-199, October, 1972.

"Indication and contraindication for interruption of pregnancy in skin diseases," by H. Schleicher, et al. DERMATOL MONATSSCHR 157:599-607, August, 1971.

"Induced abortion and marriage counseling in epilepsy," by F. Rabe MED WELT 23:330-331, March 4, 1972.

"Induced abortion and marriage counseling in multiple sclerosis," by R. C. Behrend. MED WELT 23:326-330, March 4, 1972.

"Induced abortion and marriage counseling in myasthenia," by H. G. Mertens. MED WELT 23:332-335, March 4, 1972.

"Induced abortion in the United States, 1971," by R. E.Hall. J REPROD MED 8:345-347, June, 1972.

"Induction of abortion by extra-amniotic administration of prostaglandins E2 and F2-alpha," by M. P. Embrey, et al. BR MED J 3: 146-149, July 15, 1972.

"Induction of abortion using prostaglandin F 2," by F. F. Lehmann, et al. GEBURTSHILFE FRAUENHEILKD 32:477-483, June, 1972.

"Induction of labour. Recent developments," by M. O. Pulkkinen. ANN CHIR GYNAECOL FENN 61:47-51, 1972.

"Infectious abortions of Leptospira origin in cattle," by J. Vosta, et al. VET MED 16:683-688, December, 1971.

"Infectious bovine rhinotracheitis virus-induced abortion: rapid diagnosis by fluorescent antibody technique," by D. E. Reed, et al. AM J VET RES 32:1423-1426, December, 1971.

"The influence of an anti-steroidogenic drug (aminoglutethimide phosphate) on pregnancy maintenance," by S. R. Glasser, et al. ENDOCRINOLOGY 90:1363-1370, May, 1972.

"The influence of some infectious diseases on the conceptus in northern Finland. A study based on routine serological investigation," by J. Kokkonen, et al. ANN CLIN RES 4:178-182, June, 1972.

"Influences on health professionals' attitudes," by J. P. Bourne. HOSPITALS 46:80-83, July 16, 1972.

"In-hospital care and post-hospital followup," by L. M. Tanner, et al. CLIN OBSTET GYNECOL 14:1278-1288, December, 1971.

"Injury to the kidney during paranephric blockade," by A. Kh. Zaval'niuk. SUD MED EKSPERT 15:58-59, April-June, 1972.

"Innocent human life must be protected," by J. J. Brennan. WIS MED J 71:20, August, 1972.

"Insertion of IUD after artificial interruption of pregnancy," by M. Uher, et al. CESK GYNEKOL 37:501-502, September, 1972.

"Interim report on the joint program for the study of abortion," by C. Tietze, et al. CLIN OBSTET GYNECOL 14:1317-1335, December, 1971.

"The interrelationship between sex hormone excretion and the concentration of copper, manganese, zinc, and cobalt in the placentas of women with normal and prematurely interrupted pregnancies," by P. I. Fogel. AKUSH GINEKOL 47:45-48, August, 1971.

"Interruption of late term pregnancy by intra-amnion administration of hypertonic solutions," by K. I. Braginskii. AKUSH GINEKOL 48:61-62, May, 1972.

"Interruption of late term pregnancy by intra-amnion transcervical administration of a hypertonic solution of sodium chloride," by G. A. Palladi, et al. AKUSH GINEKOL 48:58-61, May, 1972.

"Interruption of pregnancy--for and against," by H. Lochmuller. MUNCH MED WOCHENSCHR 114:1557-1560, September 15, 1972.

"Interruption of pregnancy for urological indications," by K. Geza. ORV HETIL 113:2045-2050, August 20, 1972.

"Interruption of pregnancy in the 1st trimester under neuroleptoanalgesia," by R. Muzelak, et al. CESK GYNEKOL 37:79-80, March, 1972.

"Interruption of pregnancy in women with mitral stenosis," by V. Irasek. AKUSH GINEKOL (Sofiia) 11:41-45, 1972.

"Interruption of pregnancy using F2 alpha prostaglandins," by T. Brat, et al. J GYNECOL OBSTET BIOL REPROD 1:385-387, June, 1972.

"Intra-amniotic administration of prostaglandin F 2 for abortion," by A. C. Wentz, et al. AM J OBSTET GYNECOL 113:793-803, July 15, 1972.

"Intracranial dural sinus thrombosis following intrauterine instillation of hypertonic saline," by J. A. Goldman. AM J OBSTET GYNECOL 112:1132-1133, April 15, 1972.

"Intrauterine administration of 15 (S)-15-methyl-prostaglandin F 2 for induction of abortion," by M. Bygdeman, et al. LANCET 1:1336-1337, June 17, 1972.

"Intravenous prostaglandin F 2 for therapeutic abortion," by E. J. Kirshen, et al. AM J OBSTET GYNECOL 113:340-344, June 1, 1972.

"Intravenous prostaglandin F2 for therapeutic abortion: the efficacy and tolerance of three dosage schedules," by W. E. Brenner. AM J OBSTET GYNECOL 113:1037-1045, August 15, 1972.

"Introduction of a bill for new regulations for pregnancy interruption," TIJDSCHR ZIEKENVERPL 25:784-785, July 25, 1972.

"Is abortion black genocide?" by M. Treadwell. FAM PLANN PERSPECT 4:4-5, January, 1972.

"Is abortion murder?" by R. E. Groves. NURS TIMES 68:624-625, May 18, 1972.

"Is the individual life still the highest value? (A gynecologist's thoughts on abortion and sterilization)," by H. Wagner. MED MONATSSCHR 26:303-307, July, 1972.

"Is there any justification for abortion?" by F. P. Doyle. CATH

HOSP 3:8-11, September, 1972.

"Isolation of an OLT group virus from sheep with enzootic abortions," by Kh. Z. Gaffarov, et al. VETERINARIIA 7:109-111, 1971.

"Isolation of a strain of infectious bovine rhinotracheitis virus from aborted fetuses," by Y. Shimizu, et al. NATL INST ANIM HEALTH Q 12:110-111, Summer, 1972.

"Issues of conscience," by T. M. Schorr. AM J NURS 72:61, January, 1972.

"Isthmico-cervical insufficiency as a factor in prematurity (late abortions and premature labor) and its surgical treatment," by R. Tokin. AKUSH GINEKOL (Sofiia) 8:169-177, 1969.

"Joint program for the study of abortion (JPSA): early medical complications of legal abortion," by C. Tietze, et al. STUDIES IN FAMILY PLANNING 3:97-122, June, 1972.

"Judge backs defender of fetus," NAT CATH REP 8:4, January 14, 1972.

"Kansas opponents fail to modify abortion law," HOSPITALS 46:182, March 1, 1972.

"The Karman catheter: a preliminary evaluation as an instrument for termination of pregnancies up to twelve weeks of gestation," by B. Beric, et al. AM J OBSTET GYNECOL 114:273-275, September 15, 1972.

"Ketamine for dilatation and currettage procedures: patient acceptance," by W. H. Hervey, et al. ANESTH ANALG 51:647-655, July-August, 1972.

"A key battle: outcome of next Tuesday (November 7, 1972)'s abortion referendum in Michigan will likely have national implications," by W. Mossberg. WALL ST J 180:30, November 3, 1972.

"Konflikt zwischen Katholiken und Sozialisten? Auseinandersetzung um das Abtreibungsstrafrecht in Osterreich," HERDER KORRESPONDENZ 278-281, 1972.

"L'aborto come ideologia," by G. Campanini. PRESENZA PASTORALE 243-253, 1972.

"L'avortement sur demande: des chiffres et des faits," by M. Marcotte. RELATIONS 374:242-247, September, 1972.

"La disumanita dell'aborto e il diritto," by S. Lener, S.J. CIVILTA CATTOLICA 128-144, January 15, 1972.

"Lactation following therapeutic abortion with prostaglandin F 2," by I. D. Smith, et al. NATURE (London) 240:411-412, December 15, 1972.

"Laminaria-metreurynter method of midterm abortion in Japan," by Y. Manabe, et al. OBSTET GYNECOL 40:612-615, October, 1972.

"Laminaria tent as a cervical dilator prior to aspiration-type therapeutic abortion," by C. J. Eaton, et al. OBSTET GYNECOL 39:535-537, April, 1972.

"Laminaria tent: relic of the past or modern medical device?" by B. W. Newton. AM J OBSTET GYNECOL 113:442-448, June 15, 1972.

"Large majority of public supports liberalization of abortion laws," GALLUP OPINION INDEX 13-15, September, 1972.

"Law on abortion," by M. A. Duffy. PENN BA Q 43:212, January, 1972.

"Le droit a la vie . . . . doit etre laisse a chacun," by L. Fortier. J CAN BA 3:23, October, 1972.

"Le droit de naitre; document du Conseil permanent de la Conference episcopale italienne sur l'avortement," DOC CATH 69:312-314, April 2, 1972.

"Legal abortion," by J. Lavoie. CAN MED ASSOC J 106:855 passim, April 22, 1972.

"Legal abortion," by J. D. Williamson. BR MED J 3:349-350, August 5, 1972.

"Legal abortion--the act and its effects, Part 1," by A. Hordern. MIDWIFE HEALTH VISIT 8:121-124, April, 1972.

"Legal abortion--the act and its effects, 2," by A. Hordern. MIDWIFE HEALTH VISIT 8:169-173, May, 1972.

"Legal abortion and the hospital's role," by E. B. Connell. HOSP PRACT 7:143-150, February, 1972.

"Legal abortion: a critical assessment of its risks," by J. A. Stallworthy. LANCET 2:1245-1249, December 4, 1971.

"Legal abortion effect seen long-term," AMER MED NEWS 15:12, January 17, 1972.

"Legal abortion: how safe? how available? how costly?" CONSUMER REP 37:466-470, July, 1972.

"Legal abortions: early medical complications. An interim report of the joint program for the study of abortion," by C. Tietze, et al. J REPROD MED 8:193-204, April, 1972.

"Legal induced abortion," by K. Kristoffersen. UGESKR LAEGER 134:403-404, February 21, 1972.

"Legal induced abortion. The first year under the new abortion law," by J. G. Lauritsen, et al. UGESKR LAEGER 134:405-410, February 21, 1972.

"Legal rights of the unborn," by W. W. McWhirter. ARIZ MED 29:926-929, December, 1972.

"Legalized abortion; reprint from The Missoulian January 31, 1971," by C. Brooke. C MIND 70:24-34, May, 1972.

"Let the day perish . . .," by M. J. Frazer. CATHOL NURSE 2-5, Autumn, 1972.

"Lethal chromosome abnormalities in the antenatal and perinatal stages of human development," by M. A. Petrov-Maslakov, et al. VESTN AKAD MED NAUK SSSR 27:68-77, 1972.

"Letter to Cardinal Cooke: President Nixon condemns abortion," by R. Nixon. OR 20(216)3, May 18, 1972.

"Liberalization of abortions and female sterilizations," by D. M. Potts.

CAN MED ASSOC J 105:901, November, 1971.

"Liberalized abortion: devastation--preservation," AORN J 15:91-106, April, 1972.

"The liberation of women from unwanted pregnancy," by S. L. Israel. CLIN OBSTET GYNECOL 14:1113-1123, December, 1971.

"Life and death of the law," by D. J. Keefe. HOSP PROGRESS 53: 64-74, March, 1972.

"Life in the dark age; Governor Rockefeller's veto," CHR CENT 89: 624, May 31, 1972.

"Life; the other choice," by E. Shriver. OSV 61:6, July 16, 1972.

"Lifeline--Can I help you?" by E. Anstice. NURS TIMES 68:1222-1223, September 28, 1972.

"Listeria induced abortion in pigs," by A. Weber, et al. BERL MUNCH TIERAERZTL WOCHENSCHR 85:105-107, March 15, 1972.

"Listeic abortion studies in sheep. I. Maternofetal changes," by C. O. Njoku, et al. CORNELL VET 62:608-627, October, 1972.

"Living with the Therapeutic Abortion Act of 1967," by Z. Leavy. CLIN OBSTET GYNECOL 14:1154-1164, December, 1971.

"Major surgery for abortion and sterilization," by H. Schulman. OBSTET GYNECOL 40:738-739, November, 1972.

"Male view in abortion surveyed," US MED 8:19, December 15, 1972.

"Management of recurring abortion," by H. C. McLaren. PRACTITIONER 209:661-664, November, 1972.

"Management of threatened abortion and premature delivery with Duvadilan and Dilatol," by P. Hengst, et al. Z AERZTL FORTBILD 65:850-854, August 15, 1971.

"Management of uterine perforations suffered at elective abortion," by B. N. Nathanson. AM J OBSTET GYNECOL 114:1054-1059, December 15, 1972.

"Maryland ruling permits abortion referral ads," ADV AGE 43:21, January 3, 1972.

"Mass-produced, assembly-line abortion. A prime example of unethical, unscientific medicine," by J. H. Ford. CALIF MED 117:80-84, November, 1972.

"Maternal trauma during pregnancy," by A. T. Fort. MED TRIAL TECH Q 233-242, 1972.

"McHugh: valley of death," NAT CATH REP 8:5, March 24, 1972.

"Medicaid coverage sought for legal Georgia abortions," HOSPITALS 46:116 plus, January 16, 1972.

"Medicaid funds for abortions banned by New York court," HOSPITALS 46:122, May 16, 1972.

"Medical and surgical complications of therapeutic abortions," by G. K. Stewart, et al. OBSTET GYNECOL 40:539-550, October, 1972.

"Medical ethics--malpractice and the conscience of the practitioner," by W. J. Curran. NEW ENGL J MED 285:1306-1307, December 2, 1971.

"Medical problems of abortion among adolescents," by N. Bregun-Dragic. MED PREGL 25:55-56, 1972.

"Memorandum on working of the Abortion Act," OR 6(202)12, February 10, 1972.

"Mental aspects of abortion," by L. Florean, et al. CESK GYNEKOL 37:530-531, September, 1972.

"Methods of therapeutic abortion," by H. Stamm. GEBURTSHILFE FRAUENHEILKD 32:541-547, July, 1972.

"Microbiological findings in cervical and vaginal secretions in threatened pregnancies," by E. Lindner, et al. ZENTRALBL GYNAEKOL 94:449-452, April 8, 1972.

"Mid-trimester abortion," by G. Davis, et al. LANCET 2:1026, November 11, 1972.

"Minors, ObGyn practice and the law," by D. R. Jasinski. HAWAII MED J 31:116, March-April, 1972.

"Miscarriage and abortion. Statistical studies on miscarriage in relation to family development and socioeconomic factors," by H. J. Staemmler, et al. DTSCH MED WOCHENSCHR 97:885-892, June 9, 1972.

"Miscarriage a hazard for OR nurses? research reports say it is!" RN 35:OR/ER13-14, February, 1972.

"Missouri court upholds state's abortion law," HOSPITALS 46:125, November 1, 1972.

"Monosomy 21 in spontaneous abortus," by K. Ohama, et al. HUMANGENETIK 16:267-270, 1972.

"Moral problems in genetic counseling," by J. C. Fletcher. PAST PSYCH 23:47,60, April, 1972.

"Moralists confronting abortion," by A. J. Schaller. VIE MED CAN FR 1:175-181, February, 1972.

"Moraltheologische Uberlegungen zur Abtreibung," by H. Rotter. DIAKONIA 180-185, 1972.

"Morphological study of the placenta in spontaneously interrupted pregnancies," by B. Kiutukchiev, et al. AKUSH GINEKOL (Sofiia) 10:435-439, 1971.

"The morphology and histochemistry of the fetal liver in spontaneous abortion," by G. I. Sibiriakova, et al. VOPR OKHR MATERIN DET 17:62-65, June, 1972.

"Morphology of exfoliated trophoblastic and decidual cells," by G. D. Montanari, et al. MED SCI LAW 11:200-202, October, 1971.

"Motivation in family planning," by S. Lask. NURSING MIRROR 135: 44-46, December 15, 1972.

"Movement for L.I.F.E. -- a revolution in embryo," by M. C. Shumiatcher. CAN MONTH 12,5:13-14, 1972.

"Mr. Abortion," by H. D. Dubin. NEWSWEEK 80:70. November 13, 1972.

"Mt. Carmel Mercy Hospital, Michigan, takes stand on abortion," CATH HOSP 3:8, July, 1972.

"The muddled issue of abortion; interview by H. Cargas," by N. St. John-Stevas. NAT CATH REP 9:7, November 3, 1972.

"Must the fruit of love always be saved?" by L. Kuthy. KRANKENPFLEGE 26:55, February, 1972.

"Mycotic abortion in ewes produced by Aspergillus fumigatus: intravascular and intrauterine inoculation," by A. C. Pier, et al. AM J VET RES 33:349-356, February, 1972.

"Mycotic abortions in cows," by E. P. Kremlev. VETERINARIIA 4: 89-91, April, 1971.

"Myometrial necrosis after therapeutic abortion," by A. C. Wentz, et al. OBSTET GYNECOL 40:315-320, September, 1972.

"NAACOG Statement on Abortion," SUPERV NURSE 3:14, September, 1972.

"NAACOG statement on abortions and sterilizations," JOGN NURS 1:57, June, 1972.

"NACPA on abortion," SOC JUST 65:167-168, September, 1972.

"N.E. area . . . the abortion patient and the nurse," CHRIST NURSE 39-40, April, 1972.

"Need for counseling follows abortions," by J. Wykert. PSYCHIAT NEWS 7:29 plus, February 16, 1972.

"The need for special abortion clinics," by D. Steel. SUNDAY TIMES 16, May 21, 1972.

"New abortion laws and help for nurses," by M. Heiman. AM J PSYCHIATRY 129:360, September, 1972.

"New abortion laws won't change old attitudes," by R. Shafer. MOD

HOSP 118:96-98, February, 1972.

"New abortion method," NAT CATH REP 8:17, August 4, 1972.

"New anti-abortion campaigns launched," HOSP PROGRESS 53:21, January, 1972.

"New antifertility agent--an orally active prostaglandin--ICI 74,205," by A. P. Labhsetwar. NATURE (London) 238:400-401, August 18, 1972.

"New case reporting system for therapeutic abortions introduced," by J. S. Bennett. CAN MED ASS J 106:196-198, January 22, 1972.

"New Catholic hospital code," by C. E. Curran. FAMILY PLANN PERSPECT 4:7-8, July, 1972.

"New Jersey physicians back abortion change," AMER MED NEWS 15:10, July 24, 1972.

"New Jersey's abortion law: an establishment of religion?" RUTGERS L REV 25:452, Spring, 1972.

"New laws bring new approaches. Method for the evaluation of therapeutic abortion candidates meets the requirements of California state law and the needs of patients, while conserving the time of the medical staff," by S. Loos, et al. HOSPITALS 46:76-79, July 16, 1972.

"A new method for interruption of pregnancy after the 3rd month," by R. Raichev, et al. AKUSH GINEKOL (Sofiia) 8:93-94, 1969.

"New perspectives on abortion reform," by R. B. Benjamin. WIS MED J 71:10-11, June, 1972.

"New standards for legal abortion in DDR," MED WELT 23:Suppl:37 January 29, 1972.

"New study reveals who gets legal abortions and how it's done: New York," MOD HOSP 118:47, February, 1972.

"New trends in legal abortion," by P. Kestelman. LANCET 2:1307-1308, December 16, 1972.

"New trends in therapeutic abortion," by S. L. Barron. LANCET 2: 1193, December 2, 1972.

"New trends in therapeutic abortion," by R. G. Priest. LANCET 2: 1085, November 18, 1972.

"New York State obstetricians and the new abortion law: physician experience with abortion techniques," by S. M. Wassertheil-Smoller, et al. AM J OBSTET GYNECOL 113:979-986, August 1, 1972.

"A New Yorker looks at abortion," by N. Sharkey. ST ANTH 79:10-14, February, 1972.

"New York's abortion fighters," by E. Westenhaver. NAT CATH REP 8:1 plus, February 25, 1972.

"New York's abortion law upheld by appeals court," HOSPITALS 46: 214, April 1, 1972.

"New York's abortion reform law: unanswered questions," by V. N. Duin. ALBANY L REV 37:22, 1972.

"New York's obstetricians surveyed on abortion," by R. C. Lerner, et al. FAM PLANN PERSPECT 3:56, January, 1971.

"Newer possibilities of tocolytic treatment in obstetrics," by K. H. Mosler, et al. Z GEBURTSHILFE PERINATOL 176:85-96, April, 1972.

"Newfoundland doctors concerned over abortion curb at Grace Hospital, St. John's," CAN HOSP 49:17, May, 1972.

"Newspeak wins in abortion; One-issue talk may self-defeat," AMERICA 127:305, October 21, 1972.

"Nigerian bishops condemn abortion," OR 20(216)3-4, May 18, 1972.

"Nine demographic factors and their relationship to attitudes toward abortion legalization," by D. S. Mileti, et al. SOC BIOL 19:43-50, March, 1972.

"Nixon on abortion," NAT R 24:570, May 26, 1972.

"Nixon vs. Rockefeller: the politics of abortion," by P. Hoffman. NATION 214:712-713, June 5, 1972.

"No 'unwanted child,' but 'unloving parent'," by Cardinal J. F. Dearden. CATH HOSP 3:8, March, 1972.

"Nocardia asteroides associated with swine abortion," by J. R. Cole, Jr., et al. VET MED SMALL ANIM CLIN 67:496 passim, May, 1972.

"Non-consentual destruction of the fetus: abortion or homicide?" UCLA-ALASKA L REV 1:80, Fall, 1971.

"Nonresidents have most N. Y. abortions," NAT CATH REP 8:21, March 10, 1972.

"N.O.P.: abortion survey," NEW HUMANIST 88:30-31, May, 1972.

"Nos ventres sont a nous -- avortement sur demande et feminisme de choc," by M. Marcotte. RELATIONS 376:299-303, November, 1972.

"Notes on moral theology; September 1970-March, 1971; abortion," by R.H. Springer. TH ST 32:483-487, September, 1971.

"Now I understand abortion," by R. Scheiber. OSV 61:5, July 16, 1972.

"Nurses and lawyer fight end of abortion restrictions: Santa Barbara, California," HOSP PROGRESS 53:19, February, 1972.

"Nurses Association of the American College of Obstetricians and Gynecologists takes stand on abortion," AMER J NURSING 72:1311, July, 1972.

"Nurses talk about abortion," by H. Branson. AM J NURS 72:106-109, January, 1972.

"OBG . . . abortion, family planning programs among major ACOG meeting topics," by C. Tietze. HOSP TOP 50:41-43, July, 1972.

"Observations on health care instructions given to pregnant women. Survey of women with past history of abortion," by M. Nohara. JAP J PUBLIC HEALTH NURSE 28:48-54, January, 1972.

"Observations on Leptospira hardjo infection in New South Wales," by R. J. Hoare, et al. AUST VET J 48:228-232, May, 1972.

"Obstacles to progress in family planning," by M. J. Ball. CAN MED ASS J 106:227 plus, February 5, 1972.

"Obstetrical nurses propose abortion policy," AMER MED NEWS 15:15, June 19, 1972.

"Obstetricians and legal abortions in San Francisco," by B. Behrstock, et al. CALIF MED 117:29-31, September, 1972.

"Of doctors, deterrence, and the dark figure of crime -- a note on abortion in Hawaii," by F. E. Zimring. U CHI L REV 39:699, Summer, 1972.

"Oklahoma abortion survey tabulation completed," J OKLA STATE MED ASS 65:465-466, November, 1972.

"On abortion," by P. O'Boyle. OR 40(236)9-10, October 5, 1972.

"On going to jail," by L. Bozell. TRIUMPH 7:31, January, 1972, February 21, 1972, and March 19, 1972.

"On responsibility for children not yet born," OR 12(208)8, March 23, 1972.

"On the subject of abortion: Massachusetts," by C. Moynahan. SOC JUST 65:49-53, May, 1972.

"On the uterine etiology of suspicious deaths in young women," by J. Caroff, et al. MED LEG DOMM CORPOR 4:267-272, July-September, 1971.

"Open legal abortion 'on request' is working in New York City, but is it the answer?" by A. I. Weisman. AM J OBSTET GYNECOL 112: 138-143, January 1, 1972.

"Options of the single pregnant woman," by D. D. Wachtel. R RADICAL POL ECON 4:86-106, July, 1972.

"Our attitude on the insertion of IUD immediately after artificial interruption of pregnancy," by K. Dvorak, et al. CESK GYNEKOL 37:499-501, September, 1972.

"Our experiences in interruption of advanced pregnancy," by A. Milojkovic, et al. MED ARH 26:13-16, January-February, 1972.

"Outpatient abortions," by L. Rauramo. ANN CHIR GYNAECOL FENN 61:45-46, 1972.

"Outpatient management of first trimester therapeutic abortions with and without tubal ligation," by J. A. Collins, et al. CAN MED ASSOC J 106:1077-1080, May 20, 1972.

"Ovulation following therapeutic abortion," by E. F. Boyd, Jr., et al. AM J OBSTET GYNECOL 113:469-473, June 15, 1972.

"Oxytocics used by practitioners--with special reference to induced abortions," by K. Sato. SANFUJINKA JISSAI 21:203-208, March, 1972.

"Oxytocin, 'salting out,' and water intoxication," by D. R. Gupta, et al. JAMA 220:681-683, May 1, 1972.

"The paramedic abortionist," by H. Karman. CLIN OBSTET GYNECOL 15:379-387, June, 1972.

"Participation of biogenic amines in the pathogenesis of bacterial shock," by L. S. Persianinov, et al. AKUSH GINEKOL 47:3-7, November, 1971.

"Parts of Kansas abortion statute held unconstitutional," NEWSLETTER (Amer Soc Hosp Attorneys) 5:3-4, May, 1972.

"Past and present," OR 8(204)3, February 24, 1972.

"A pastoral approach to abortion," by J. F.Hickey. J REPROD MED 8:355-358, June, 1972.

"Pastoral letter on abortion; July 26, 1972," by J. Garner. OR 48(244) 3, November 30, 1972.

"Pathomorphology and pathogenesis of streptococcal abortion in cows," by V. Jelev, et al. ZENTRALBL VETERINAERMED 18:610-616, October, 1971.

"Patterns of abortion and contraceptive usage," by D. M. Potts. R SOC HEALTH J 91:294-296, November-December, 1971.

"Perplexities for the would-be liberal in abortion," by A. J. Dyck. J REPROD MED 8:351-354, June, 1972.

"Personal business (abortion)," edited by W. Flanagan. BUS W 65-66, July 22, 1972.

"Personal experience at a legal abortion center," AM J NURS 72:110-112, January, 1972.

"Physicians' attitudes toward abortion," by L. A. LoSciuto, et al. J REPROD MED 9:70-74, August, 1972.

"'Pill,' IUD, sterilization reduce unwanted births," AMER MED NEWS 15:10-11, August 14, 1972.

"Pine-needle (Pinus ponderosa)-induced abortion in range cattle," by A. H. Stevenson, et al. CORNELL VET 62:519-524, October, 1972.

"Placental lactogen levels as guide to outcome of threatened abortion," by P. A. Niven, et al. BR MED J 3:799-801, September 30, 1972.

"Planning family planning," by J. K. Russell. LANCET 1:310-311, February 5, 1972.

"Plasma volume, electrolyte, and coagulation factor changes following intra-amniotic hypertonic saline infusion," by W. E. Easterling, Jr., et al. AM J OBSTET GYNECOL 113:1065-1071, August 15, 1972.

"Policy position on abortion: Canadian Public Health Association," CAN J PUBLIC HEALTH 63:370-371, July-August, 1972.

"Politics of abortion," by S. Alexander. NEWSWEEK 80:29, October 2, 1972.

"The politics of abortion (United States)," by W.M. Hern. PROGRESSIVE 36:26-29, November, 1972.

"Poll says Catholics back abortion," NAT CATH REP 8:6, September 15, 1972.

"Pollution of the operating-theatre suite by anaesthetic gases," by J. Bullough. LANCET 1:1337, June 17, 1972.

"A positive alternative to abortion in England," OR 20(216)3, May 18, 1972.

"Possible guidelines for problem pregnancy counseling," by L. Scott. PAST PSYCH 23:41-49, May, 1972.

"Post-abortion group therapy," by G. M. Burnell, et al. AM J PSYCHIATRY 129:220-223, August, 1972.

"Post abortum acute renal insufficiency treated by daily dialysis," by V. Jovanovic, et al. SRP ARH CELOK LEK 98:1453-1458, December, 1970.

"Postabortum sacroiliac arthritis," by G. Robinet, et al. BULL FED SOC GYNECOL OBSTET LANG FR 23:424-425, September-October, 1971.

"Power to start and end a life," ECONOMIST 245:45, December 2, 1972.

"Preabortion evaluation: decision-making, preparation and referral," by L. M. Tanner, et al. CLIN OBSTET GYNECOL 14:1273-1277, December, 1971.

"Preabortion evaluation: selection of patients for psychiatric referral," by J. R. Bragonier, et al. CLIN OBSTET GYNECOL 14:1263-1270, December, 1971.

"Pre-emptive abortion; menstrual extractions," NEWSWEEK 80:69, July 24, 1972.

"Pregnancy, abortion, and the developmental tasks of adolescence," by C. Schaffer, et al. J AM ACAD CHILD PSYCHIATRY 11:511-536, July, 1972.

"Pregnancy and labor after cerclage," by M. Vitse, et al. BULL FED SOC GYNECOL OBSTET LANG FR 23:425-426, September-October, 1971.

"Pregnancy and labor in women with ABO incompatibility," by A. B. Saturaksia. AKUSH GINEKOL 47:51-53, August, 1971.

"Pregnancy damage and birth-complications in the children of paraplegic women," by H. Goller, et al. PARAPLEGIA 10:213-217, November, 1972.

"Pregnancy interruption. What is my function as a nurse?" by C. Guller. Z KRANKENPFL 65:173-174, May, 1972.

"Pregnancy interruption and origin of extrauterine pregnancy," by A. Cernoch. CAS LEK CESK 111:285-287, March 24, 1972.

"Pregnancy interruption due to polyneuritis," by G. K. Kohler, et al. MED WELT 23:1762-1766, November 18, 1972.

"Pregnancy interruption from the radiologist's viewpoint," by V. Bohringer. RADIOL DIAGN 13:187-191, 1972.

"Pregnancy termination: the impact of new laws. An invitational symposium," J REPROD MED 6:274-301, June, 1971.

"Prehumane, humane, posthumane and inhumane human life," by W. S. Stekhoven. TIJDSCHR ZIEKENVERPL 25:674-676, June 27, 1972.

"Prelinimary attempts to terminate pregnancy by immunological attack on uterine protein," by J. C. Daniel, Jr. EXPERIENTIA 28:700-701, June 15, 1972.

"Premature placental detachment: physiopathology and therapeutic management," by B. Neme. MATERN INFANC 30:127-134, April-June, 1971.

"Prenatal diagnosis of genetic disease," by T. Friedmann. SCI AM 225:34-42, November, 1971.

"Prenatal losses in border Leicester-Merino cross ewes in Victoria," by D. J. Cannon, et al. AUST VET J 47:323-325, July, 1971.

"Preparing students for abortion care," by D. Malo-Juvera. NURS J INDIA 63:223-224 plus, July, 1972.

"President Nixon condemns abortion," by R. Nixon. SOC JUST 65:88, June, 1972.

"Preventing unwanted pregnancies: role of the hospital," by R. J.

Pion. POSTGRAD MED 51:172-175, January, 1972.

"Prevention of pregnancy and pregnancy interruption," by E. Erb. Z KRANKENPFL 65:167-170, May, 1972.

"Prevention of pregnancy and pregnancy interruption," by A. Trenkel. Z KRANKENPFL 65:170-172, May, 1972.

"Prevention of Rh immunization after abortion with Anti-Rh (D)-immunoglobulin," by J. A. Goldman, et al. OBSTET GYNECOL 40: 366-370, September, 1972.

"Prevention of Rh immunization in abortions," by J. Goldman, et al. HAREFUAH 81:514-515, November 15, 1971.

"Prevention of unwanted pregnancies," by E. F. Daily. AM J OBSTET GYNECOL 113:1148, August 15, 1972.

"Preventive control of the Lesch-Nyhan syndrome," by P. J. Van Heewsijk, et al. OBSTET GYNECOL 40:109-113, July, 1972.

"Preventive treatment of spontaneous abortion, such as it results from the study of mechanism of contraction and relaxation of uterine muscle," by K. Kato, et al. GYNECOL PRAT 23:89-94, 1972.

"The problem of abortion," by J. Williamson. R SOC HEALTH J 92: 85-87 passim, April, 1972.

"The problem of abortion from the medical viewpoint," by H. Husslein. WIEN MED WOCHENSCHR 2:Suppl:3-7, November, 1971.

"Problem pregnancy. A perspective on abortion and the quality of human life," by S. A. Plummer. ROCKY MT MED J 69:64-66, November, 1972.

"Problemi attuali dell'aborto: l'aspetto giuridica," by D. Tettamanzi. RIVISTA DEL CLERO ITALIANO 213-324, 1972.

"Problems of abortion from the radiobiological indication viewpoint," by K. Neumeister, et al. DTSCH GESUNDHEITSW 27:549-553, March 23, 1972.

"Problems of abortion patients after one-day stay studied at Vancouver General Hospital," CAN NURSE 68:16, April, 1972.

"Problems of our population trend and the artificial interruption of pregnancy in practice," by A. Kotasek. CESK GYNEKOL 37:565-568, October, 1972.

"Problems of our population trends and the abortion law in practice," by R. Houdek. CESK GYNEKOL 37:582-583, October, 1972.

"Problems of our population trends and the abortion law in practice," by K. Schmidt, et al. CESK GYNEKOL 37:583-584, October, 1972.

"Procedural due process limitations on state abortion statutes," MARQ L REV 55:137, Winter, 1972.

"The prognostic and therapeutic value of chorionic hormones in the prevention of early abortions," by M. Chartier, et al. REV FR GYNECOL OBSTET 67:203-208, April, 1972.

"Pro-life activities committee set up," NAT CATH REP 9:15, November 24, 1972.

"Prospective study of fertility in the District of Sao Paulo. I. Comparison of retrospective and prospective methods to estimate the rates of spontaneous and induced abortions," by M. L. Milanesi, et al. BOL OF SANIT PANAM 72:234-243, March, 1972.

"Prostaglandin E 2: analysis of effects on pregnancy and corpus luteum in hamsters and rats," by A. P. Labhsetwar. ACTA ENDOCRINOL 170:Suppl:3-32, 1972.

"Prostaglandin-oxytocin enhancement," by M. Seppala, et al. BR MED J 1:747, March 18, 1972.

"Prostaglandin-oxytocin enhancement and potentiation and their clinical applications," by A. Gillespie. BR MED J 1:150-152, January 15, 1972.

"Prostaglandins and abortion," by M. Seppala. DUODECIM 88:1029-1031, 1972.

"Prostaglandins and therapeutic abortion," by P. G. Gillett. J REPROD MED 8:329-334, June, 1972.

"Prostaglandins in fertility control," by J. S. Carrel. SCIENCE 175:1279, March 17, 1972.

"Prostaglandins in human reproduction," by V. Vakhariya, et al. MICH MED 71:777-784, September, 1972.

"Prostaglandins in inducing labour and abortion," by Z. Polishuk. HAREFUAH 80:332-333, March 15, 1971.

"Proteins of the blood serum in patients with pyoseptic diseases following infected abortion (electrophoresis on polyacrylamide gel)," by M. I. Kotliar, et al. AKUSH GINEKOL 48:73-74, March, 1972.

"Proteinuria in toxaemia and abruptio placentae," by P. R. MacLean, et al. J OBSTET GYNAECOL BR COMMONW 79:321-326, April, 1972.

"A Protestant minister's view of abortion," by W. E. Wygant, Jr. JOURNAL OF RELIGION AND HEALTH 269-277, 1972.

"Psychiatric aftermaths of the 1967 Abortion Act," by A. Hordern. PROC R SOC MED 65:158-160, February, 1972.

"Psychiatric aspects of abortion," by A. C. Gullattee. J NATL MED ASSOC 64:308-311, July, 1972.

"Psychiatric complications of therapeutic abortion," by R. O. Pasnau. OBSTET GYNECOL 40:252-256, August, 1972.

"Psychiatrists and abortion," by H. P. Dunn, et al. NZ MED J 74:411-412, December, 1971.

"Psychiatrists' attitudes to abortion," by J. C. Little. BR MED J 1: 110, January 8, 1972.

"Psychologic issues in therapeutic abortion," by C. Nadelson. WOMAN PHYSICIAN 27:12-15, Januray, 1972.

"The psychological antecedent and consequences of abortion," by J. L. Maes. J REPROD MED 8:341-344, June, 1972.

"The psychological reaction of patients to legalized abortion," by J. D. Osofsky, et al. AM J ORTHOPSYCHIATRY 42:48-60, January, 1972.

"Psychological reaction to therapeutic abortion. II. Objective response," by K. R. Niswander, et al. AM J OBSTET GYNECOL 114: 29-33, September 1, 1972.

"Psychosocial aspects of induced abortion. Its implications for the woman, her family and her doctor. 1.," by B. Raphael. MED J AUST 2:35-40, July 1, 1972.

"Psychosocial aspects of induced abortion. Its implications for the woman, her family and her doctor. 2.," by B. Raphael. MED J AUST 2:98-101, July 8, 1972.

"Psychosocial aspects of selective abortion," by E. J. Lieberman. BIRTH DEFECTS 7:20-21, April, 1971.

"Psychosocial sequelae of therapeutic abortion in young unmarried women," by J. S. Wallerstein, et al. ARCH GEN PSYCHIATRY 27:828-832, December, 1972.

"Psychosomatic aspects of the reform of the abortion law (218)," by H. Poettgen. GEBURTSHILFE FRAUENHEILKD 32:493-500, June, 1972.

"Public agency reaches out to women tn crisis," by S. A. MacMullen. PUBLIC WELFARE 30:2-4, Spring, 1972.

"Public health and the law. Presidential morality, abortion, and federal-state law," by W. J. Curran. AM J PUBLIC HEALTH 61: 1042-1043, May, 1971.

"Public health perspective on the limitation of births," by W. B. Jones, Jr., et al. NC MED J 33:688-691, August, 1972.

"Public opinion trends: Elective abortion and birth control services to teenagers," by R. Pomeroy, et al. FAMILY PLANN PERSPECT 4: 44-55, October, 1972.

"Puerperal inflammations and late complications after legal abortions," by A. Cernoch. CAS LEK CESK 111:765-768, August 18, 1972.

"Punishment: the hidden issue in abortion," by F. H. Hoffman. CONSULTANT 12:65-67, July, 1972.

"The putting into effect of the artificial abortion act in Warsaw in the years 1957-1966; an analysis," by K. Waszynski. GINEKOL POL 43:371-376, 1972.

"Q: What, doctor is the difference between you and Adolph Hitler . .," TRIUMPH 7:18-20 plus, February, 1972.

"The quality of life as opposed to the right to life," by H. I. Posin, et al. AM J PSYCHIATRY 129:358-360, September, 1972.

"Question fetus experiments," NAT CATH REP 8:23, March 17, 1972.

"Rcn Congress report. First session: The abortion act. Part 1.," NURS MIRROR 134:9, March 31, 1972.

"Recht auf Leben: Moraltheologische Erwagungen zur Diskussion um Art. 218 StGB," by K. Demmer. THEOLOGIE UND GLAUBE 1-22, 1972.

"Recommended program guide for abortion services: American Public Health Association," AMER J PUBLIC HEALTH 62:1669-1671, December, 1972.

"Reduction in fertility due to induced abortions: a simulation model (India)," by K. Venkatacharya. DEMORGAPHY 9:339-352, August, 1972.

"Reductions in complications due to induced abortions noted," HOSPITALS 46:19, December 1, 1972.

"Reflections on abortion. Research and new solutions," by F. Hanon. REV INFIRM 22:139-145, February, 1972.

"Reflections on legalized abortion," by P. Piraux. INFIRMIERE 49: 24-25, December, 1971.

"Reflexiones sobre el aborto," by A. E. Lopez. RAZON Y FE 143-154, February, 1972.

"Reforming the abortion law," TABLET 226:119-122, February 5, 1972.

"Der Regierungsentwurf zur Reform des Art. 218," HERDER KORRESPONDENZ 110-111, 1972.

"Relationship between placental alkaline phosphatase phenotypes and the frequency of spontaneous abortion in previous pregnancies," by L. Beckman, et al. HUM HERED 22:15-17, 1972.

"Relationship between prevalence of sterilization by surgery and pregnancy, parity and induced abortion," JAP J PUBLIC HEALTH NURSE 27:50-56, December, 1971.

"The relationship of amniotic fluid sodium to the latent period of saline abortion," by H. Schulman, et al. OBSTET GYNECOL 39: 679-682, May, 1972.

"The relaxant and antispasmotic effects of streptidin on smooth muscles," by O. Altinkurt. TURK HIJ TECR BIYOL DERG 30:242-244, 1970.

"Release of prostaglandin F 2 following injection of hypertonic saline for therapeutic abortion: a preliminary study," by B. Gustavii, et al. AM J OBSTET GYNECOL 114:1099-1100, December 15, 1972.

"The renal lesions of toxaemia and abruptio placentae studied by light and electron microscopy," by D. Thomson, et al. J OBSTET GYNAECOL BR COMMONW 79:311-320, April, 1972.

"Repeated abortion. Enzyme and chromosome anomalies in the couple," by J. Grozdea, et al. NOUV PRESSE MED 1:1234, April 29, 1972.

"Repeated early spontaneous abortions and maternal autosomal translocation t(Bq plus, Cq minus)," by A. Broustet, et al. BORD MED 5:669-672, March, 1972.

"Report on therapeutic abortions for fiscal 1971," by J. K. Seegar, Jr. MD STATE MED J 21:32-35, February, 1972.

"Resolving ethical conflicts in a surgical suite in which abortions are performed," AORN J 16:15, September, 1972.

"Respect Life Week in U.S.A.," OR 37(233)4, September 14, 1972.

"Respectable killing, by K. D. Whitehead. A review," by D. W. Cooper. NAT R 24:1415-1416, December 22, 1972.

"Restoration of nidation in aureomycin-treated mice," by D. Boucher.

C R SOC BIOL 163:1131-1134, 1969.

"Results of surgical treatment of cervical incompetence in pregnancy," by F. Glenc, et al. POL TYG LEK 27:834-836, May 29, 1972.

"Results of a year's liberal regulation of abortion in the State of New York," by F. K. Beller. MED WELT 23:471-472, March 25, 1972.

"Retarded embryonic development and pregnancy termination in ovariectomized guinea-pigs: progesterone deficiency and decidual collapse," by R. Deanesly. J REPROD FERTIL 28:241-247, February, 1972.

"Retinal reflectance dye dilution: cardiac output during disseminated embolism and fibrination," by C. L. Schneider, et al. BIBL ANAT 10:592-599, 1969.

"Revised standards on abortion issued by American Public Health Association task force," NATIONS HEALTH 2:1 plus, December, 1972.

"Rhesus sensitization in abortion," by P. S. Gavin. OBSTET GYNECOL 39:37-40, January, 1972.

"Rh-immune globulin in induced abortion: utilization in a high-risk population," by R. G. Judelsohn, et al. AM J OBSTET GYNECOL 114:1031-1034, December 15, 1972.

"Right not to be born," J TENN MED ASS 65:250, March, 1972.

"Right to abortion," TIDSKR SVER SJUKSKOT 39:6-7, February 24, 1972.

"The right to abortion: a psychiatric view," GROUP ADV PSYCHIATRY 7:203-227, October, 1969.

"The right to be born," by E. Shriver. MARRIAGE 54:8-12, June, 1972.

"Right to life," by L. Adams. CATH HOSP 3:2, July, 1972.

"The right to life: the Harvard statement; continued from the Boston Globe, October 29, 1971," by A. Dyck. C DGST 36:29-32, March, 1972.

"Right to life has a message for New York state Legislators," by F. C. Shapiro. N Y TIMES MAG 10-11 plus, August 20, 1972; Discussion 23, September 10, 1972.

"Right to life: new strategy needed," TRIUMPH 7:46, April, 1972.

"Rights of the unborn - - a CAS looks at abortion," by T. T. Daley. CAN WEL 48:19-21, May-June, 1972.

"The rising tide of abortion," by N. St. John-Stevas. TABLET 226:98, February 5, 1972.

"Risk pregnancy in women examined before conception and treated for habitual abortion," by A. Zwinger, et al. CESK GYNEKOL 37:232-233, May, 1972.

"The risks of abortion," CAN MED ASSOC J 106:295-298, February 19, 1972.

"Risks of legal abortion," by R. Goodlin. LANCET 1:97, January 8, 1972.

"Rockefeller vetoes abortion repeal," NAT CATH REP 8:21, May 16, 1972.

"The role of the federal government," by B. Packwood. CLIN OBSTET GYNECOL 14:1212-1224, December, 1971.

"The role of induced abortion in the changing pattern of birth control in the Netherlands," by P. E. Treffers. NED TIJDSCHR GENEESKD 116:1459-1466, August 12, 1972.

"Role of local government in therapeutic abortions," by C. F. Coffelt. CLIN OBSTET GYNECOL 14:1197-1203, December, 1971.

"The role of Planned Parenthood-World Population in abortion," by G. Langmyhr. CLIN OBSTET GYNECOL 14:1190-1196, December, 1971.

"The role of private counseling for problem pregnancies," by J. H. Anwyl. CLIN OBSTET GYNECOL 14:1225-1229, December, 1971.

"The role of the university hospital in solving the logistic problems of legal abortion," by E. W. Overstreet. CLIN OBSTET GYNECOL

14:1243-1247, December, 1971.

"The Royal College of Psychiatrists' memorandum on the Abortion Act in practice," BR J PSYCHIATRY 120:449-451, April, 1972.

"Rubella and medical abortion," by E. Hervet, et al. NOUV PRESSE MED 1:379-380, February 5, 1972.

"Rubella reinfection during early pregnancy: a case report," by R. L. Northrop, et al. OBSTET GYNECOL 38:524-526, April, 1972.

"Rubella serology and abortions in Finland," by T. Vesikari, et al. LANCET 2:1375, December 23, 1972.

"Rubella vaccination and termination of pregnancy," by H. J. Mair, et al. BR MED J 4:271-273, November 4, 1972.

"SA abortion law; its implications on our society," by E. G. Cleary. AUSTRALAS NURSES J 1:12, July, 1972.

"Saline abortion," by E. M. Stim. OBSTET GYNECOL 40:247-251, August, 1972.

"Scores abortion code," NAT CATH REP 8:13, August 18, 1972.

"Scottish abortion statistics - - 1970," HEALTH BULL 30:27-35, January, 1972.

"Second-trimester abortion after vaginal termination," by D. M. Potts. LANCET 2:133, July 15, 1972.

"Second-trimester abortion after vaginal termintaion of pregnancy," by A. J. Margolis, et al. LANCET 2:431-432, August 26, 1972.

"Second-trimester abortion after vaginal termination of pregnancy," by C. S. Wright, et al. LANCET 1:1278-1279, June 10, 1972.

"A secular case against abortion on demand," by R. Stith. COMM 95: 151-154, November 12, 1971; Reply by J. Ducore. 95:468-469, February 18, 1972; Rejoinder 95:469-470, February 18, 1972.

"Seesaw response of a young unmarried couple to therapeutic abortion," by J. Wallerstein, et al. ARCH GEN PSYCHIATRY 27:251-

254, August, 1972.

"Selective abortion, gametic selection, and the X chromosome," by G. R. Fraser. AM J HUM GENET 24:359-370, July, 1972.

"Septic abortion masquerading as thrombotic thrombocytopenic purpura," by M. Yudis, et al. AM J OBSTET GYNECOL 111:350-352, October 1, 1971.

"Septic abortions," by A. Marzuki, et al. MED J MALAYA 26:77-83, December, 1971.

"Serotonin content and excretion of 5-hydroxyindoleacetic acid during threatened abortion at early and late stages," by Z. V. Urazaeva, et al. AKUSH GINEKOL 48:65-66, May, 1972.

"Serum ceruloplamsin, 1 -antitrypsin, 2 -macroglobulin and iron and T 3 binding proteins during hypertonic saline-induced abortion," by K. Willman, et al. ACTA OBSTET GYNECOL SCAND 51:161-163, 1972.

"Serum human chorionic gonadotropin, human chorionic somatomammotropin, and progesterone following intra-amniotic injection of hypertonic urea," by H. R. Raud, et al. AM J OBSTET GYNECOL 113:887-894, August 1, 1972.

"Serum levels of oestradiol-17 dehydrogenase in normal and abnormal pregnancies," by G. Plotti, et al. J OBSTET GYNAECOL BR COMMONW 79:603-611, July, 1972.

"Sex education at Duke: The development, implementation, and expansion of a medical school program," by M. Shangold, et al. BULL AM COLL NURSE MIDWIVES 17:4-10, February, 1972.

"Sexually transmitted diseases," by J. K. Oates. NURS TIMES 68:832-834, July 6, 1972.

"Should abortions be performed in doctors' offices?" by S. Neubardt, et al. FAM PLANN PERSPECT 4:4-7, July, 1972.

"Significance of aerobic vibrios in the etiology of abortions and sterility in cows," by V. F. Shatalov. VETERINARIIA 9:97-99, August, 1971.

"Significance of cervical cerclage for the child," by G. Mau. Z GEBURTSHILFE PERINATOL 176:331-342, August, 1972.

"The significance of fibrinolysis in abortion," by H. Soma. J TOKYO MED COLL 28:343-350, March, 1970.

"Significance of immunologic conflict in the development of pregnancy complications (literature review)," by D. V. Umbrumiants. AKUSH GINEKOL 48:41-46, January, 1972.

"Silicone-plastic cuff for the treatment of the incompetent cervix in pregnancy," by E. E. Yosowitz, et al. AM J OBSTET GYNECOL 113:233-238, May 15, 1972.

"Simultaneous vena cava inferior syndrome and utero-placental apoplexy," by E. Veszely, et al. ORV HETIL 112:2652-2653, October 31, 1971.

"Sixty years age," NURS J INDIA 62:385, December, 1971.

"Slavery and abortion; continued from a press release distributed by Minnesota Citizens Concerned for Life, August 18, 1972," by W. Schaller. C DGST 37:24-26, December, 1972.

"The social effects of legal abortion," by R. A. Schwartz. AM J PUBLIC HEALTH 62:1331-1335, October, 1972.

"Social indication in pregnancy interruption," by W. Becker. THER GGW 111:587-588 passim, April, 1972.

"Social perspectives: abortion and female behavior," by W. P. Nagan. VALPARAISO UNIV LAW R 6:286-314, Spring, 1972.

"Social work service to abortion patients," by A. Ullmann. SOC CASEWORK 53:481-487, October, 1972.

"Society for Developmental Biology backs 'right to abortion'," J AMER MED ASS 221:646, August 14, 1972.

"Some Catholics on abortion," by E. Miller. LIGUORIAN 60:8, October, 1972.

"Some clinical-physiological indices in children born of mothers with habitual abortion," by A. K. Svetlova, et al. VOPR OKHR MATERIN DET 16:64-70, May, 1971.

"Some problems in the evaluation of women for therapeutic abortion," by D. S. Werman, et al. CAN PSYCHIATR ASSOC J 17:249-251, June, 1972.

"Some thoughts on the illegitimate child," by J. M. Lomax-Simpson. HEALTH VISIT 45:66-68, March, 1972.

"Some thoughts on medical evaluation and counseling of applicants for abortion," by A. J. Margolis. CLIN OBSTET GYNECOL 14:1255-1257, December, 1971.

"Sonar in the management of abortion," by H. P. Robinson. J OBSTET GYNAECOL BR COMMONW 79:90-94, January, 1972.

"S.P.U.C.: its people and their sayings," NEW HUMANIST 88:15-17, May, 1972.

"Spontaneous abortion in wild-caught rhesus monkeys, Macaca mulatta," by A. T. Hertig, et al. LAB ANIM SCI 21:510-519, August, 1971.

"Spontaneous abortions in women-carriers of the phenylketonuria gene," by M. G. Bliumina. AKUSH GINEKOL 48:52-55, May, 1972.

"Sporadic triploid and hexaploid cells in embryonic tissue. Negative relationship to maternal intake of oral contraceptives," by T. Kajii, et al. ANN GENET 15:11-18, March, 1972.

"Staff reactions to abortion. A psychiatrist's view," by H. D. Kibel. OBSTET GYNECOL 39:128-133, January, 1972.

"State of the menstrual and child-bearing functions of pregnant women involved in the production of caprolactam," by L. Z. Nadezhdina, et al. GIG TR PROF ZABOL 15:43-44, November, 1971.

"The state of the reproductive systems in women with thyrotoxicosis, before and after pathogenetic treatment," by M. Sh. Sadykova. AKUSH GINEKOL 47:43-46, July, 1971.

"Statement on abortions and sterilizations: Nurses Association of the American College of Obstetricians and Gynecologists," JOGN

NURSING 1:57, June, 1972.

"A statement on abortion by one hundred professors of obstetrics," AM J OBSTET GYNECOL 112:992-993, April 1, 1972.

"A statement on abortion in Victoria," MED J AUST 1:443, February 26, 1972.

"A statement on abortion in Victoria," by J. R. Coulter. MED J AUST 1:32-33, January 1, 1972.

"A statement on abortion in Victoria," by J. R. Coulter. MED J AUST 1:550, March 11, 1972.

"A statement on abortion in Victoria," by L. Hemingway, et al. MED J AUST 1:608, March 18, 1972.

"A statement on abortion in Victoria," by B. A. Smithurst, et al. MED J AUST 1:240-241, January 29, 1972.

"Stellungnahme Munsteraner Theologen zu 218," Z EV ETHIK 15:380-381, November, 1971.

"Stop the death merchants," by L. Bozell. TRIUMPH 7:19, October, 1972, 31, November, 1972, 18-19, December, 1972.

"Straflose Schwangerschaftsunterbrechung?" by P. Kaufmann. REF 21:155-162, March, 1972.

"Study of applicants for abortion at the Royal Northern Hospital, London," by C. Ingham, et al. J BIOSOC SCI 4:351-369, July, 1972.

"Study of cellular immunity in couples with habitual abortion," by J. Gordillo, et al. GINECOL OBSTET MEX 31:325-328, March, 1972.

"Study of maternal mortality," J KY MED ASSOC 70:168, March, 1972.

"A study of Title 19 coverage of abortion," by H. M. Wallace, et al. AM J PUBLIC HEALTH 62:1116-1122, August, 1972.

"Subsequent gestational morbidity after various types of abortion," by D. T. Liu, et al. LANCET 2:431, August 26, 1972.

"Suction curettage," by A. Sikkel. NED TIJDSCHR GENEESKD

116:1757-1758, September 23, 1972.

"Sudden death of feticide," NAT R 24:1407, December 22, 1972.

"Suicide American style: the danger of birth rate decline," by J. Diamond. LIGUORIAN 60:45-49, April, 1972.

"Supreme Court resumes abortion hearings," HOSP PROGRESS 53: 22-23, November, 1972.

"Supreme Court to consider woman's right to abortion," HOSP PROG 53:10-11 plus, March, 1972.

"Surgical management of abortion," by J. F. Palomaki, et al. N ENGL J MED 287:752-754, October, 1972.

"Surgical sterilization and interruption of pregnancy as means of fertility regulation," by W. Dalicho. BEITR GERICHTL MED 29: 344-350, 1972.

"Surgical treatment of abruptio placentae," by J. Kosowsky, et al. ZENTRALBL GYNAEKOL 94:754-756, June 10, 1972.

"Surgical treatment of pregnant women with habitual abortion caused by cervix insufficiency," by J. Bocev. AKUSH GINEKOL 47:69-70, April, 1971.

"Surveillance of legal abortions in the United States, 1970," by J. P. Bourne, et al. JOGN NURS 1:11-22, June, 1972.

"A survey of Milwaukee obstetricians and gynecologists attitudes toward abortion," by P. Halverson, et al. WIS MED J 71:134-139, April, 1972.

"Survey of the present statutory and case law on abortion: the contradictions and the problems," U ILL L F 1972:177, 1972.

"Survey on the incidence of criminal abortion in Sofia," by D. Vasilev. AKUSH GINEKOL (Sofiia) 10:271-278, 1971.

"Susceptibility of Alveonasus lahorensis neumann ticks to the agent of enzootic abortion of sheep," by I. I. Terskikh, et al. VOPR VIRUSOL 17:430-432, July-August, 1972.

"Symposium: Abortion and the Law," CASE W RES L REV 23:705-895, Summer, 1972.

"Syndrome of multiple osseous defects," by J. Kucera. LANCET 1: 260-261, January 29, 1972.

"Teaching social conscience," by D. Rottenberg. TODAYS HEALTH 50:40-43 plus, September, 1972.

"Teenage mothers," by J. E. Hodgson. MINN MED 55:49, January, 1972.

"Teen-age pregnancy and the problem of abortion: American Academy of Pediatrics," PEDIATRICS 49:303-304, February, 1972.

"The teenage sexual revolution and the myth of an abstinent past," by P. Cutright. FAMILY PLANN PERSPECT 4:24-31, January, 1972.

"Teen birth control information requested," US MED 8:3 plus, November 15, 1972.

"Temporary submucosal cerclage for cervical incompetence: report of forty-eight cases," by C. L. Jennings, Jr. AM J OBSTET GYNECOL 113:1097-1102, August 15, 1972.

"Termination of a mid-trimester pregnancy," by J. O. Greenhalf. NURS MIRROR 134:34-36, June 2, 1972.

"Termination of pregnancy," by D. Bluett. BR MED J 2:228, April 22, 1972.

"Termination of pregnancy," by E. J. Hill. NZ MED J 74:412, December, 1971.

"Termination of pregnancy," by H. C. McLaren. BR MED J 2:714, June 17, 1972.

"Termination of pregnancy," by P. Moxon. BR MED J 2:655, June 10, 1972.

"Termination of pregnancy," by J. Slome. LANCET 2:881-882,October 21, 1972.

"Termination of pregnancy by continuous intrauterine infusion of prostaglandins," by A. W. Miller, et al. LANCET 2:5-7, July 1, 1972.

"Termination of pregnancy during the mid-trimester by intra-amniotic injection of urea," by J. O. Greenhalf. BR J CLIN PRACT 26:24-26, January, 1972.

"The termination of pregnancy in adolescent women," by R. U. Hausknecht. PEDIATR CLIN NORTH AM 19:803-810, August, 1972.

"Termination of pregnancy in the unmarried," by E. M. Briggs, et al. SCOTT MED J 17:399-400, December, 1972.

"Termination of pregnancy in the unmarried," by M. C. Macnaughton. SCOTT MED J 17:381-382, December, 1972.

"Termination of second trimester pregnancy with 15 methylanalogues of prostaglandins E 2 and F 2," by S. M. Karim, et al. J OBSTET GYNAECOL BR COMMONW 79:737-743, August, 1972.

"Therapeutic abortion and ultrasound," by K. E. Hodge. CAN MED ASSOC J 105:1021, November 20, 1971.

"Therapetuic abortion by intra-amniotic injection of prostaglandins," by G. Roberts, et al. BR MED J 4:12-14, October 7, 1972.

"The Therapeutic Abortion Committee," by I. M. Cushner. CLIN OBSTET GYNECOL 14:1248-1254, December, 1971.

"Therapeutic abortion conflict and resolution," by R. Zahourek. AORN J 16:114-119, October, 1972.

"Therapeutic abortion: government figures show big increase in 1971," CAN MED ASS J 106:1131, May 20, 1972.

"Therapeutic abortion in the Maori," by V. G. Deobhakta. NZ MED J 75:174, March, 1972.

"Therapeutic abortion in the Maori in psychiatric perspective," by L. K. Gluckman. NZ MED J 75:22-24, January, 1972.

"Therapeutic abortion in Maryland, 1968-1970," by R. J. Melton, et al. OBSTET GYNECOL 39:923-930, June, 1972.

"Therapeutic abortion is more than an operation," by L. J. Dunn. AORN J 16:120-123, October, 1972.

"Therpaeutic abortion: middle-class privilege or curse," by F. G. Surawicz. J AM MED WOM ASSOC 27:590-597, November, 1972.

"Therapeutic abortion practices in Chicago hospitals -- vagueness, variation, and violation of the law," by P. Broeman, et al. L & SOC ORDER 1971:757, 1971.

"Therapeutic abortion: the role of state government. I.," by R. D. Lamm. CLIN OBSTET GYNECOL 14:1204-1207, December, 1971.

"Therapeutic abortion: the role of state government. II.," by A. L. Seltzer, et al. CLIN OBSTET GYNECOL 14:1208-1211, December, 1971.

"Therapeutic abortion trends in the United States," by A. Heller. CURR PSYCHIATR THER 12:171-184, 1972.

"Therapeutic abortion: two important judicial pronouncements," by S. A. Strauss. S AFR MED J 46:275-279, March 11, 1972.

"Therapeutic abortion with the use of prostaglandin F 2. A study of efficacy, tolerance, and plasma levels with intravenous administration," by P. G. Gillett, et al. AM J OBSTET GYNECOL 112:330-338, February 1, 1972.

"Therapeutic abortion without inpatient hospitalization. An early experience with 325 cases," by I. M. Golditch, et al. CALIF MED 116:1-3, March, 1972.

"Therapeutic abortions in Virginia," by M. I. Shanholtz. VA MED MON 99:876-878, August, 1972.

"Thesen zur Schwangerschaftsunterbrechung?" by M. Stahli. REF 21: 162-169, March, 1972.

"Thomson on abortion," by R. A. Brody. PHIL PUB AFFAIRS 1:335-340, Spring, 1972.

"Those against legal abortion," by E. Hackett. AUSTRALAS NURSES J 1:15, August, 1972.

"Thoughts after viewing an abortion; continued from the National Observer, December 18, 1971," by E. Roberts, Jr. C DGST 36:6-8, April, 1972.

"Thoughts for the New Year," by L. Valvanne. KATILOLEHTI 77:52, February, 1972.

"Threatened abortion," by E. Pirvulescu. MUNCA SANIT 20:133-135, March, 1972.

"Threatened abortions, immature and premature birth in women infected with Toxoplasma gondii," by K. Nowosad, et al. WIAD PARAZYTOL 18:265-267, 1972.

"3 cases of defibrination in the course of retro-placental hematomas," by M. Samama, et al. BULL FED SOC GYNECOL OBSTET LANG FR 23:368-378, September-October, 1971.

"Three phases of the abortion process and its influence on women's mental health," by N. Kapor-Stanulovic. AM J PUBLIC HEALTH 62: 906-907, July, 1972.

"Three years' experience of the abortion act," by A. G. W. Weir. NURS J INDIA 62:395-396, December, 1971.

"Three years' experience of the working of the Abortion Act in Britain," by C. Pannell. NZ MED J 76:117-119, August, 1972.

"Three years of the Abortion Act: gynecological and psychiatric aftermaths," by D. Baird. PROC R SOC MED 65:160-162, February, 1972.

"A time for dialogue on abortion," by A. Swidler. NAT CATH REP 9: 7, December 1, 1972.

"Tiny gold valves to control fertility in men and laparoscopies for women," LIFE 73:54-56, July 28, 1972.

"Toronto Archbishop appeals for anti-abortion campaign," OR 22(218)4, June 1, 1972.

"Torts -- the Illinois wrongful death act held inapplicable to a viable fetus," LOYOLA U L J 3:402, Summer, 1972.

"Toward a family planning program in psychiatric hospitals," by V. D. Abernethy, et al. AMER J PUBLIC HEALTH 62:1638-1646, December, 1972.

"The tragic results of abortion in England," by N. St. John-Stevas. LINACRE 39:30-38, February, 1972.

"Transabdominal cervico-uterine suture," by R. A. Watkins. AUST NZ J OBSTET GYNAECOL 12:62-64, February, 1972.

"Transcervical intra-amnionic administration of a 20 per cent sodium chloride solution for artificial interruption of late term pregnancy," by A. A. Lebedev, et al. AKUSH GINEKOL 48:55-58, May, 1972.

"Transplacental haemorrhage in induced abortion," by W. B. Costley, et al. LANCET 1:843, April 15, 1972.

"Transplacental haemorrhage in induced abortion," by S. Murray, et al. LANCET 1:954-955, April 29, 1972.

"Treatment of habitual abortion by the Mitchell-Bardavil method," by V. I. Finik. AKUSH GINEKOL 48:61-63, February, 1972.

"Treatment of habitual miscarriages with long-acting steroid hormones," by M. D. Moiseenko, et al. VOPR OKHR MATERIN DET 17:60-62, June, 1972.

"Treatment of septic soap abortion," by G. Gerisch, et al. ZENTRALBL GYNAEKOL 94:520-523, April 22, 1972.

"Treatment of threatened abortion and premature labor with isoxsuprine hydrochloride," by P. Scillieri, et al. ARCH OSTET GINECOL 76: 129-137, 1971.

"Trends in therapeutic abortion in San Francisco," by P. Goldstein, et al. AM J PUBLIC HEALTH 62:695-699, May, 1972.

"A trial of cyproheptadine in habitual abortion," by E. Sadovsky, et al. ISR J MED SCI 81:623-625, May, 1972.

"Trisomy 14 in spontaneous abortus," by T. Kajii, et al. HUMANGENETIK 15:265-267, 1972.

"Tu ne tueras pas! L'interruption de grossesse selon l'Eglise catholique," by Ch. Robert. ESPRIT ET VIE 33-48, 1972.

"Tubingen theologian condemned by bishop; interview by Konkret (periodical)," by N. Greinacher. OR 22(218)4, June, 1972.

"Twisted logic; proposals to legalize abortion," CHR TODAY 17:24-25, December 22, 1972.

"Two-minute abortion is here--are we ready?" MED WORLD NEWS 13:15-17, May 12, 1972.

"2,000 Catholic abortions," NAT CATH REP 8:13, August 18, 1972.

"2 weeks make a big difference," by G. Janny, et al. ORV HETIL 113: 537-538, February 27, 1972.

"UK 'Conscience Clause' examined," AUSTRALAS NURSES J 1:15, August, 1972.

"Ultrasonic diagnosis in abortion," by H. R. Schulte, et al. ZENTRALBL GYNAEKOL 94:513-519, April 22, 1972.

"UN reports abortion is world's commonest form of birth control," HOSP ADMIN CAN 14:13, May, 1972.

"Unborn child," by N. Jeffcoate. NURSING MIRROR 134:10-14, April April 28, 1972.

"Uneasy abortion. A policy for change: 5.," by M. Simms. OBSERVER 18, May 28, 1972.

"Unofficial abortion; menstrual extraction," TIME 100:47, September 11, 1972.

"Unusual complication during pregnancy interruption by vacuum extraction," by K. Mirkov, et al. AKUSH GINEKOL (Sofiia) 11:85-86, 1972.

"Unusual findings in cesarean section," by L. Pozsonyi. ORV HETIL 113:573-574, March 5, 1972.

"Unwanted by whom; reprint from Catholic Currents, February 1, 1972," by W. Sayers. FAM DGST 27:2-5, August, 1972.

"Update on abortion in Michigan," by E. B. Keemer, Jr. J NATL MED ASSOC 64:518-519, November, 1972.

"U.S. bishops clash with national commission on abortion proposal," HOSP PROGRESS 53:23-24, May, 1972.

"U.S. courts strike down restrictive abortion laws. British nurses ask special hospital abortion units," AMER J NURSING 72:867, May, 1972.

"Use of choriogonin in threatened abortion," by Ia. M. Gel'man, et al. PEDIATR AKUSH GINEKOL 71:40-42, September-October, 1971.

"Use of conception control methods before pregnancies terminating in birth or a requested abortion in New York City municipal hospitals," by E. F. Daily, et al. AMER J PUBLIC HEALTH 62:1544-1545, November, 1972.

"The use of human chorionic gonadotropin levels in assessing the prognosis of threatened abortion," by P. R. Grob, et al. PRACTITIONER 209:79-81, July, 1972.

"Use of maninaria tents with saline abortion," by J. H. Lischke, et al. LANCET 1:49, January 1, 1972.

"The use of prostaglandin E 2 for therapeutic abortion," by S. M. Karim, et al. J OBSTET GYNAECOL BR COMMONW 79:1-13, January, 1972.

"Use of rheohysterography in pregnancy," by V. N. Kuznetsov. AKUSH GINEKOL 48:64, January, 1972.

"Use of sigetin for the prevention of perinatal mortality and morbidity after the 1st half of complicated pregnancy (experimental and clinical data)," by N. G. Kosheleva. AKUSH GINEKOL 47:40-43, March, 1971.

"Uterine distention and hypertension," by R. C. Goodlin. AM J OBSTET GYNECOL 112:1133-1134, April 15, 1972.

"Uterine stimulation. Prostaglandins," by M. P. Embrey. PROC R SOC MED 64:1018-1020, October, 1971.

"Uteroplacental apoplexia with acute defibrination syndrome. Therapeutical discussion of 3 cases," by R. Palliez, et al. BULL FED SOC GYNECOL OBSTET LANG FR 23:411-414, September-October, 1971.

"Utero-placental apoplexy complicated by defibrination," by A. Grand, et al. NOUV PRESSE MED 1:733-736, March 11, 1972.

"Vacuum aspiration in the management of abortions," by V. E. Aimakhu. INT SURG 57:13-16, January, 1972.

"Vacuum aspiratiosn at a hospital outpatient clinic," by R. Fahraeus. LAKARTIDNINGEN 69:4665-4670, October 4, 1972.

"Value of placenta examination in spontaneous abortions of the 1st trimester," by J. Cohen. REV FR GYNECOL OBSTET 67:123-126, February-March, 1972.

"Value of pregnanetriol determination in threatened abortion," by S. Sonnino, et al. RASS INT CLIN TER 52:191-196, February 29, 1972.

"The value of studying the abortus in teratology," by V. P. Kulazhenko, et al. ARKH PATOL 34:50-55, 1972.

"The value of studying acidophilic and kariopicnotic indices in abnormal pregnancies," by H. Venegas, et al. REV CHIL OBSTET GINECOL 34:14-16, 1969.

"Value of the systematic determination of teratogenic factors in latent infections of the so-called abortive diseases (preliminary note)," by P. Bierent. BULL SOC PATHOL EXOT 64:423-428, July-August, 1971.

"The value of ultrasonic B-scanning in diagnosis when bleeding is present in early pregnancy," by T. R. Varma. AM J OBSTET GYNECOL 114:607-612, November 1, 1972.

"Varicelliform eruption, vasculitis, spontaneous abortion, giardiasis and eosinophilia," by S. M. Bierman. ARCH DERMATOL 106:122-123, July, 1972.

"Vascular disorders in habitual abortion," by P. DeAgustin, et al. ACTA OBSTET GINECOL HISP LUSIT 19:475-488, December, 1971.

"Vesical sclerosis with reflux due to caustic injection treated by utetero-ceco-cystoplasty," by J. Auvert, et al. J UROL NEPHROL 73:476-482, June, 1967.

"Very early abortion using syringe as vacuum source," by H. Karman, et al. LANCET 1:1051-1052, May 13, 1972.

"Virological studies of the central nervous system of horse fetuses and findings in mares suffering from central nervous system disease following abortion caused by equine herpesvirus 1," by K. Petzoldt, et al. SCHWEIZ ARCH TIERHEILKD 114:129-139, February, 1972.

"Voluntary interruption of pregnancy: its psychiatric and contraceptive correlates," by S. L. Corson, et al. J REPROD MED 8:151-154, March, 1972.

"Washington: first in the performance of illegal (?) abortions," by D. C. Crain. MED ANN DIST COLUMBIA 41:1-2, August, 1972.

"Ways to cut U.S. birth rate - - findings of an official study," US NEWS WORLD REP 72:64, March 27, 1972.

"What causes miscarriages?" GOOD H 174:171, June, 1972.

"What happens when abortion is available on demand," MED WORLD NEWS 13:57-58, November 3, 1972.

"What is LIFE?" NEW HUMANIST 88:192-194, September, 1972.

"What sisters should know about abortion; interview by D. Durken," by P. Marx. SISTERS 43:519-531, May, 1972.

"What will abortion regulations be if law is reformed? Here are clues," by J. W. Eliot. MICH MED 71:959-962, November, 1972.

"When does human life start?" by H. Berger. OSTERR SCHWETERNZTG 25:143-146, June, 1972.

"When your patient is pregnant," EMERGENCY MED 4:99-101 plus, April, 1972.

"Who wants abortion reform?" TRANS-ACTION 8:14, May, 1971.

"Why I favour abortion," by H. Calderot. AUSTRALAS NURSES J

1:9, July, 1972.

"Wirksamer Schutz fur das ungeborene Leben - Aufgabe von Recht und Gesellschaft," by F. G. von Westphalen. DIAKONIA 27-37, 1972.

"Women obstetricians in New York and the state abortion law," by S. Wassertheil-Smoller, et al. HEALTH SERV REP 87:328-335, April, 1972.

"Women who seek therapeutic abortion: a comparison with women who complete their pregnancies," by C. V. Ford, et al. AM J PSYCHIATRY 129:546-552, November, 1972.

"Women's lib pill," by D. Gould. NEW STATESM 84:542, October 20, 1972.

"Xeroderma pigmentosum; a rapid sensitive method for prenatal diagnosis," by J. D. Regan, et al. SCIENCE 174:147-150, October 8, 1971.

"Youth--and the VAD," by L. Porritt. NZ NURS J 65:4, August, 1972.

"Y.W.C.A. v. Kugler, 342 F Supp 1048," MISS L J 43:728, November, 1972.

"Zur Diskussion um den Art. 218," by A. Leenen. MANN IN DER KIRCHE 21-27, January-February, 1972.

PERIODICAL LITERATURE

SUBJECT INDEX

ABNORMALTIES
see: Complications

ABORTION (GENERAL)
"Abortion," by A. L. Ferguson. S AFR MED J 46:1194, August 26, 1972.

"Abortion," by J. M. Malone. AM J OBSTET GYNECOL 114:280, September 15, 1972.

"Abortion," by S. A. Nigro, et al. JAMA 219:1068-1069, February 21, 1972.

"On abortion," by P. O'Boyle. OR 40(236)9-10, October 5, 1972.

"The beginning: the end," by J. A. Fitzgerald. NY STATE J MED 72:2457-2459, October 1, 1972.

"Business as usual," by M. Lawrence. TRIUMPH 7:15, June, 1972.

"Inconsistency or misunderstanding?" by H. S. Morris. CAN MED ASSOC J 106:857-858, April, 1972.

ABORTION ACT
see: Laws and Legislation

ABORTION: BULGARIA
"Survey on the incidence of criminal abortion in Sofia," by D. Vasilev. AKUSH GINEKOL (Sofiia) 10:271-278, 1971.

ABORTION: CANADA
"Abortion in Canada," by J. Kettle. CAN DOCTOR 38:55-56, July, 1972.

"Abortion rate up in Canada," HOSP ADMIN CAN 14:17, July, 1972.

"Attitudes toward abortion of married women in metropolitan Toronto," by T. R. Balakrishnan, et al. SOC BIOL 19:35-42, March, 1972.

"British Columbia hospital receives abortion study grant," CAN HOSP 49:11, March, 1972.

"Canadian Nurses' Association position on family planning and related health care," CAN NURSE 68:11, August, 1972.

"Care and treatment of therapeutic abortion patients in Canadian hospitals: January 1 to September 30, 1971," HOSP ADMIN CAN 14:25-31, March, 1972.

"Newfoundland doctors concerned over abortion curb at Grace Hospital, St. John's," CAN HOSP 49:17, May, 1972.

"Policy position on abortion: Canadian Public Health Association," CAN J PUBLIC HEALTH 63:370-371, July-August, 1972.

"A statement on abortion in Victoria," MED J AUST 1:443, February 26, 1972.

"A statement on abortion in Victoria," by J. R. Coulter. MED J AUST 1:32-33, January 1, 1972.

"A statement on abortion in Victoria," by J. R. Coulter. MED J AUST 1:550, March 11, 1972.

"A statement on abortion in Victoria," by L. Hemingway, et al. MED J AUST 1:608, March 18, 1972.

"A statement on abortion in Victoria," by B. A. Smithurst, et al. MED J AUST 1:240-241, January 29, 1972.

"Toronto Archbishop appeals for anti-abortion campaign," OR 22 (218)4, June 1, 1972.

ABORTION: CHINA
"Birth control appears successful in China despite its low esteem in Marxist theory," SCI NEWS 102:51-52, July 22, 1972.

ABORTION: EUROPE
"Abortion--United Kingdom style," by R. J. Brigden. SUPERVISOR NURSE 3:78-79, April, 1972.

"Anesthetic practice and pregnancy. Controlled survey of women anaesthetists in the United Kingdom," by R. P. Knill-Jones, et al. LANCET 1:1326-1328, June 17, 1972.

"The demographic effects of legal abortion in eastern Europe," by B. Kapotsy. EUROPEAN DEMOGRAPHIC INFO BUL 3:193-207, November 4, 1972.

"The fertility response to abortion reform in eastern Europe: demographic and economic implications," by R. J. McIntyre. AM ECONOMIST 16:45-65, Fall, 1972.

ABORTION: FINLAND
"The influence of some infectious diseases on the conceptus in northern Finland. A study based on routine serological investigation," by J. Kokkonen, et al. ANN CLIN RES 4:178-182, June, 1972.

"Rubella serology and abortions in Finland," by T. Vesikari, et al. LANCET 2:1375, December 23, 1972.

ABORTION: FRANCE
"Power to start and end a life," ECONOMIST 245:45, December 2, 1972.

ABORTION: GERMANY
"Abortion law in East Germany," AMER MED ASS 221:516, July 31, 1972.

"Abortion on demand in East Germany," CAN DOCTOR 38:18, August, 1972.

"Arztliche Uberlegungen zur reform des 218," by H. Hepp. STIMM

ABORTION: GERMANY

ZEIT 189:375-392, June, 1972.

"On responsibility for children not yet born," OR 12(208)8, March 23, 1972.

"Past and present," OR 8(204)3, February 24, 1972.

ABORTION: GREAT BRITAIN

"The abortion Act--Scotland 1968," HEALTH BULL 27:60-74, July, 1969.

"Abortion: defining G P's attitudes," NEW HUMANIST 88:74-76, June, 1972.

"Abortion teaser," by R. Wilson. SPECTATOR 755, May 13, 1972.

"Abortion touts," by D. Gould. NEW STATESM 83:165-166, February 11, 1972.

"After the Act," by H. L. A. Hart, et al. GUARDIAN 9, May 3, 1972.

"Birth-control plan for Britain," LANCET 1:675, March 25, 1972.

"Britain and Spain; abortion, ltd.," ECONOMIST 234:55, May 20, 1972.

"A challenge to abortionists: the Liverpool rally," by N. St. John-Stevas. TABLET 226:394, April 29, 1972.

"The need for special abortion clinics," by D. Steel. SUNDAY TIMES 16, May 21, 1972.

"N. O. P.: abortion survey," NEW HUMANIST 88:30-33, May, 1972.

"A positive alternative to abortion in England," OR 20(216)3, May 18, 1972.

"The rising ride of abortion," by N. St. John-Stevas. TABLET 226: 98, February 5, 1972.

"Scottish abortion statistics--1970," HEALTH BULL 30:27-35, January, 1972.

ABORTION: GREAT BRITAIN

"Study of applicants for abortion at the Royal Northern Hospital, London," by C. Ingham, et al. J BIOSOC SCI 4:351-369, July, 1972.

"Three years' experience of the working of the Abortion Act in Britain," by C. Pannell. NZ MED J 76:117-119, August, 1972.

"The tragic results of abortion in England," by N. St. John-Stevas. LINACRE 39:30-38, February, 1972.

"Uneasy abortion. A policy for change: 5.," by M. Simms. OBSERVER 18, May 28, 1972.

"U. S. courts strike down restrictive abortion laws. British nurses ask special hospital abortion units," AMER J NURSING 72:867, May, 1972.

ABORTION: JAPAN

"Laminaria-metreurynter method of midterm abortion in Japan," by Y. Manabe, et al. OBSTET GYNECOL 40:612-615, October, 1972.

ABORTION: LATIN AMERICA

"Prospective study of fertility in the District of Sao Paulo. I. Comparison of retrospective and prospective methods to estimate the rates of spontaneous and induced abortions," by M. L. Milanesi, et al. BOL OF SANIT PANAM 72:234-243, March, 1972.

ABORTION: NETHERLANDS

"The role of induced abortion in the changing pattern of birth control in the Netherlands," by P. E. Treffers. NED TIJDSCHR GENEESKD 116:1459-1466, August 12, 1972.

ABORTION: NEW ZEALAND

"Therapeutic abortion in the Maori," by V. G. Deobhakta. NZ MED J 75:174, March, 1972.

"Therapeutic abortion in the Maori in psychiatric perspective," by L. K. Gluckman. NZ MED J 75:22-24, January, 1972.

ABORTION: NORWAY

"Declaration of Oslo: statement on therapeutic abortion--World

Medical Assembly," WORLD MED J 19:30, March-April, 1972.

ABORTION: ROMANIA

"Fertility effects of the abolition of legal abortion in Romania," by M. S. Teitelbaum. POPULATION STUDIES 26:405-417, November, 1972.

ABORTION: SPAIN

"Abortion, Ltd.," ECONOMIST 243:55, May 20, 1972.

ABORTION: SWEDEN

"Abortion and contraception in Sweden 1870-1970," by H. Sjovall. Z RECHTSMED 70:197-209, 1972.

ABORTION: USSR

"The putting into effect of the artificial abortion act in Warsaw in the years 1957-1968; An anaylsis," by K. Waszynski. GINEKOL POL 43:371-376, 1972.

ABORTION: UNITED STATES

"Abortion and life's intrinsic value (emphasis on practice of abortion in New York City under liberalized statutes)," by D. C. Anderson. WALL ST J 179:8, April 7, 1972.

"Abortion consent rule struck down in District of Columbia: husband's consent not required," AMER MED NEWS 15:18, July 10, 1972.

"Abortion data for North Carolina," TEX MED 68:21, August, 1972.

"Abortion issue; move to repeal New York state's liberalized law," TIME 99:23, May 22, 1972.

"Abortion law in South Carolina," SC L REV 24:425, 1972.

"Abortion: Missouri HB 1470," by W. Brennan. SOC JUST 65:129-132, July-August, 1972.

"Abortion pay limits upheld in New York," AMER MED NEWS 15:15, February 28, 1972.

"Abortion; work of Clergy counseling service for problem pregnancies,

Los Angeles and Birthright of Chicago," by C. Remsberg, et al. SEVENTEEN 31:140-141 plus, September, 1972.

"Abortion yes or no: nurses organize both ways: New York," AMER J NURSING 72:416 plus, March, 1972.

"Abortions among women on public assistance in Hawaii: implications for practice," by K. T. Kumabe. AM J PUBLIC HEALTH 62:1538-1543, November, 1972.

"Acute identity crisis hits hospital abortion staff--morality the issue: North Carolina Memorial Hospital, Chapel Hill," US MED 8:8-9, May 15, 1972.

"Anti-abortion law upheld by Indiana Supreme Court," AMER MED NEWS 15:17, August 14, 1972.

"Appeals court blocks suit to ban abortions in New York City," HOSPITALS 46:164, February 1, 1972.

"Attitudes toward abortion among young black (based on a study of 300 young Negro women in Baltimore, Md.)," by F. F. Furstenburg, Jr. STUDIES IN FAMILY PLANNING 3:66-69, April, 1972.

"Attitudes toward abortion law reform at the University of Michigan Medical Center," by D. Hickok, et al. MICH MED 71:327-329, April, 1972.

"Attitudes toward abortion: a survey of Milwaukee obstetricians and gynecologists," by P. Halverson, et al. WIS MED J 71:134-139, April, 1972.

"Backlash on abortion; move to repeal New York state's liberal law," NEWSWEEK 79:32, May 22, 1972.

"Baltimore hospital abortion patient given $90,000 in damages," HOSPITALS 46:133, November 1, 1972.

"Birth control among the unmarried in Massachusetts: the Supreme Court speaks in varied tongues," by W. J. Curran. NEW ENGL J MED 286:1198-1199, June 1, 1972.

"Birthright New York: continued from the Lamp, October, 1971," by N. Sharkey. C DGST 36:100-103, February, 1972.

"Bitter abortion battle; Pennsylvania," TIME 100:32, December 11, 1972.

"Black physicians' experience with abortion requests and opinion about abortion law change in Michigan," by E. L. Hill, et al. J NATL MED ASSOC 64:52-58, January, 1972.

"California abortion statistics for 1971," by W. M. Ballard. CALIF MED 116:55, April, 1972.

"Colorado parish survey reveals laity's opinions," NAT CATH REP 8:7, May 12, 1972.

"Connecticut abortion laws ruled unconstitutional," CHR CENT 89: 539, May 10, 1972.

"The death peddlers. N. Y. appeals court rules against fetus," NAT CATH REP 8:21, March 10, 1972.

"Effects of a liberalized abortion law in New York City," by J. Pakter, et al. MT SINAI J MED NY 39:535-543, November-December, 1972.

"18 month experience in New York City with a liberalized abortion law," by J. Pakter. NY MED 28:333 plus, September, 1972.

"Federal court in New York invalidates order banning abortions for indigents under Medicaid," HOSPITALS 46:25, September 16, 1972.

"Fight for life: Missouri, March 8, 1972," by J. Doyle, et al. SOC JUST 65:89-94, June, 1972.

"Figures and fetuses; findings of New York TV surveys," by R. J. Neuthaus. COMMONWEAL 97:175-178, November 24, 1972.

"Florida abortion law--reform or regression in 1972," U FLA L REV 24:346, Winter, 1972.

ABORTION: UNITED STATES

"Florida's century-old antiabortion law declared unconstitutional," HOSPITALS 46:43, March 1, 1972.

"Georgia board rules Medicaid will cover abortion fees," RN 35:19, March, 1972.

"Governor signs Connecticut's new abortion law," HOSPITALS 46: 25, June 16, 1972.

"Hospital opposing abortions returns Hill-Burton money: Mercy Hospital in New Orleans," HOSPITALS 46:147, June 1, 1972.

"Implementation of therapeutic abortion in the Kaiser Hospital-Southern California Permanente medical group," by A. Saltz. CLIN OBSTET GYNECOL 14:1230-1236, December, 1971.

"Indiana Supreme Court upholds state abortion law," by M. McKernan, Jr. SOC JUST 65:197-199, October, 1972.

"Kansas opponents fail to modify abortion law," HOSPITALS 46:182, March 1, 1972.

"A key battle: outcome of next Tuesday (November 7, 1972)'s abortion referendum in Michigan will likely have national implications," by W. Mossberg. WALL ST J 180:30, November 3, 1972.

"Maryland ruling permits abortion referral ads," ADV AGE 43:21, January 3, 1972.

"Medicaid coverage sought for legal Georgia abortions," HOSPITALS 46:166 plus, January 16, 1972.

"Medicaid funds for abortions banned by New York court," HOSPITALS 46:122, May 16, 1972.

"Missouri court upholds state's abortion law," HOSPITALS 46:125, November 1, 1972.

"Mt. Carmel Mercy Hospital, Michigan, takes stand on abortion," CATH HOSP 3:8, July, 1972.

"New Jersey physicians back abortion change," AMER MED NEWS 15:10, July 24, 1972.

"New Jersey's abortion law: an establishment of religion?" RUTGERS L REV 25:452-475, Spring, 1972.

"New laws bring new approaches. Method for the evaluation of therapeutic abortion candidates meets the requirements of California state law and the needs of patients, while conserving the time of the medical staff," by S. Loos, et al. HOSPITALS 46:76-79, July 16, 1972.

"New study reveals who gets legal abortions and how it's done: New York," MOD HOSP 118:47, February, 1972.

"New York State obstetricians and the new abortion law: physician experience with abortion techniques," by S. M. Wassertheil-Smoller, et al. AM J OBSTET GYNECOL 113:979-986, August 1, 1972.

"A New Yorker looks at abortion," by N. Sharkey. ST ANTH 79:10-14, February, 1972.

"New York's abortion fighters," by E. Westenhaver. NAT CATH REP 8:1 plus, February 25, 1972.

"New York's abortion law upheld by appeals court," HOSPITALS 46:214, April 1, 1972.

"New York's abortion reform law: unanswered questions," by V. N. Duin. ALBANY L REV 37:22, 1972.

"New York's obstetricians surveyed on abortion," by R. C. Lerner, et al. FAM PLANN PERSPECT 3:56, January, 1971.

"Nonresidetns have most N. Y. abortions," NAT CATH REP 8:21, March 10, 1972.

"Nurses and lawyer fight end of abortion restrictions: Santa Barbara, California," HOSP PROGRESS 53:19, February, 1972.

"Obstetricians and legal abortions in San Francisco," by B. Behrstock, et al. CALIF MED 117:29-31, September, 1972.

"Of doctors, deterrence, and the dark figure of crime--a note on abortion in Hawaii," by F. E. Zimring. U CHI L REV 39:699, Summer, 1972.

"Oklahoma abortion survey tabulation completed," J OKLA STATE MED ASS 65:465-466, November, 1972.

"On the subject of abortion: Massachusetts," by C. Moynahan. SOC JUST 65:49-53, May, 1972.

"Open legal abortion 'on request' is working in New York City, but is it the answer?" by A. I. Weisman. AM J OBSTET GYNECOL 112:138-143, January 1, 1972.

"Parts of Kansas abortion statute held unconstitutional," NEWSLETTER (Amer Soc Hosp Attorneys) 5:3-4, May, 1972.

"Results of a year's liberal regulation of abortion in the state of New York," by F. K. Beller. MED WELT 23:471-472, March 25, 1972.

"Right to life has a message for New York state legislators," by F. C. Shapiro. N Y TIMES MAG 10-11 plus, August 20, 1972; Discussion 23 plus, September 10, 1972.

"Slavery and abortion: continued from a press release distributed by Minnesota Citizens Concerned for Life, August 18, 1972," by W. Schaller. C DGST 37:24-26, December, 1972.

"A survey of Milwaukee obstetricians and gynecologists attitudes toward abortion," by P. Halverson, et al. WIS MED J 71:134-139, April, 1972.

"Therapeutic abortion in Maryland, 1968-1970," by R. J. Melton, et al. OBSTET GYNECOL 39:923-930, June, 1972.

"Therapeutic abortion practices in Chicago hospitals--vagueness, variation, and violation of the law," by P. Broeman, et al.

L & SOC ORDER 1971:757, 1971.

"Therapeutic abortions in Virginia," by M. I. Shanholtz. VA MED MON 99:876-878, August, 1972.

"Torts--the Illinois wrongful death act held inapplicable to a viable fetus," LOYOLA U L J 3:402, Summer, 1972.

"Trends in therapeutic abortion in San Francisco," by P. Goldstein, et al. AM J PUBLIC HEALTH 62:695-699, May, 1972.

"Update on abortion in Michigan," by E. B. Keemer, Jr. J NATL MED ASSOC 64:518-519, November, 1972.

"Use of conception control methods before pregnancies terminating in birth or a requested abortion in New York City municipal hospitals," by E. F. Daily, et al. AMER J PUBLIC HEALTH 62:1544-1545, November, 1972.

"Washington: first in the performance of illegal (?) abortions," by D. C. Crain. MED ANN DIST COLUMBIA 41:1-2, August, 1972.

"Women obstetricians in New York and the state abortion law," by S. Wassertheil-Smoller, et al. HEALTH SERV REP 87:328-335, April, 1972.

ALYLESTENOL

"Alylestenol (Gestanone) in the treatment of threatened abortion," by D. Vasilev. AKUSH GINEKOL (Sofiia) 10:413-419, 1971.

"Experiences in the therapy of spontaneous and habitual abortions with the oral administration of Gestanon A," by B. Beric, et al. MED PREGL 24:505-507, 1971.

AMINOGLUTETHIMIDE PHOSPHATE

"The influence of an anti-steroidogenic drug (aminoglutethimide phosphate) on pregnancy maintenance," by S. R. Glasser, et al. ENDOCRINOLOGY 90:1363-1370, May, 1972.

ANESTHESIA
  see also: Induced Abortion
    Therapeutic Abortion

"Anaesthetic practice and pregnancy. Controlled survey of women anaesthetists in the United Kingdom," by R. P. Knill-Jones, et al. LANCET 1:1326-1328, June 17, 1972.

"Anesthesia for early artificial interruption of pregnancy," by R. S. Mikhaleva. AKUSH GINEKOL 47:61, December, 1971.

"Anesthesia in minor gynecologic surgery with trichloroethylene," by V. S. Lesiuk. AKUSH GINEKOL 48:70-71, April, 1972.

"Anesthesia, pregnancy and pollution," BR J ANAESTH 44:541, June, 1972.

"Anesthesiology grand rounds Yale-New Haven Hospital. Placental abruption with **coagulopathy**," CONN MED 36:238-241, April, 1972.

"Anesthetic-induced abortion?" by D. H. Carr. ANESTHESIOLOGY 35:335, October, 1971.

"Anesthetics as a cuase of abortion," by T. H. Corbett. FERTIL STERIL 23:866-869, November, 1972.

"Effects of termination of pregnancy and general anesthesia on acid-base equilibrium in blood," by J. Denk, et al. WIAD LEK 25:500-503, March 15, 1972.

"Experience with the use of promedol in anesthesia for artificial abortion," by Z. P. Drozdovskaia, et al. AKUSH GINEKOL 47:61-62, December, 1971.

"Pollution of the operating-theatre suite by anaesthetic gases," by J. Bullough. LANCET 1:1337, June 17, 1972.

BEHAVIOR
  see: Sociology, Behavior and Abortion

BIBLIOGRAPHY

"Abortion," CLW 44:177-179, October, 1972

BIRTH CONTROL

see also: Family Planning

"Agonizing dilemma: abortion and birth control and the Catholic hospital," CATH HOSP 3:1-2, September, 1972.

"Birth control among the unmarried in Massachusetts: the Supreme Court speaks in varied tongues," by W. J. Curran. NEW ENGL J MED 286:1198-1199, June 1, 1972.

"Birth control appears successful in China despite its low esteem in Maxrist theory," SCI NEWS 102:51-52, July 22, 1972.

"Birth control: the establishment chimes in," ECONOMIST 243:24 plus, April 8, 1972.

"Birth control for teen-agers--is it legal?" by C. A. Gravenor, Jr. CAN DOCTOR 38:103-104, October, 1972.

"Birth control in the USA," INT HOSP REV 9:32, November 4, 1971.

"Birth-control plan for Britain," LANCET 1:675, March 25, 1972.

"Birth control usage among abortion patients," by J. G. Hill. J KANS MED SOC 73:295-301 passim, June, 1972.

"Domiciliary midwives and birth control advice 1970-1971," by M. Waite. NURSING TIMES 68:193-195, December 7, 1972.

"The effect of legislation for interruption of pregnancy on the level of birth rate," by G. Stoimenov, et al. AKUSH GINEKOL (Sofiia) 11:1-7, 1972.

"Health visitors and birth control advice 1970-1971," by M. Waite. NURSING TIMES 68:157-159, October 12, 1972; 161-164, October 19, 1972.

"Public health perspective on the limitation of births," by W. B.

Jones, Jr., et al. N C MED J 33:688-691, August, 1972.

"Public opinion trends: Elective abortion and birth control services to teenagers," by R. Pomeroy, et al. FAMILY PLANN PERSPECT 4:44-55, October, 1972.

"The role of induced abortion in the changing pattern of birth control in the Netherlands," by P. E. Treffers. NED TIJDSCHR GENEESKD 116:1459-1466, August 12, 1972.

"Teen birth control information requested," US MED 8:3 plus, November 15, 1972.

"UN reports abortion is world's commonest form of birth control," HOSP ADMIN CAN 14:13, May, 1972.

"Use of conception control methods before pregnancies terminating in birth or a requested abortion in New York City municipal hospitals," by E. F. Daily, et al. AMER J PUBLIC HEALTH 62:1544-1545, November, 1972.

"Ways to cut U. S. birth rate--findings of an official study," US NEWS WORLD REP 72:64, March 27, 1972.

BISHYDROXYCOUMARIN

"Attempted abortion by the use of bishydroxycoumarin," by N. S. De Jager, et al. CAN MED ASSOC J 107:50 passim, July 8, 1972.

BLOOD

"ABO blood groups and abortion," BR MED J 4:314-315, November 11, 1972.

"ABO incompatibility as a cause of spontaneous abortion: evidence from abortuses," by K. Takano, et al. J MED GENET 9:144-150, June, 1972.

"Analysis of prostaglandin F 2 and metabolites in blood during constant intravenous infusion of progestaglandin F 2 in the human female," by F. Beguin, et al. ACTA PHYSIOL SCAND 86:430-432, November, 1972.

BLOOD

"Changes in the concentration of copper and ceruloplasmin, and cholinesterase activity in the blood in threatened abortion," by L. I. Priakhina. AKUSH GINEKOL 47:61-63, April, 1971.

"The clinical problems of fibrinolysis between the utero-placental and the feto-placental units in relation to the abortion," by K. Oyanagi. J TOKYO MED COLL 28:757-776, September, 1970.

"Erythocyte diameter in mothers of premature infants," by C. Hadnagy, et al. THER GGW 110:1511-1512 passim, October, 1971.

"Fetal blood typing after induced abortion," by S. Shah, et al. OBSTET GYNECOL 40:724-727, November, 1972.

"Placental lactogen levels as guide to outcome of threatened abortion," by P. A. Niven, et al. BR MED J 3:799-801, September 30, 1972.

"Plasma volume, electrolyte, and coagulation factor changes following intra-amniotic hypertonic saline infusion," by W. E. Easterling, Jr., et al. AM J OBSTET GYNECOL 113:1065-1071, August 15, 1972.

"Pregnancy and labor in women with ABO incompatibility," by A. B. Saturskaia. AKUSH GINEKOL 47:51-52, August, 1971.

"Proteins of the blood serum in patients with pyoseptic diseases following infected abortion (electrophoresis on polyacrylamide gel)" by M. I. Kotilar, et al. AKUSH GINEKOL 48:73-74, March, 1972.

"Retinal reflectance dye dilution: caridac output during disseminated embolism and fibrination," by C. L. Schneider, et al. BIBL ANAT 10:592-599, 1969.

"The significance of fibrinolysis in abortion," by H. Soma. J TOKYO MED COLL 28:343-350, March, 1970.

BLOOD TYPES AND ABORTION
see: Blood

CERVICAL INCOMPETENCE AND INSUFFICIENCY

"Cervical **fistula:** a complication of midtrimester abortion," by R. Goodlin, et al. OBSTET GYNECOL 40:82-84, July, 1972.

"Cervical mucus, vaginal cytology and steroid excretion in recurrent abortion," by R. R. MacDonald, et al. OBSTET GYNECOL 40: 394-402, September, 1972.

"Cervicovaginal fistula as a result of saline abortion," by R. T. Gordon. AM J OBSTET GYNECOL 112:578-579, February 15, 1972.

"Characteristics of uterine contractile activity in isthmico-cervical insufficiency," by G. M. Lisovskaia, et al. AKUSH GINEKOL 48:63, January, 1972.

"Experiences with cerclage," by G. Ruzicska, et al. ORV HETIL 112:1628-1631, July 11, 1971.

"Isthmico-cervical insufficiency as a factor in prematurity (late abortions and premature labor) and its surgical treatment," by R. Tokin. AKUSH GINEKOL (Sofiia) 8:169-177, 1969.

"Results of surgical treatment of cervical incompetence in pregnancy," by F. Glenc, et al. POL TYG LEK 27:834-836, May 29, 1972.

"Significance of cervical cerclage for the child," by G. Mau. Z GEBURTSHILFE PERINATOL 176:331-342, August, 1972.

"Silicone-plastic cuff for the treatment of the incompetent cervix in pregnancy," by E. E. Yosowitz, et al. AM J OBSTET GYNECOL 113:233 -238, May 15, 1972.

"Surgical treatment of pregnant women with habitual abortion caused by cervix insufficiency," by J. Bocev. AKUSH GINEKOL 47:69-70, April, 1971.

"Temporary submucosal cerclage for cervical incompetence: report of forty-eight cases," by C. L. Jennings, Jr. AM J OBSTET GYNECOL 113:1097-1102, August 15, 1972.

CESAREAN SECTION
see: Complications

CHORIOGONIN
"Use of choriogonin in threatened abortion," by Ia. M. Gel'man, et al. PEDIATR AKUSH GINEKOL 71:40-42, September-October, 1971.

CLINICAL ASPECTS
"A clinical and pathologic survey of 91 cases of spontaneous abortion," by J. Brotherton, et al. FERTIL STERIL 23:289-294, April, 1972.

"Clinical aspects, pathogenesis and prevention of animal toxoplasmosis (with special reference to toxoplasmosis abortion in sheep)," by J. K. Beverley. MONATSH VET MED 26:893-900, December 1, 1971.

"Clinical experiences in induced abortion using vacuum extraction and the metranoikter," by J. Hoffman, et al. ZENTRALBL GYNAEKOL 94:913-917, July 22, 1972.

"The clinical problems of fibrinolysis between the utero-placental and the feto-placental units in relation to the abortion," by K. Oyanagi. J TOKYO MED COLL 28:757-776, September, 1970.

"A clinical study on prognosticating threatened abortions by vaginal cytogram in the first trimester of pregnancy," by J. Aoki. ACTUAL PHARMACOL 23:257-266, 1970; also in J JAP OBSTET GYNECOL SOC 24:257-266, April, 1972.

"Early abortion and clinical findings in women having an abortion," by P. Drac. ZENTRALBL GYNAEKOL 94:918-921, July 22, 1972.

"Epidemiological and clinical factors in premature detachment of the normally inserted placenta," by A. Barone, et al. MINERVA GINECOL 23:623-625, August, 1971.

"Experience with therapeutic abortion clinic. Methods and complications," by R. Egdell. DEL MED J 44:207-212, August, 1972.

CLINICAL ASPECTS

"Implementation of the Abortion Act: report on a year's working of abortion clinics and operating sessions," by A. E. Buckle, et al. BR MED J 3:381-384, August 12, 1972.

"Prostaglandin-oxytocin enhancement and potentiation and their clinical applications," by A. Gillespie. BR MED J 1:150-152, January 15, 1972.

COMPLICATIONS

see also: Hemorrhage

"Abdominal aspiration hysterotomy," by D. T. Liu. LANCET 2:654, September 23, 1972.

"Abortion recidivism. A problem in preventive medicine," by J. J. Rovinsky. OBSTET GYNECOL 39:649-659, May, 1972.

"Air embolism and maternal death from therapeutic abortion," by R. A. Munsick. OBSTET GYNECOL 39:688-690, May, 1972.

"Anesthesiology grand rounds Yale-New Haven Hospital. Placental abruption with coagulopathy," CONN MED 36:238-241, April, 1972.

"Arias-Stella phenomenon in spontaneous and therapeutic abortion," by S. G. Silverberg. AM J OBSTET GYNECOL 112:777-780, March 15, 1972.

"Bacterial endocarditis with 'associated bacteria'," by E. Bergogne-Berezin, et al. NOUV PRESSE MED 1:271-272, January 22, 1972.

"Bronchospasm complicating intravenous prostaglandin F 2a for therapeutic abortion," by J. I. Fishburne, et al. OBSTET GYNECOL 39:892-896, June, 1972.

"Clinical aspects, pathogenesis and prevention of animal toxoplasmosis (with special reference to toxoplasmosis abortion in sheep)," by J. K. Beverley. MONATSH VET MED 26:893-900, December 1, 1971.

"Coexistence of abortion in tubal pregnancy with incipient prolapse of uterine myoma," by A. Cieplak. POL TYG LEK 27:1403-1404, September 4, 1972.

"Complications of cervical suture," by A. Adoni, et al. HAREFUAH 83:146-147, August 15, 1972.

"Congenital malformations and refused termination," by T. J. David, et al. LANCET 1:1123, May 20, 1972.

"Consumptive coagulopathy associated with intra-amniotic infusion of hypertonic salt," by F. K. Beller, et al. AM J OBSTET GYNECOL 112:534-543, February 15, 1972.

"Consumptive coagulopathy with generalized hemorrhage after hypertonic saline-induced abortion. A case report," by D. R. Halbert, et al. OBSTET GYNECOL 39:41-44, January, 1972.

"Course and late effects of acute renal insufficiencies post partum and post abortum," by P. Zech, et al. J MED LYON 51:251 passim, January 20, 1970.

"Defibrination in saline abortion," by R. Schwartz, et al. OBSTET GYNECOL 40:728-737, November, 1972.

"Defibrination syndrome after intra-amniotic infusion of hypertonic saline," by A. E. Weiss, et al. AM J OBSTET GYNECOL 113: 868-874, August 1, 1972.

"Defibrinogenation after intra-amniotic injection of hypertonic saline," by J. L. Spivak, et al. N ENGL J MED 287:321-323, August 17, 1972.

"Divergence of opinion on placental damage due to hypertonic saline-induced abortion," by Y. Manabe, et al. AM J OBSTET GYNECOL 114:1107-1108, December 15, 1972.

"Early abortion and clinical findings in women having an abortion," by P. Drac. ZENTRALBL GYNAEKOL 94:918-921, July 22, 1972.

"Early abortion and Mycoplasma infection," by E. Caspi, et al.

ISR J MED SCI 8:122-127, February, 1972.

"Early complications of pregnancy interruptions according to our records," by B. Jakubovska, et al. CESK GYNEKOL 37:532-533, September, 1972.

"Early somatic complications in abortion," by P. Atterfelt, et al. LAKARTIDNINGEN 69:241-246, January 12, 1972.

"Effects of administration of Furosemide in acute postabortum renal insufficiency," by T. Burghele, et al. ACTA UROL BELG 39: 315-321, July, 1971.

"Effects of exchange transfusion on hemostatic disorders during septic shock after abortion," by C. Gibert, et al. REV MED SUISSE ROMANDE 91:689-696, October, 1971.

"Effects of haemodialysis on dynamics of some antibiotics in blood of patients with kidney insufficiency complicated by purulent infection," by M. I. Kuzin, et al. BULL SOC INT CHIR 31:298-303, July-August, 1972.

"Emergency care in injuries of the uterus during abortion," by N. A. Zakhar'eva. VOPR OKHR MATERIN DET 16:77-79, May, 1971.

"Epidemiological and clinical factors in premature detachment of the normally inserted placenta," by A. Barone, et al. MINERVA GINECOL 23:623-625, August, 1971.

"Fever and bacteremia associated with hypertonic saline abortion," by C. R. Steinberg, et al. OBSTET GYNECOL 39:673-678, May, 1972.

"Fever as a cause of abortion," by F. Dietzel, et al. MED KLIN 67:387-390, March 17, 1972.

"Folic acid deficiency and abruptio placentae," by M. H. Hall. J OBSTET GYNAECOL BR COMMONW 79:222-225, March, 1972.

"Habitual abortion and toxoplasmosis. Is there a relationship?" by P. M. Southern, Jr. OBSTET GYNECOL 39:45-47, January, 1972.

"Histamine reactivity of the skin in women with habitual abortion," by B. Kiutukchiev, et al. AKUSH GINEKOL (Sofiia) 11:13-36, 1972.

"Immediate mordibity on large abortion service: the first year's experience," by L. A. Walton. N Y STATE J MED 72:919-921, April 15, 1972.

"Immunologic indices and serum protein fractions in patients with peritonitis and sepsis following non-hospital abortions," by N. N. Kulikova, et al. AKUSH GINEKOL 47:14-18, November, 1971.

"Incidence of abortion in a group of young patients with rheumatic cardiopathy," by R. M. Del Bosque, et al. GINECOL OBSTET MEX 32:167-171, August, 1972.

"Incidence of chromosome abnormalities in spontaneous abortion and study of the risk in subsequent pregnancies," by J. G. Boue. REV FR GYNECOL OBSTET 67:182-187, February-March, 1972.

"Incidence of congenital transmission of Chagas' disease in abortion," by A. L. Bittencourt, et al. REV INST MED TROP SAO PAULO 14:257-259, July-August, 1972.

"Indication and contraindication for interruption of pregnancy in skin diseases," by H. Schleicher, et al. DERMATOL MONATSSCHR 157:599-607, August, 1971.

"Induced abortion and marriage counseling in epilepsy," by F. Rabe. MED WELT 23:330-331, March 4, 1972.

"Induced abortion and marriage counseling in multiple sclerosis," by R. C. Behrend. MED WELT 23:326-330, March 4, 1972.

"Induced abortion and marriage counseling in myasthenia," by H. G. Mertens. MED WELT 23:332-335, March 4, 1972.

"The influence of some infectious diseases on the conceptus in northern Finland. A study based on routine serological investigation," by J. Kokkonen, et al. ANN CLIN RES 4:178-182, June, 1972.

COMPLICATIONS

"Injury to the kidney during paranephric blockade," by A. Kh. Zaval'nluk. SUD MED EKSPERT 15:58-59, April-June, 1972.

"Interruption of pregnancy for urological indications," by K. Geza. ORV HETIL 113:2045-2050, August 20, 1972.

"Interruption of pregnancy in women with mitral stenosis," by V. Irasek. AKUSH GINEKOL (Sofiia) 11:41-45, 1972.

"Intracranial dural sinus thrombosis following intrauterine instillation of hypertonic saline," by J. A. Goldman, et al. AM J OBSTET GYNECOL 112:1132-1133, April 15, 1972.

"Joint program for the study of abortion (JPSA): early medical complications of legal abortion," by C. Tietze, et al. STUDIES IN FAMILY PLANNING 3:97-122, June, 1972.

"Legal abortions: early medical complications. An interim report of the joint program for the study of abortion," by C. Tietze, et al. J REPROD MED 8:193-204, April, 1972.

"Lethal chromosome abnormalities in the antenatal and perinatal stages of human development," by M. A. Petrov-Maslakov, et al. VESTN AKAD MED NAUK SSSR 27:68-77, 1972.

"Medical and surgical complications of therapeutic abortions," by G. K. Stewart, et al. OBSTET GYNECOL 40:539-550, October, 1972.

"Myometrial necrosis after therapeutic abortion," by A. C. Wentz, et al. OBSTET GYNECOL 40:315-320, September, 1972.

"On the uterine etiology of suspicious deaths in young women," by J. Caroff, et al. MED LEG DOMM CORPOR 4:267-272, July-September, 1971.

"Participation of biogenic amines in the pathogenesis of bacterial shock," by L. S. Persianinov, et al. AKUSH GINEKOL 47:3-7, November, 1971.

"Post abortum acute renal insufficiency treated by daily dialysis," by V. Jovanovic, et al. SRP ARH CELOK LEK 98:1453-1458, December, 1970.

"Postabortum sacroiliac arthritis," by G. Robinet, et al. BULL FED SOC GYNECOL OBSTET LANG FR 23:424-425, September-October, 1971.

"Pregnancy damage and birth-complications in the children of paraplegic women," by H. Goller, et al. PARAPLEGIA 10:213-217, November, 1972.

"Pregnancy interruption due to polyneuritis," by G. K. Kohler, et al. MED WELT 23:1762-1766, November 18, 1972.

"Pre-emptive abortion: menstrual extractions," NEWSWEEK 80:69-July 24, 1972.

"Premature placental detachment: physiopathology and therapeutic management," by B. Neme. MATERN INFANC 30:127-134, April-June, 1971.

"Proteinurai in toxaemia and abruptio placentae," by P. R. MacLean, el al. J OBSTET GYNAECOL BR COMMONW 79:321-326, April, 1972.

"Puerperal inflammations and late complications after legal abortions," by A. Cernoch. CAS LEK CESK 111:765-768, August 18, 1972.

"Reductions in complications due to induced abortions noted," HOSPITALS 46:19, December 1, 1972.

"The renal lesions of toxaemia and abruptio placentae studied by light and electron microscopy," by D. Thomson, et al. J OBSTET GYNAECOL BR COMMONW 79:311-320, April, 1972.

"Rubella and medical abortion," by E. Hervet, et al. NOUV PRESSE MED 1:379-380, February 5, 1972.

"Rubella reinfection during early pregnancy: a case report," by R. L. Northrop, et al. OBSTET GYNECOL 39:524-536, April, 1972.

"Rubella serology and abortions in Finland," by T. Vesikari, et al. LANCET 2:1375, December 23, 1972.

"Rubella vaccination and termination of pregnancy," by H. J. Mair, et al. BR MED J 4:271-273, November 4, 1972.

"Second-trimester abortion after vaginal termination," by D. M. Potts. LANCET 2:133, July 15, 1972.

"Second-trimester abortion after vaginal termination of pregnancy," by A. J. Margolis, et al. LANCET 2:431-432, August 26, 1972.

"Second-trimester abortion after vaginal termination of pregnancy," by C. S. Wright, et al. LANCET 1:1278-1279, June 10, 1972.

"Significance of immunologic conflict in the development of pregnancy complications (literature review)," by D. V. Umbrumiants. AKUSH GINEKOL 48:41.46, January, 1972.

"Simultaneous vena cava inferior syndrome and utero-placental apoplexy," by E. Veszely, et al. ORV HETIL 112:2652-2653, October 31, 1971.

"Some clinical-physiological indices in children born of mothers with habitual abortion," by A. K. Svetlova, et al. VOPR OKHR MATERIN DET 16:64-70, May, 1971.

"State of the menstrual and child-bearing functions of pregnant women involved in the production of caprolactam," by L. Z. Nadezhdina, et al. GIG TR PROF ZABOL 15:43-44, November, 1971.

"The state of the reproductive systems in women with thyrotoxicosis, before and after pathogenetic treatment," by M. Sh. Sadykova. AKUSH GINEKOL 47:43-46, July, 1971.

"Subsequent gestational morbidity after various types of abortion," by D. T. Liu, et al. LANCET 2:431, August 26, 1972.

"Surgical treatment of abruptio placentae," by I. Kosowsky, et al. ZENTRALBL GYNAEKOL 94:754-756, June 10, 1972.

"Threatened abortions, immature and premature birth in women infected with Toxoplasma gondii," by K. Nowosad, et al. WIAD PARAZYTOL 18:265-267, 1972.

"Three cases of defibrination in the course of retro-placental hematomas," by M. Samama, et al. BULL FED SOC GYNECOL OBSTET LANG FR 23:368-378, September-October, 1971.

"Transplacental haemorrhage in induced abortion," by W. B. Costley, et al. LANCET 1:843, April 15, 1972.

"Transplacental haemorrhage in induced abortion," by S. Murray, et al. LANCET 1:954-955, April 29, 1972.

"Unusual complication during pregnancy interruption by vacuum extraction," by K. Mirkov, et al. AKUSH GINEKOL (Sofiia) 11:85-86, 1972.

"Unusual findings in cesarean section," by L. Pozsonyi. ORV HETIL 113:573-574, March 5, 1972.

"Use of sigetin for the prevention of perinatal mortality and morbidity after the 1st half of complicated pregnancy (experimental and clinical data)," by N. G. Kosheleva. AKUSH GINEKOL 47:40-43, March, 1971.

"Uteroplacental apoplexia with acute defibrination syndrome. Therapeutical discussion of 3 cases," by R. Palliez, et al. BULL FED SOC GYNECOL OBSTET LANG FR 23:411-414, September-October, 1971.

"Utero-placental apoplexy complicated by defibrination," by A. Grand, et al. NOUV PRESSE MED 1:733-736, March 11, 1972.

"The value of studying acidophilic and kariopicnotic indices in abnormal pregnancies," by H. Venegas, et al. REV CHIL OBSTET GINECOL 34:14-16, 1969.

"Value of the systematic determination of teratogenic factors in latent infections of the so-called abortive diseases (preliminary note)," by P. Bierent. BULL SOC PATHOL EXOT 64:423-428,

July-August, 1971.

"Varicelliform eruption, vasculitis, spontaneous abortion, giardiasis and eosinophilia," by S. M. Bierman. ARCH DERMATOL 106:122-123, July, 1972.

"Vascular disorders in habitual abortion," by P. De Agustin, et al. ACTA OBSTET GINECOL HISP LUSIT 19:475-488, December, 1971.

CONTRACEPTION

"Abortion and contraception in scripture," by C. E. Cerling, Jr. CHRISTIAN SCHOLAR'S REVIEW 42-58, Fall, 1971.

"Abortion and contraception in Sweden 1870-1970," by H. Sjovall. Z RECHTSMED 70:197-209, 1972.

"Abortion or contraception?" by P. J. Huntingford. R SOC HEALTH J 91:292-294, November-December, 1971.

"Abortion or contraception," by C. Verdoux. REV INFIRM 22:117-121, February, 1972; also in Z KRANKENPFL 65:279-281 passim, July, 1972.

"Contraception, abortion, demography," by H. De Saint-Blanquat. REV INFIRM 22:107-115, February, 1972.

"Contraception, abortion, prostaglandins and sterilization," by J. H. Ravina. NOUV PRESSE MED 1:989-990, August 26, 1972.

"Contraception or abortion?" DIST NURS 14:262, March, 1972.

"Contraception or abortion?" NURS TIMES 69:249-250, February 24, 1972.

"Contraception or abortion? (a). Usage of contraception and abortion," by G. Chamberlain. R SOC HEALTH J 92:191-194, August, 1972.

"Contraception or abortion? (b). Is abortion a form of contraception?" by H. Gordon. R SOC HEALTH J 92:194-197, August, 1972.

"Contraception or abortion? (e). Termination of pregnancy," by H. R. Arthur. R SOC HEALTH J 92:204-207, August, 1972.

"Contraceptive antecedents to early and late therapeutic abortions," by W. Oppel, et al. AM J PUBLIC HEALTH 62:824-827, June, 1972.

"Experiences with the insertion of IUD after artificial abortion," by M. Tichy, et al. CESK GYNEKOL 37:502-503, September, 1972.

"Experiences with the insertion of intrauterine contraception pessaries of DANA type immediately after artificial abortion," by K. Poradovsky, et al. CESK GYNEKOL 37:497-499, September, 1972.

"Immediate postabortal intrauterine contraceptive device insertion: a double-blind study," by A. Goldsmith, et al. AM J OBSTET GYNECOL 112:957-962, April 1, 1972.

"Increasing consumer participation in professional goal setting: contraception and therapeutic abortion," by R. W. Tichauer, et al. J AM MED WOMENS ASSOC 27:365 passim, July, 1972.

"Insertion of IUD after artificial interruption of pregnancy," by M. Uher, et al. CESK GYNEKOL 37:501-502, September, 1972.

"Our attitude on the insertion of IUD immediately after artificial interruption of pregnancy," by K. Dvorak, et al. CESK GYNEKOL 37:499-501, September, 1972.

"Patterns of abortion and contraceptive usage," by D. M. Potts. R SOC HEALTH J 91:294-296, November-December, 1971.

"'Pill,' IUD, sterilization reduce unwanted births," AMER MED NEWS 15:10-11, August 14, 1972.

"Sporadic triploid and hexaploid cells in embryonic tissue. Negative relationship to maternal intake of oral contraceptives," by T. Kajii, et al. ANN GENET 15:11-18, March, 1972.

"Voluntary interruption of pregnancy: its psychiatric and contraceptive correlates," by S. L. Corson, et al. J REPROD MED 8:151-154, March, 1972.

CYPROHEPTADINE

"A trial of cyproheptadine in habitual abortion," by E. Sadovsky, et al. ISR J MED SCI 81:623-625, May, 1972.

DEMOGRAPHY

see also: Population

"Contraception, abortion, demography," by H. de Saint-Blanquat. REV INFIRM 22:107-115, February, 1972.

"The demographic effects of legal abortion in eastern Europe," by B. Kaptsy. EUROPEAN DEMOGRAPHIC INFO BUL 3:193-207, November 4, 1972.

"The fertility response to abortion reform in eastern Europe: demographic and economic implications," by R. J. McIntyre. AM ECONOMIST 16:45-65, Fall, 1972.

"Nine demographic factors and their relationship to attitudes toward abortion legalization," by D. S. Mileti, et al. SOC BIOL 19:43-50, March, 1972.

DIAGNOSIS

"An abuse of prenatal diagnosis," by M. A. Stenchever. JAMA 221: 408, July 24, 1972.

"Ancedotal contribution to the study of in-utero retention of the dead fetus in the 1st trimester of pregnancy," by C. Guiran. BULL FED SOC GYNECOL OBSTET LANG FR 23:473-475, September-October, 1971.

"Changes in chorionic gonadotropins time as a test for the prognosis of threatened abortion in the 1st trimester," by P. De Patre. MINERVA MED 63:549-553, February 7, 1972.

"Colpocytogram and some indices of hormone levels in women with threatened abortion," by O. S. Badiva. PEDIATR AKUSH GINEKOL 4:38-41, July-August, 1971.

"Evaluation of the immunologic method of determining chorionic gonadotropin in the diagnosis of threatened abortion in its early stages," by V. M. Savitskii, et al. PEDIATR AKUSH GINEKOL 71:38-40, September-October, 1971.

"Fractionated analysis of human chorionic gonadotropins and ultrasonic studies. Supplementary methods for the diagnosis and differential diagnosis of abortions," by H. Wallner, et al. Z ALLGEMEINMED 48:75-79, January 20, 1972.

"Monosomy 21 in spontaneous abortus," by K. Ohama, et al. HUMANGENETIK 16:267-270, 1972.

"Morphological study of the placenta in spontaneously interrupted pregnancies," by B. Kiutukchiev, et al. AKUSH GINEKOL (Sofiia) 10:435-439, 1971.

"The morphology and histochemistry of the fetal liver in spontaneous abortion," by G. I. Sibiriakova, et al. VOPR OKHR MATERIN DET 17:62-65, June, 1972.

"Morphology of exfoliated trophoblastic and decidual cells," by G. D. Montanari, et al. MED SCI LAW 11:200-202, October, 1971.

"Prenatal diagnosis of genetic disease," by T. Friedmann. SCI AM 225:34-42, November, 1971.

"The prognostic and therapeutic value of chorionic hormones in the prevention of early abortions," by M. Chartier, et al. REV FR GYNECOL OBSTET 67:203-208, April, 1972.

"Septic abortion masquerading as thrombotic thrombocytopenic purpura," by M. Yudis, et al. AM J OBSTET GYNECOL 111: 350-352, October 1, 1971.

"Sonar in the management of abortion," by H. P. Robinson. J OBSTET GYNAECOL BR COMMONW 79:90-94, January, 1972.

"Therapeutic abortion and ultrasound," by K. E. Hodge. CAN MED ASSOC J 105:1021, November 20, 1971.

DIAGNOSIS

"Ultrasonic diagnosis in abortion," by H. R. Schulte, et al. ZENTRALBL GYNAEKOL 94:513-519, April 22, 1972.

"The use of human chorionic gonadotropin levels in assessing the prognosis of threatened abortion," by P. R. Grob, et al. PRACTITIONER 209:79-81, July, 1972.

"Use of rheohysterography in pregnancy," by V. N. Kuznetsov. AKUSH GINEKOL 48:64, January, 1972.

"The value of ultrasonic B-scanning in diagnosis when bleeding is present in early pregnancy," by T. R. Varma. AM J OBSTET GYNECOL 114:607-612, November 1, 1972.

"Xeroderma pigmentosum: a rapid sensitive method for prenatal diagnosis," by J. D. Regan, et al. SCIENCE 174:147-150, October 8, 1971.

DILATOL

"Management of threatened abortion and premature delivery with Duvadilan and Dilatol," by P. Hengst, et al. Z AERZTL FORTBILD 65:850-854, August 15, 1971.

DRUG THERAPY

see: Induced Abortion
Surgical Treatment and Management
Techniques of Abortion
Under Specific Drugs

DUVADILAN

"Management of threatened abortion and premature delivery with Duvadilan and Dilatol," by P. Hengst, et al. Z AERZTL FORTBILD 65:850-854, August 15, 1971.

EDTA

"Excellent effect of sodium-citrate-ETDA combination therapy in severe lead poisoning during pregnancy," by K. Abendroth. DTSCH GESUNDHEITSW 26:2130-2131, November 4, 1971.

EDUCATION AND ABORTION

"Sex education at Duke: the development, implementation, and expansion of a medical school program," by M. Shangold, et al. BULL AM COLL NURSE MIDWIVES 17:4-10, February, 1972.

"Sexually transmitted diseases," by J. K. Oates. NURS TIMES 68: 832-834, July 6, 1972.

EPILESPY

see: Complications

FAMILY PLANNING

see also: Sociology, Behavior and Abortion

"Birth: organic selection or technologic design?" by O. C. Schroeder, Jr. POSTGRAD MED 51:53-55, June, 1972.

"Birthright moves ahead," OR 30(226)5, July 27, 1972.

"Birthright New York: continued from the Lamp, October, 1971," by N. Sharkey. C DGST 36:100-103, February, 1972.

"Canadian Nurses' Association position on family planning and related health care," CAN NURSE 68:11, August, 1972.

"Family planning and abortion," LANCET 2:748-749, October 7, 1972.

"Family planning and abortion," by D. Munday. LANCET 2:1308, December 16, 1972.

"Family planning and abortion," by M. Simms. LANCET 2:1085, November 18, 1972.

"Family planning in health services," WHO CHRON 26:73-79, February, 1972.

"Motivation in family planning," by S. Lask. NURSING MIRROR 135:44-46, December 15, 1972.

"OBG . . . abortion, family planning programs among major ACOG meetign topics," by C. Tietze. HOSP TOP 50:41-43, July, 1972.

FAMILY PLANNING

"Obstacles to progress in family planning," by M. J. Ball. CAN MED ASS J 106:227 plus, February 5, 1972.

"Planning family planning," by J. K. Russell. LANCET 1:310-311, February 5, 1972.

"The role of Planned Parenthood-World Population in abortion," by G. Langmyhr. CLIN OBSTET GYNECOL 14:1190-1196, December, 1971.

"Toward a family planning program in psychiatric hospitals," by V. D. Abernethy, et al. AMER J PUBLIC HEALTH 62:1638-1646, December, 1972.

FEES AND PUBLIC ASSISTANCE

see also: Sociology, Behavior and Abortion

"Abortion: financial impact on the patient," by C. Muller. CLIN OBSTET GYNECOL 14:1302-1312, December, 1971.

"Abortion pay limits upheld in New York," AMER MED NEWS 15:15, February 28, 1972.

"Abortion rate up in Canada," HOSP ADMIN CAN 14:17, July, 1972.

"Abortion study finds risks lower for patients not getting public aid," US MED 8:6-7, March 15, 1972.

"Abortions among women on public assistance in Hawaii: implications for practice," by K. T. Kumabe. AMER J PUBLIC HEALTH 62:1538-1543, November, 1972.

"Federal court in New York invalidates order banning abortions for indigents under Medicaid," HOSPITALS 46:25, September 16, 1972.

"Fee charged for the artificial interruption of pregnancy," by K. Jiratko. CESK GYNEKOL 37:586, October, 1972.

"Fee charged for the interruption of pregnancy," by V. Kelensky. CESK GYNEKOL 37:585-586, October, 1972.

FEES AND PUBLIC ASSISTANCE

"Free abortions for all? Report of Commission on Population Growth and the American Future," TIME 99:71, March 27, 1972.

"Freestanding abortion clinics," by C. Tietze. N ENGL J MED 286:432, February 24, 1972.

"Georgia board rules Medicaid will cover abortion fees," RN 35:19, March, 1972.

"Legal abortion: how safe? how available? how costly?" CONSUMER REP 37:466-470, July, 1972.

"Medicaid coverage sought for legal Georgia abortions," HOSPITALS 46:116 plus, January 16, 1972.

"Medicaid funds for abortions banned by New York court," HOSPITALS 46:122, May 16, 1972.

"Public agency reaches out to women in crisis," by S. A. MacMullen. PUBLIC WELFARE 30:2-4, Spring, 1972.

FETUS

"Abortion. The fetal indications. Several reflections," by E. Hervet. NOUV PRESSE MED 1:375-377, February 5, 1972.

"Abortion, fetal indications. Various considerations," by E. Hervet. J SCI MED LILLE 90:176-178, April, 1972.

"Aborting a fetus: the legal right, the personal choice," by S. Lessard. WASHINGTON MO 4:29-37, August, 1972.

"Ancedotal contribution to the study of in-utero retention of the dead fetus in the 1st trimester of pregnancy," by G. Guiran. BULL FED SOC GYNECOL OBSTET LANG FR 23:473-475, September-October, 1971.

"A case of osseus tissue from the fetus residue remaining for 19 years in the uterine wall," by O. I. Stupko, et al. PEDIATR AKUSH GINEKOL 31:62, 1969.

"Dermatoglyphics associated with fetal wastage," by L. I. Rose, et al. N ENGL J MED 287:451-452, August 31, 1972.

"Fetal indications for therapeutic abortion," by A. C. Christakos. NC MED J 33:115-119, February, 1972.

"Fetus exitus," MD 16:261 plus, April, 1972.

"Non-consentual destruction of the fetus: abortion or homicide?" UCLA-ALASKA L REV 1:80, Fall, 1971.

"Question fetus experiments," NAT CATH REP 8:23, March 17, 1972.

"Sudden death of feticide," NAT R 24:1407, December 22, 1972.

"The value of studying the abortus in teratology," by V. P. Kulazhenko, et al. ARKH PATOL 34:50-55, 1972.

FUROSEMIDE

"Effects of administration of Furosemide in acute postabortum renal insufficiency," by T. Burhgele, et al. ACTA UROL BELG 39: 315-321, July, 1971.

GENETICS

"A case of fecundity disorders: chromosomal discussion," by H. Dar, et al. REV FR GYNECOL OBSTET 67:193-194, February-March, 1972.

"Chromosome aberrations and spontaneous abortions," by A. M. Kuliev. AKUSH GINEKOL 47:38-40, April, 1971.

"Chromosome aberrations in oogenesis and embryogenesis of mammals and man," by G. Rohrborn. ARCH TOXIKOL 28:115-119, 1971.

"Chromosome studies in selected spontaneous abortions. IV. Unusual cytogenetic disorders," by D. H. Carr, et al. TERATOLOGY 5:49-56, February, 1972.

"Chromosome studies on spontaneous and threatened abortions," by T. Ikeuchi, et al. JAP J HUM GENET 16:191-197, March, 1972.

"Cytogenetic aspects of induced and spontaneous abortions," by D. H. Carr. CLIN OBSTET GYNECOL 15:203-219, March, 1972.

"Cytogenetic effect of DDB," by B. Ia. Ekshtat, et al. GIG SANIT 36:26-29, December, 1971.

"Eugenic abortion," by C. P. Kindregan. SUFFOLK U L REV 6:405, Spring, 1972.

"Fetal wastage and maternal masochism," by L. Y. Hsu, et al. OBSTET GYNECOL 40:98-103, July, 1972.

"Incidence of chromosome abnormalities in spontaneous abortion and study of the risk in subsequent pregnancies," by J. G. Boue. REV FR GYNECOL OBSTET 67:183-187, February-March, 1972.

"Lethal chromosome abnormalities in the antenatal and perinatal stages of human development," by M. A. Petrov-Maslakov, et al. VESTN AKAD MED NAUK SSSR 27:68-77, 1972.

"Moral problems in genetic counseling," by J. C. Fletcher. PAST PSYCH 23:47-60, April, 1972.

"Prenatal diagnosis of genetic disease," by T. Friedmann. SCI AM 225:34-42, November, 1971.

"Repeated abortion. Enzyme and chromosome anomalies in the couple," by J. Grozdea, et al. NOUV PRESSE MED 1:1234, April 29, 1972.

"Repeated early spontaneous abortions and maternal autosomal translocation t(Bq plus, Cq minus)," by A. Broustet, et al. BORD MED 5:669-672, March, 1972.

"Selective abortion, gametic selection, and the X chromosome," by G. R. Fraser. AM J HUM GENET 24:359-370, July, 1972.

"Spontaneous abortions in women-carriers of the phenylketonuria gene," by M. G. Bliumina. AKUSH GINEKOL 48:52-55, May, 1972.

GYNAECOLOGY

"Advances in obstetrics and gnyaecology," by V. R. Tindall. PRACTITIONER 209:437-443, October, 1972.

"Developing applications of prostaglandins in obstetrics and gynecology," by J. W. Hinman. AM J OBSTET GINECOL 113:130-138, May 1, 1972.

"Effects of legal abortion on gynaecology," by A. H. John, et al. BR MED J 3:99-102, July 8, 1972.

"Gynaecological aftermaths of the 1967 Abortion Act," by M. Brudenell. PROC R SOC MED 65:155-158, February, 1972.

"Three years of the Abortion Act: gynecological and psychiatric aftermaths," by D. Baird. PROC R SOC MED 65:160-162, February, 1972.

HABITUAL ABORTION

"Causes of infertility," by R. Gergova, et al. CESK GYNEKOL 37: 529-530, September, 1972.

"Cervical mucus, vaginal cytology and steroid excretion in recurrent abortion," by R. R. MacDonald, et al. OBSTET GYNECOL 40:394-402, September, 1972.

"Chromosome aberrations and spontaneous abortions," by A. M. Kuliev. AKUSH GINEKOL 47:38-40, April, 1971.

"The course of pregnancy and labor in women with previous abortions," by A. Atanasov, et al. AKUSH GINEKOL (Sofiia) 10:456-459, 1971.

"Experiences in the therapy of spontaneous and habitual abortions with the oral administration of Gestanon A," by B. Beric, et al. MED PREGL 24:505-507, 1971.

"Experiences with cerclage," by R. Ruzicska, et al. ORV HETIL 112:1628-1631, July 11, 1971.

"Figlu test in habitual abortion and missed abortion," by O. Sacco, et al. ARCH OSTET GINECOL 75:484-491, December, 1970.

"Habitual abortion and toxoplasmosis. Is there a relationship?" by P. M. Southern, Jr. OBSTET GYNECOL 39:45-47, January, 1972.

"Histamine reactivity of the skin in women with habitual abortion," by B. Kiutukchiev, et al. AKUSH GINEKOL (Sofiia) 11:31-36, 1972.

"Isthmico-cervical insufficiency as a factor in prematurity (late abortions and premature labor) and its surgical treatment," by R. Tokin. AKUSH GINEKOL (Sofiia) 8:169-177, 1969.

"Management of recurring abortion," by H. C. McLaren. PRACTITIONER 209:661-664, November, 1972.

"Repeated abortion. Enzyme and chromosome anomalies in the couple," by J. Grozdea, et al. NOUV PRESSE MED 1:1234, April 29, 1972.

"Repeated early spontaneous abortions and maternal autosomal translocation t(Bq plus, Cq minus)," by A. Broustet, et al. BORD MED 5:669-672, March, 1972.

"Risk pregnancy in women examined before conception and treated for habitual abortion," by A. Zwinger, et al. CESK GYNEKOL 37:232-233, May, 1972.

"Some clinical-physiological indices in children born of mothers with habitual abortion," by A. K. Svetiova, et al. VOPR OKHR MATERIN DET 16:64-70, May, 1971.

"The state of the reproductive systems in women with thyrotoxicosis, before and after pathogenetic treatment," by M. Sh. Sadykova. AKUSH GINEKOL 47:43-46, July, 1971.

"Study of cellular immunity in couples with habitual abortion," by J. Gordillo, et al. GINECOL OBSTET MEX 31:325-328, March, 1972.

"Surgical treatment of pregnant women with habitual abortion caused by cervix insufficiency," by J. Bocev. AKUSH GINEKOL 47:69-70, April, 1971.

"Temporary submucosal cerclage for cervical incompetence: report of forty-eight cases," by C. L. Jennings, Jr. AM J OBSTET GYNECOL 113:1097-1102, August 15, 1972.

"Transabdominal cervico-uterine suture," by R. A. Watkins. AUST NZ J OBSTET GYNAECOL 12:62-64, February, 1972.

"Treatment of habitual abortion by the Mitchell-Bardavil method," by V. I. Finik. AKUSH GINEKOL 48:61-63, February, 1972.

"A trial of cyproheptadine in habitual abortion," by E. Sadovsky, et al. ISR J MED SCI 81:623-625, May, 1972.

"Vascular disorders in habitual abortion," by P. De Agustin, et al. ACTA OBSTET GINECOL HISP LUSIT 19:475-488, December, 1971.

HEMORRHAGE

see also: Complications

"Blood loss and changes in total blood volume during induced abortion," by R. Raicheva. AKUSH GINEKOL (Sofiia) 10:284-286, 1971.

"Coagulation changes after hypertonic saline infusion for late abortions," by F. D. Brown, et al. OBSTET GYNECOL 39:538-543, April, 1972.

"Concealed accidental haemorrhage," by M. N. Malathy. NURS J INDIA 63:75 plus, March, 1972.

"Fatal embolism following abortion and surgery," by E. S. Redfield, et al. JAMA 220:1745-1746, June 26, 1972.

"The value of ultrasonic B-scanning in diagnosis when bleeding is present in early pregnancy," by T. R. Varma. AM J OBSTET GYNECOL 114:607-612, Novembe1 1, 1972.

HISTORY

"Abortion and contraception in Sweden 1870-1970," by H. Sjovall. Z RECHTSMED 70:197-209, 1972.

"Dr. Andre Hellegers: in the year 2000 abortion will be considered backward," by R. Simanski. NAT CATH REP 8:5-6, October 5, 1972.

"18th century medical dissertations on anatomy at the Rostock University. 2. Inaugural address of Wilhelm Friedrich Zander on abortion (1748)," by H. G. Wischhusen, et al. ANAT ANZ 130: 277-284, 1972.

"Sixty years ago," NURS J INDIA 62:385, December, 1971.

HORMONES

"Colpocytogram and some indices of hormone levels in women with threatened abortion," by O. S. Badiva. PEDIATR AKUSH GINEKOL 4:38-41, July-August, 1971.

"Hormone levels during prostaglandin F 2 infusions for therapeutic abortion," by L. Speroff, et al. J CLIN ENDOCRINOL METAB 34:531-536, March, 1972.

"Hormone therapy of threatened abortion," by S. Stojanov. ZENTRALBL GYNAEKOL 94:1323-1326, October 7, 1972.

"The interrelationship between sex hormone excretion and the concentration of copper, manganese, zinc, and cobalt in the placentas of women with normal and prematurely interrupted pregnancies," by P. I. Fogel. AKUSH GINEKOL 47:45-48, August, 1971.

"The prognostic and therapeutic value of chorionic hormones in the prevention of early abortions," by M. Chartier, et al. REV FR GYNECOL OBSTET 67:203-208, April, 1972.

"Treatment of habitual miscarriages with long-acting steroid hormones," by M. D. Moiseenko, et al. VOPR OKHR MATERIN DET 17:60-62, June, 1972.

HOSPITALS AND ABORTION

"Abortion clinics: hospital hot spots," by J. Battaglai. HOSP WORLD 1:12 plus, January, 1972.

"Abortions in all hospitals by 1975," CAN HOSP 49:9, March, 1971.

"Baltimore hospital abortion patient given $90,000 in damages," HOSPITALS 46:133, November 1, 1972.

"Design complements patients' needs: Planned Parenthood Family Planning Center's abortion clinic, New York City," HOSPITALS 46:42 plus, September 16, 1972.

"The experience of two county hospitals in implementation of therapeutic abortion," by J. R. Bragonier, et al. CLIN OBSTET GYNECOL 14:1237-1242, December, 1971.

"Hospital opposing abortions returns Hill-Burton money: Mercy Hospital in New Orleans," HOSPITALS 48:147, June 1, 1972.

"In-hospital care and post-hospital followup," by L. M. Tanner, et al. CLIN OBSTET GYNECOL 14:1278-1288, December, 1971.

"Legal abortion and the hospital's role," by E. B. Connell. HOSP PRACT 7:143-150, February, 1972.

"Mt. Carmel Mercy Hospital, Michigan, takes stand on abortion," CATH HOSP 3:8, July, 1972.

"New Catholic hospital code," by C. E. Curran. FAMILY PLANN PERSPECT 4:7-8, July, 1972.

"Outpatient abortions," by L. Rauramo. ANN CHIR GYNAECOL FENN 61:45-46, 1972.

"Outpatient management of first trimester therapeutic abortions with and without tubal ligation," by J. A. Collins, et al. CAN MED ASSOC J 106:1077-1080, May 20, 1972.

"Preventing unwanted pregnancies: role of the hospital," by R. J. Pion. POSTGRAD MED 51:172-175, January, 1972.

HOSPITALS AND ABORTION

"The role of the university hospital in solving the logistic problems of legal abortion," by E. W. Overstreet. CLIN OBSTET GYNECOL 14:1243-1247, December, 1971.

"Vacuum aspirations at a hospital outpatient clinic," by R. Fahraeus. LAKARTIDNINGEN 69:4665-4670, October 4, 1972.

IMMUNITY AND ABORTION

"Antinuclear factor in a patient with recurrent abortions," by C. Abrahams, et al. S AFR MED J 46:844, June 17, 1972.

"Antinuclear factor in 2 patients with recurrent abortions," by C. Abrahams, et al. LANCET 1:498-499, February 26, 1972.

"Characteristics of nonspecific immunity during pregnacny, after abortions and labor," by F. D. Aniskova, et al. VOPR OKHR MATERIN DET 16:60-63, May, 1971.

"Danger of Rh-isoimmunization in induced abortion and its prevention using anti-Rh (D) immunoglobulin," by G. Bajtal, et al. ZENTRALBL GNYAEKOL 94:922-925, July, 1972.

"Do Rh-negative women with an early spontaneous abortion need Rh immune prophylaxis?" by R. D. Visscher, et al. AM J OBSTET GYNECOL 113:158-165, May 15, 1972.

"Immunologic indices and serum protein fractions in patients with peritonitis and sepsis following non-hospital abortions," by N. N. Kulikova, et al. AKUSH GINEKOL 47:14-18, November, 1971.

"Preliminary attempts to terminate pregnancy by immunological attack on uterine protein," by J. C. Daniel, Jr. EXPERIENTIA 28:700-701, June 15, 1972.

"Prevention of Rh immunization after abortion with Anti-Rh (D)-immunoglobulin," by J. A. Goldman, et al. OBSTET GYNECOL 40:366-370, September, 1972.

"Prevention of Rh immunization in abortions," by J. Goldman, et al. HAREFUAH 81:514-515, November 15, 1971.

IMMUNITY AND ABORTION

"Rhesus sensitization in abortion," by P. S. Gavin. OBSTET GYNECOL 39:37-40, January, 1972.

"Rh-immune globulin in induced abortion: utilization in a high-risk population," by R. G. Judelsohn, et al. AM J OBSTET GYNECOL 114:1031-1034, December 15, 1972.

"Significance of immunologic conflict in the development of pregnancy complications (literature review)," by D. V. Umbrumiants. AKUSH GINEKOL 48:41-46, January, 1972.

"Study of cellular immunity in couples with habitual abortion," by J. Gordillo, et al. GINECOL OBSTET MEX 31:325-328, March, 1972.

INDUCED ABORTION

see also: Techniques of Abortion

"Abdominal aspiration hysterotomy," by D. T. Liu. LANCET 2:654, September 23, 1972.

"Abortion and Islam," by H. Hathout. J MED LIBAN 25:237-239, 1972.

"Abortion and morality," by P. R. Ehrlich, et al. CAN NURSE 68:37, June, 1972.

"Abortion by aspiration technic," by T. B. Cheikh, et al. TUNIS MED 2:119-120, March-April, 1971.

"Abortion counseling," by J. D. Asher. AM J PUBLIC HEALTH 62: 686-688, May, 1972.

"Abortion counseling and behavioral change," by B. Dauber, et al. FAM PLANN PERSPECT 4:23-27, April, 1972.

"Abortion deaths," BR MED J 4:295, November 4, 1972.

"Abortion deaths," by H. C. McLaren. BR MED J 3:826, September 30, 1972.

"Abortion; do attitudes of nursing personnel affect the patient's perception of care?'' by M. W. Harper, et al. NURS RES 21:327-331, July-August, 1972.

''Abortion during the 1st trimester by means of polyclinical vacuum aspiration without anesthesia,'' NED TIJDSCHR GENEESKD 116:165, January 22, 1972.

''The abortion explosion,'' by J. F. Hulka. NC MED J 33:957-959, November, 1972.

''Abortion . . . human aspects,'' by D. Goyette. INFIRM CAN 14:30-34, June, 1972.

''Abortion in a general practice. The fourth baby syndrome,'' by E. J. Hopkins, et al. PRACTITIONER 208:528-533, April, 1972.

''Abortion in psychological perspective,'' by H. P. David. AM J ORTHOPSYCHIATRY 42:61-68, January, 1972.

''Abortion law,'' by J. Newlinds. MED J AUST 2:627, September 9, 1972.

''Abortion operations--the right to opt out,'' AUSTRALAS NURSES J 1:17, April, 1972.

''Abortion or contraception?'' by P. J. Huntingford. R SOC HEALTH J 91:292-294, November-December, 1971.

''Abortion or contraception,'' by C. Verdoux. REV INFIRM 22:117-121, February, 1972; also in Z KRANKENPFL 65:279-281 passim, July, 1972.

''Abortion, psychiatry, and the quality of life,'' by Z. M. Lebensohn. AM J PSYCHIATRY 128:946-951, February, 1972.

''Abortion recidivism. A problem in preventive medicine,'' by J. J. Rovinsky. OBSTET GYNECOL 39:649-659, May, 1972.

''Abortion reform,'' by R. G. Bubeck. J AM OSTEOPATH ASSOC 71: 842-845, June, 1972.

"Abortion: use of prostaglandins and epidural analgesia," by I. Craft. LANCET 2:41, July 1, 1972.

"Abortion with extra-amniotic prostaglandins," by J. E. Bruce. LANCET 2:380, August 19, 1972.

"Abortion with extra-amniotic prostaglandins," by M. P. Embrey, et al. LANCET 2:654-655, September 23, 1972.

"Abortion with prostaglandins," by B. Alderman. LANCET 2:279, August 5, 1972.

"Abortions and acute identity crisis in nurses," by W. F. Char, et al. AM J PSYCHIATRY 128:952-957, February, 1972.

"Abortions regaining objectivity or rationalization?" by E. F. Kal, et al. AM J PSYCHIATRY 129:484-485, October, 1972.

"The action of PGF 2 prostaglandin on the pregnant uterus," by F. Szontagh, et al. ORV HETIL 113:919-922, April 16, 1972.

"Ambulatory abortion: experience with 26,000 cases (July 1, 1970, to August 1, 1971)," by B. N. Nathanson. N ENGL J MED 286: 403-407, February 24, 1972.

"Analysis of prostaglandin F 2 and metabolites in blood during constant intravenous infusion of prostaglandin F 2 in the human female," by F. Beguin, et al. ACTA PHYSIOL SCAND 86:430-432, November, 1972.

"Anesthesia for early artificial interruption of pregnancy," by R. S. Mikhaleva. AKUSH GINEKOL 47:61, December, 1971.

"Anesthesia in minor gynecologic surgery with trichloroethylene," by V. S. Lesiuk. AKUSH GINEKOL 48:70-71, April, 1972.

"Anesthetic-induced abortion?" by D. H. Carr. ANESTHESIOLOGY 35:335, October, 1971.

"Anticipatory guidance for abortion," by L. W. Tinnin, et al. MD STATE MED J 21:73, May, 1972.

"Artificial interruption of pregnancy and extrauterine pregnancy," by A. Cernoch. ZENTRALBL GYNAEKOL 93:1784-1791, December 25, 1971.

"Attitude of the woman to artificial interruption of pregnancy and the gynecologist's tasks," by J. Kveton, et al. CESK GYNEKOL 37: 533-534, September, 1972.

"Blood loss and changes in total blood volume during induced abortion," by R. Raicheva. AKUSH GINEKOL (Sofiia) 10:284-286, 1971.

"A case of osseus tissue from the fetus residue remaining for 19 years in the uterine wall," by O. I. Stupko, et al. PEDIATR AKUSH GINEKOL 31:62, 1969.

"Cervicovaginal fistula as a result of saline abortion," by R. T. Gordon. AM J OBSTET GYNECOL 112:578-579, February 15, 1972.

"Changes in serum and urinary electrolytes," by T. C. Wong, et al. NY STATE J MED 72:564-577, March 1, 1972.

"Clinical experiences in induced abortion using vacuum extraction and the metranoikter," by J. Hoffman, et al. ZENTRALBL GYNAEKOL 94:913-917, July 22, 1972.

"Coagluation changes after hypertonic saline infusion for late abortions," by F. D. Brown, et al. OBSTET GYNECOL 39:538-543, April, 1972.

"Comparative studies on effects of previous pregnancy interruption, spontaneous abortion and term labor on the incidence of immature and premature labors," by S. Rozewicki, et al. WIAD LEK 25:31-38, January, 1972.

"Congenital malformations and refused termination," by T. J. David, et al. LANCET 1:1123, May 20, 1972.

"Consumptive coagulopathy associated with intra-amniotic infusion of hypertonic salt," by F. K. Keller, et al. AM J OBSTET

GYNECOL 112:534-543, February 15, 1972.

"Consumptive coagulopathy with generalized hemorrhage after hypertonic saline-induced abortion, a case report," by D. R. Halbert, et al. OBSTET GYNECOL 39:41-44, January, 1972.

"Contraception or abortion?" DIST NURS 14:262, March, 1972.

"Contraception or abortion?" NURS TIMES 69:249-250, February 24, 1972.

"Correlates of repeat induced abortions," by M. B. Bracken, et al. OBSTET GYNECOL 40:816-825, December, 1972.

"Counseling the abortion patient is more than talk," by C. Keller, et al. AM J NURS 72:102-106, January, 1972.

"Cytogenetic aspects of induced and spontaneous abortions," by D. H. Carr. CLIN OBSTET GYNECOL 15:203-219, March, 1972.

"Cytogenetic effect of DDB," by B. Ia. Ekshtat, et al. GIG SANIT 36:26-29, December, 1971.

"Danger of Rh-isoimmunization in induced abortion and its prevention using anti-Rh (D) immunoglobulin," by G. Bajtai, et al. ZENTRALBL GYNAEKOL 94:922-925, July 22, 1972.

"Defibrination in saline abortion," by R. Schwartz, et al. OBSTET GYNECOL 40:728-737, November, 1972.

"Defibrination syndrome after intra-amniotic infusion of hypertonic saline," by A. E. Weiss, et al. AM J OBSTET GYNECOL 113: 868-874, August 1, 1972.

"Defibrinogenation after intra-amniotic injection of hypertonic saline," by J. L. Spivak, et al. N ENGL J MED 287:321-323, August 17, 1972.

"Delayed after effects of medically induced abortion," by H. Warnes. CAN PSYCHIATR ASSOC J 16:537-541, December, 1971.

"Design complements patients' needs," HOSPITALS 46:42-43 passim passim, September 16, 1972.

"Developing applications of prostaglandins in obstetrics and gynecology," by J. W.Hinman. AM J OBSTET GYNECOL 113:130-138, May 1, 1972.

"Developing professional parameters: nursing and social work roles in the care of the induced abortion patient," by L. M. Tanner. CLIN OBSTET GYNECOL 14:1271-1272, December, 1972.

"Divergence of opinion on placental damage due to hypertonic saline-induced abortion," by Y. Manabe, et al. AM J OBSTET GYNECOL 114:1107-1108, December 15, 1972.

"Early abortion without cervical dilation: pump or syringe aspiration," by A. J. Margolis, et al. J REPROD MED 9:237-240, November, 1972.

"Early complications of pregnancy interruption according to our records," by B. Jakubovska, et al. CESK GYNEKOL 37:532-533, September, 1972.

"Early somatic complications in abortion," by P. Atterfelt, et al. LAKARTIDNINGEN 69:241-246, January 12, 1972.

"Effect of intraamniotic sodium concentration on saline induced abortion," by R. R. Weiss, et al. OBSTET GYNECOL 40:243-246, August, 1972.

"Effect of the method of induced abortion (curettage, v. aspiration) on feto-maternal isoimmunization," by M. Asztalos, et al. ZENTRALBL GYNAEKOL 94:926-930, July 22, 1972.

"8 cases of therapetuic abortion in advanced pregnancy by injections of hypertonic saline serum," by T. B. Cheikh, et al. TUNIS MED 2:117-118, March-April, 1971.

"Elective abortion. Woman in crisis," by N. Leiter. NY STATE J MED 72:2908-2910, December 1, 1972.

INDUCED ABORTION

"Excellent effect of sodium-citrate-EDTA-combination therapy in severe lead poisoning during pregnancy," by K. Abendroth. DTSCH GESUNDHEITSW 26:2130-2131, November 4, 1971.

"Experience with the use of promedol in anesthesia for artificial abortion," by Z. P. Drozdovskaia, et al. AKUSH GINEKOL 47: 61-62, December, 1971.

"Experiences with the insertion of intrauterine contraception pessaries of DANA type immediately after artificial abortion," by K. Poradovsky, et al. CESK GYNECOL 37:497-499, September, 1972.

"Experiences with the insertion of IUD after artificial abortion," by M. Tichy, et al. CESK GYNEKOL 37:502-503, September, 1972.

"Factors associated with delay in seeking induced abortions," by M. B. Bracken, et al. AM J OBSTET GYNECOL 113:301-309, June 1, 1972.

"Factors associated with instillation-abortion time during saline-instillation abortion," by M. B. Bracken, et al. AM J OBSTET GYNECOL 114:10-12, September 1, 1972.

"Factors responsible for delay in obtaining interruption of pregnancy," by G. B.Mallory, Jr, et al. OBSTET GYNECOL 40:556-562, October, 1972.

"Fetal blood typing after induced abortion," by S. Shah, et al. OBSTET GYNECOL 40:724-727, November, 1972.

"Fever and bacteremia assoicated with hypertonic saline abortion," by C. R. Steinberg, et al. OBSTET GYNECOL 39:673-678, May, 1972.

"Harmfulness of the interruption of pregnancy in primigravidae," by K. Balak. CESK GYNEKOL 37:585, October, 1972.

"Hazard of saline abortion," by N. R. Kaplan. JAMA 221:89, July 3, 1972.

"Hemotherapeutic safeguarding of induced abortion in inborn proconvertin insufficiency (hemagglutination factor VII) using exchange plasmapheresis," by S. Valnicek, et al. ZENTRALBL GYNAEKOL 94:931-935, July 22, 1972.

"Hormone therapy of threatened abortion," by S. Stojanov. ZENTRALBL GYNAEKOL 94:1323-1326, October 7, 1972.

"How safe is abortion?" by S. V. Sood. LANCET 1:380, February 12, 1972.

"Immediate morbidity on large abortion service. The first year's experience," by L. A. Walton. NY STATE J MED 72:919-921, April 15, 1972.

"Implementation of legal abortion: a national problem. Epilogue," by J. R. Marshall. CLIN OBSTET GYNECOL 14:1336-1338, December, 1971.

"Induced abortion and marriage counseling in multiple sclerosis," by R. C. Behrend. MED WELT 23:326-330, March 4, 1972.

"Induced abortion and marriage counseling in myasthenia," by H. G. Mertens. MED WELT 23:332-335, March 4, 1972.

"Induced abortion in the United States, 1971," by R. E. Hall. J REPROD MED 8:345-347, June, 1972.

"Induction of abortion by extra-amniotic administration of prostaglandins E2 and F2-alpha," by M. P. Embrey, et al. BR MED J 3:146-149, July 15, 1972.

"Induction of labour. Recent developments," by M. O. Pulkkinen. ANN CHIR GYNAECOL FENN 61:47-51, 1972.

"The influence of an anti-steroidogenic drug (aminoglutethimide phopshate) on pregnancy maintenance," by S. R. Glasser, et al. ENDOCRINOLOGY 90:1363-1370, May, 1972.

"Insertion of IUD after artificial interruption of pregnancy," by M. Uher, et al. CESK GYNEKOL 37:501-502, September, 1972.

"The interrelationship between sex hormone excretion and the concentration of copper, manganese, zinc, and cobalt in the placentas of women with normal and prematurely interrupted pregnancies," by P. I. Fogel. AKUSH GINEKOL 47:45-48, August, 1971.

"Interruption of late term pregnancy by intra-amnion administration of hypertonic solutions," by K. I. Braginskii. AKUSH GINEKOL 48: 61-62, May, 1972.

"Interruption of late term pregnancy by intra-amnion transcervical administration of a hypertonic solution of sodium chloride," by G. A. Palladi, et al. AKUSH GINEKOL 48:58-61, May, 1972.

"Interruption of pregnancy--for and against," by H. Lochmuller. MUNCH MED WOCHENSCHR 114:1557-1560, September 15, 1972.

"Interruption of pregnancy in women with mitral stenosis," by V. Irasek. AKUSH GINEKOL (Sofiia) 11:41-45, 1972.

"Interruption of pregnanyy using F2 alpha prostaglandins," by T. Brat, et al. J GYNECOL OBSTET BIOL REPROD 1:385-387, June, 1972.

"Intra-amniotic administration of prostaglandin F 2 for abortion," by A. C. Wenz, et al. AM J OBSTET GYNECOL 113:793-803, July 15, 1972.

"Intracranial dural sinus thrombosis following intrauterine instillation of hypertonic saline," by J. A. Goldman, et al. AM J OBSTET GYNECOL 112:1132-1139, April 15, 1972.

"Intrauterine administration of (S)-15-methyl-prostaglandin F 2 for induction of abortion," by M. Bygdeman, et al. LANCET 1:1336-1337, June 17, 1972.

"Is abortion murder?" by R. E. Groves. NURS TIMES 68:624-625, May 18, 1972.

"Issues of conscience," by T. M. Schorr. AM J NURS 72:61, January, 1972.

"The Karman catheter: a preliminary evaluation as an instrument for termination of pregnancies up to twelve weeks of gestation," by B. Beric, et al. AM J OBSTET GYNECOL 114:273-275, September 15, 1972.

"Lactation following therapeutic abortion with prostaglandin F 2," by I. D. Smith, et al. NATURE (London) 240:411-412, December 15, 1972.

"Laminaria tent: relic of the past or modern medical device?" by B. W. Newton. AM J OBSTET GYNECOL 113:442-448, June 15, 1972.

"Legal abortion--the act and its effects. 2.," by A. Hordern. MIDWIFE HEALTH VISIT 8:169-173, May, 1972.

"Legal induced abortion," by K. Kristoffersen. UGESKR LAEGER 134:403-404, February 21, 1972.

"Legal induced abortion. The first year under the new abortion law," by J. G. Lauritsen, et al. UGESKR LAEGER 134:405-410, February 21, 1972.

"Let the day perish . . .," by M. J. Frazer. CATHOL NURSE 2-5, Autumn, 1972.

"Mental aspects of abortion," by L. Florean, et al. CESK GYNEKOL 37:530-531, September, 1972.

"Mid-trimester abortion," by G. Davis, et al. LANCET 2:1026, November 11, 1972.

"Moralists confronting abortion," by A. J. Schaller. VIE MED CAN FR 1:175-181, February, 1972.

"New antifertility agent--an orally active prostaglandin--ICI 74,205," by A. P. Labhsetwar. NATURE (London) 238:400-401, August 18, 1972.

"A new method for interruption of pregnancy after the 3rd month," by R. Raichev, et al. AKUSH GINEKOL (Sofiia) 8:93-94, 1969.

"Our attitude on the insertion of IUD immediately after artificial interruption of pregnancy," by K. Dvorak, et al. CESK GYNEKOL 37:499-501, September, 1972.

"Our experience in interruption of advanced pregnancy," by A. Milojkovic, et al. MED ARH 26:13-16, January-February, 1972.

"Oxytocin, 'salting out,' and water intoxication," by D. R. Gupta, et al. JAMA 220:681-683, May 1, 1972.

"Oxytocics used by practitioners--with special reference to induced abortions," by K. Sato. SANFUJINKA JISSAI 21:203-208, March, 1972.

"The paramedic abortionist," by H. Karman. CLIN OBSTET GYNECOL 15:379-387, June, 1972.

"A pastoral approach to abortion," by J. F. Hickey. J REPROD MED 8:355-358, June, 1972.

"Perplexities for the would-be liberal in abortion," by A. J. Dyck. J REPROD MED 8:351-354, June, 1972.

"Physicians' attitudes toward abortion," by L. A. LoSciuto, et al. J REPROD MED 9:70-74, August, 1972.

"Post abortum acute renal insufficiency treated by daily dialysis," by V. Jovanovic, et al. SPR ARH CELOK LEK 98:1453-1457, December, 1970.

"Preabortion evaluation: decision-making, preparation and referral," by L. M. Tanner, et al. CLIN OBSTET GYNECOL 14:1273-1277, December, 1971.

"Pre-emptive abortion," NEWSWEEK 80:69, July 24, 1972.

"Pregnancy interruption. What is my function as a nruse?" by C. Guller. Z KRANKENPFL 65:173-174, May, 1972.

"Pregnancy interruption and origin of extrauterine pregnancy," by A. Cernoch. CAS LEK CESK 111:285-287, March 24, 1972.

"Pregnancy interruption from the radiologist's viewpoint," by V. Bohringer. RADIOL DIAGN 13:187-191, 1972.

"Pregnancy termination: the impact of new laws. An invitational symposium," J REPROD MED 6:274-301, June, 1971.

"Prehumane, humane, posthumane and inhumane human life," by W. S. Stekhoven. TIJDSCHR ZIEKENVERPL 25:674-676, June 27, 1972.

"Prevention of pregnancy and pregnancy interruption, I.," by E. Erb. Z KRANKENPFL 65:167-170, May, 1972.

"Prevention of pregnancy and pregnancy interruption, II.," by A. Trenkel. Z KRANKENPFL 65:170-172, May, 1972.

"The problem of abortion from the medical viewpoint," by H. Husslein. WIEN MED WOCHENSCHR 2:Suppl:3-7, November, 1971.

"Problems of our population trend and the artificial interruption of pregnancy in practice," by A. Kotasek. CESK GYNEKOL 37: 565-568, October, 1972.

"Prospective study of fertility in the District of Sao Paulo. I. Comparison of retrospective and prospective methods to estimate the rates of spontaneous and induced abortions," by M. L. Milanesi, et al. BOL OF SANIT PANAM 72:234-243, March, 1972.

"Prostaglandin E 2: analysis of effects on pregnancy and corpus luteum in hamsters and rats," by A. P. Labhsetwar. ACTA ENDOCRINOL 170:Suppl:3-32, 1972.

"Prostaglandin-oxytocin enhancement and potentiation and their clinical applications," by A. Gillespie. BR MED J 1:150-152, January 15, 1972.

"Prostaglandins and abortion," by M. Seppala. DUODECIM 88:1029-1031, 1972.

"Prostaglandins in fertility control," by J. S. Carrel. SCIENCE 175:1279, March 17, 1972.

INDUCED ABORTION

"Prostaglandins in human reproduction," by V. Vakhariya, et al. MICH MED 71:777-784, September, 1972.

"Prostaglandins in inducing labour and abortion," by Z. Polishuk. HAREFUAH 80:332-333, March 15, 1971.

"Psychiatric aspects of abortion," by A. C. Gullattee. J NATL MED ASSOC 64:308-311, July, 1972.

"Psychiatrists' attitudes to abortion," by J. C. Little. BR MED J 1:110, January 8, 1972.

"The psychological antecedent and consequences of abortion," by J. L. Maes. J REPROD MED 8:341-344, June, 1972.

"Psychosocial aspects of induced abortion. Its implications for the woman, her family and her doctor. 1.," by B. Raphael. MED J AUST 2:35-40, July 1, 1972.

"Psychosocial aspects of induced abortion. Its implications for the woman, her family and her doctor. 2.," by B. Raphael. MED J AUST 2:98-101, July 8, 1972.

"Public health and the law. Presidential morality, abortion, and federal-state law," by W. J. Curran. AM J PUBLIC HEALTH 61: 1042-1043, May, 1971.

"The quality of life as opposed to the right to life," by H. I. Posin, et al. AM J PSYCHIATRY 129:358-360, September, 1972.

"Reduction in fertility due to induced abortions: a simulation model," by K. Venkatacharya. DEMOGRAPHY 9:339-352, August, 1972.

"Reductions in complications due to induced abortions noted," HOSPITALS 46:19, December 1, 1972.

"Relationship between prevalence of steriliaztion by surgery and pregnancy, parity and induced abortion," JAP J PUBLIC HEALTH NURSE 27:50-56, December, 1971.

"The relationship of amniotic fluid sodium to the latent period of saline abortion," by H. Schulman, et al. OBSTET GYNECOL 39:679-682, May, 1972.

"Rh-immune globulin in induced abortion: utilization in a high-risk population," by R. G. Judelsohn, et al. AM J OBSTET GYNECOL 114:1031-1034, December 15, 1972.

"The right to abortion: a psychiatric view," GROUP ADV PSYCHIATRY 7:203-227, October, 1969.

"The role of induced abortion in the changing pattern of birth control in the Netherlands," by P. E. Treffers. NED TIJDSCHR GENEESKD 116:1459-1466, August 12, 1972.

"Saline abortion," by E. M. Stim. OBSTET GYNECOL 40:247-251, August, 1972.

"Second-trimester abortion after vaginal termination of pregnancy," by A. J. Margolis, et al. LANCET 2:431-432, August 26, 1972.

"Second-trimester abortion after vaginal termination of pregnancy," by C. S. Wright, et al. LANCET 1:1278-1279, June 10, 1972.

"Serum ceruloplasmin, 1 -antitrypsin, 2 -macroglobulin and iron and T 3 binding proteins during hypertonic saline-induced abortion," by K. Willman, et al. ACTA OBSTET GYNECOL SCAND 51:161-163, 1972.

"Serum human chorionic gonadotropin, human chorionic somatomammotropin, and progesterone following intra-amniotic injection of hypertonic urea," by H. R. Raud, et al. AM J OBSTET GYNECOL 113:887-894, August 1, 1972.

"Should abortions be performed in doctors' offices?" by S. Neubardt, et al. FAM PLANN PERSPECT 4:4-7, July, 1972.

"Social indication in pregnancy interruption," by W. Becker. THER GGW 111:587-588 passim, April, 1972.

"Sporadic tripioid and hexapioid cells in embryonic tissue. Negative relationship to maternal intake of oral contraceptives," by T.

Kajii, et al. ANN GENET 15:11-18, March, 1972.

"A study of Title 19 coverage of abortion," by H. M. Wallace, et al. AM J PUBLIC HEALTH 62:1116-1122, August, 1972.

"Surgical management of abortion," by J. F. Palomaki, et al. N ENGL J MED 287:752-754, October 12, 1972.

"Surgical sterilization and interruption of pregnancy as means of fertility regulation," by W. Dalicho. BEITR GERICHTL MED 29:344-350, 1972.

"Termination of pregnancy," by D. Bluett. BR MED J 2:228, April 22, 1972.

"Termination of pregnancy," by H. C. McLaren. BR MED J 2:714, June 17, 1972.

"Termination of pregnancy," by P. Moxon. BR MED J 2:655, June 10, 1972.

"Termination of pregnancy," by J. Slome. LANCET 2:881-882, October 21, 1972.

"Termination of pregnancy by continuous intrauterine infusion of prostaglandins," by A. W. Miller, et al. LANCET 2:5-7, July 1, 1972.

"Termination of pregnancy during the mid-trimester by intra-amniotic injection of urea," by J. O. Greenhalf. BR J CLIN PRACT 26: 24-26, January, 1972.

"Transcervical intra-amniotic administration of a 20 per cent sodium chloride solution for artificial interruption of late term pregnancy," by A. A. Lebedev, et al. AKUSH GINEKOL 48:55-58, May, 1972.

"Transplacental haemorrhage in induced abortion," by W. B. Costley, et al. LANCET 1:843, April 15, 1972.

"Transplacental haemorrhage in induced abortion," by S. Murray, et al. LANCET 1:954-955, April 28, 1972.

"2 weeks make a big difference," by G. Janny, et al. ORV HETIL 113:537-538, February 27, 1972.

"Unusual complication during pregnancy interruption by vacuum extraction," by K. Mirkov, et al. AKUSH GINEKOL (Sofiia) 11:85-86, 1972.

"Unusual findings in cesarean section," by L. Pozsonyi. ORV HETIL 113:573-574, March 5, 1972.

"Use of maninaria tents with saline abortion," by J. H. Lischke, et al. LANCET 1:49, January 1, 1972.

"Uterine distention and hypertension," by R. C. Goodlin. AM J OBSTET GYNECOL 112:1133-1134, April 15, 1972.

"Uterine stimulation. Prostaglandins," by M. P. Embrey. PROC R SOC MED 64:1018-1020, October, 1971.

"Very early abortion using syringe as vacuum source," by H. Karman, et al. LANCET 1:1051-1052, May 13, 1972.

"Voluntary interruption of pregnancy: its psychiatric and contraceptive correlates," by S. L. Corson, et al. J REPROD MED 8: 151-154, March, 1972.

"When does human life start?" by H. Berger. OSTERR SCHWESTER-NTG 25:143-146, June, 1972.

"Why I favour abortion," by H. Calderot. AUSTRALAS NURSES J 1:9, July, 1972.

INFECTION
see: Complications

ISOXSUPRINE HYDROCHLORIDE

"Treatment of threatened abortion and premature labor with isoxsuprine hydrochloride," by P. Scillieri, et al. ARCH OSTET GINECOL 76:129-137, 1971.

IUCD
see: Contraception

KETAMINE
"Ketamine for dilatation and currettage procedures: patient acceptance," by W. H. Hervey, et al. ANESTH ANALG 51:647-655, July-August, 1972.

LAW ENFORCEMENT
see: Laws and Legislation

LAWS AND LEGISLATION
"Aborting a fetus: the legal right, the personal choice," by S. Lessard. WASHINGTON MONTHLY 4:29-37, August, 1972.

"Abortion act," by C. B. Goodhart. BR MED J 2:714, June 17, 1972.

"The Abortion Act -- Scotland, 1968," HEALTH BULL 27:60-74, July, 1969.

"Abortion and legislation," by A. M. Dourlen-Rollier. REV INFIRM 22:133-137, February, 1972.

"Abortion and life's intrinsic value (emphasis on practice of abortion in New York city under liberalized statutes," by D. C. Anderson. WALL ST J 179:8, April 7, 1972.

"Abortion and the religious liberty clauses," by J. S. Oteri, et al. HARV CIVIL RIGHT L REV 7:559, May, 1972.

"Abortion and sterilization. Comment on the outline of a fifth law for the reform of the criminal law 5th StRG from 14 February 1972 (BR-print. 58-72) prepared by the Commission on Questions of Rights," by H. Ehrhardt. NEVRENARZT 43:338-340, June, 1972.

"Abortion consent rule struck down in District of Columbia: husband's consent not required," AMER MED NEWS 15:18, July 10, 1971.

"Abortion controversy. Remarks. L. B. Cummings; Statement. J. L. Nellis; Remarks. A. L. Scanlan; Remarks. J. V. Gartian, Jr.,"

DCB J 39:17, January-April, 1972.

"Abortion controversy: the law's response," CHI-KENT L REV 48: 191, Fall-Winter, 1971.

"Abortion: inalienable right," by N. Shainess. NY STATE J MED 72:1772-1775, July 1, 1972.

"The abortion issue," by B. J. Ficarra. NY STATE J MED 72:2460-2463, October 1, 1972.

"Abortion issue: move to repeal New York state's liberalization law," TIME 99:23, May 22, 1972.

"Abortion law," by H. P. Dunn. NZ MED J 75:229-230, April, 1972.

"Abortion law," by J. Newlinds. MED J AUST 2:627, September 9, 1972.

"Abortion law," by J. Woolnough. MED J AUST 2:338-339, August 5, 1972.

"Abortion law in East Germany," J AMER MED ASS 221:516, July 31, 1972.

"Abortion law in South Carolina," SC L REV 24:425, 1972.

"The abortion--law mill. Parts 1-6," by B. J. George, Jr. NEW YORK LAW JOURNAL 167:1 plus, May 10-July 26, 1972.

"Abortion law reform and repeal: legislative and judicial developments," by R. Roemer. CLIN OBSTET GYNECOL 14:1165-1180, December, 1971.

"Abortion law reform: the English experience," by H. L. A. Hart. M U L R 8:388, May, 1972.

"Abortion laws in the federal courts--the Supreme Court as supreme platonic guardian," by H. Sigworth. IND LEGAL F 5:130, Fall, 1971.

LAWS AND LEGISLATION

"Abortion laws in other countries," by E. Strutz. GEBURTSHILFE FRAUENHEILKD 32:407-414, May, 1972.

"Abortion laws still in ferment," by R. J. Trotter. SCI NEWS 101:75- January 29, 1972.

"Abortion...legal aspects," by N. Isaac. INFIRM CAN 14:27-29, June, 1972.

"Abortion: a legal cop out," NEW ENGLAND L REV 7:311, Spring, 1972.

"Abortion: legal dilemma," J KANS MED SOC 73:19, June, 1972.

"Abortion: legal morass of American jurisprudence," J MISS STATE MED ASS 13:59-61, February, 1972.

"Abortion, ltd.," ECONOMIST 243:55, May 20, 1972.

"Abortion: new laws bring new approaches," by S. Loos, et al. HOSPITALS 46:76-79, July 16, 1972.

"Abortion: Missouri HB 1470," by W. Brennan. SOC JUST 65:129-132, July-August, 1972.

"Abortion on demand," by E. B. Grogone. LANCET 1:45-46, January 1, 1972.

"Abortion on demand in East Germany," CAN DOCTOR 38:18, August, 1972.

"Abortion on request: the physician's view," by A. F. Guttmacher. AM BIOL TEACH 34:514-517, December, 1972.

"Abortion: on whose demand?" AMERICA 126:335, April 1, 1972.

"Abortion operations--the right to opt out," AUSTRALAS NURSES J 1:17, April, 1972.

"Abortion: opinion aside, you should know all the facts," BUS W 65, July 22, 1972.

"Abortion, the patient, the physician and the law. The first year's experience," by E. S. Gendel. J KANS MED SOC 73:18-19, January, 1972.

"Abortion reform," by R. G. Bubeck. J AM OSTEOPATH ASSOC 71: 842-845, June, 1972.

"Abortion reform," by M. Fishbein. MED WORLD NEWS 13:68, June 2, 1972.

"Abortion rulings reported," NEWSLETTER (Amer Soc Attorneys) 5:3-5, June, 1972.

"Abortion: a special demand," JAMA 221:400, July 24, 1972.

"Abortion today," by G. Papola. OR 12(208)9-10, March 23, 1972.

"Abortion under the law," SCI AM 227:51, July, 1972.

"Abortion: where it's at, where it's going?" by B. Tierney. J CAN BA 3:26, April, 1972.

"Abortion: who should certify the need?" edited by J. B. McClements. DEL MED J 44:231-232, August, 1972.

"Abortive politics," ECONOMIST 243:62, May 13, 1972.

"Aborto procurato e legislazione statuale," by S. Lener. CIVILTA CATTOLICA 328-342, February 19, 1972.

"Abortus provocatus legislation," by W. S. Stekhoven. NED TIJDSCHR GENEESKD 116:203-205, January 29, 1972.

"The absence of sweat: abortion on demand," by W. Bausch. US CATH 37:39-40, April, 1972.

"Acute fatal poisionng with silver nitrate following an abortion attempt," by G. Reinhardt, et al. ARCH KRIMINOL 148:69-78, September-October, 1971.

"The aetiology of abortion in a rural community," by P. R. Grob.

J R COLL GEN PRACT 22:499-507, August, 1972.

"After the Act," by H. L. A. Hart, et al. GUARDIAN 9, May 3, 1972.

"Against the tide of abortion laws," MED WORLD NEWS 13:7-8, February 18, 1972.

"Allegations, actions, and ad interim," by D. S. Wert. PA MED 74: 59-62, May, 1971.

"American Academy of Pediatrics. Committee on Youth. Teen-age pregnancy and the problem of abortion," PEDIATRICS 49:303-304, February, 1972.

"Anti-abortion law upheld by Indiana Supreme Court," AMER MED NEWS 15:17, August 14, 1972.

"Appeals court blocks suit to ban abortions in New York City," HOSPITALS 46:164, February 1, 1972.

"Article 218 of the Legal Code," by I. von Troschke. DTSCH KRANKENPFLEGEZ 25:127-129, March, 1972.

"Arztliche Uberlegungen zur reform des 218," by H. Hepp. STIMM ZEIT 189:375-392, June, 1972.

"Attitudes toward abortion law reform at the University of Michigan Medical Center," by D. Hickok, et al. MICH MED 71:327-329, April, 1972.

"Back abortion reform," NAT CATH REP 8:4, April 7, 1972.

"Birth control among the unmarried in Massachusetts: the Supreme Court speaks in varied tongues," by W. J. Curran. NEW ENGL J MED 286:1198-1199, June 1, 1972.

"Birth control for teen-agers - - is it legal?" by C. A. Gravenor, Jr. CAN DOCTOR 38:103-104, October, 1972.

"Bitter abortion battle in Pennsylvania," TIME 100:32, December 11, 1972.

"Black physicians' experience with abortion requests and opinion about abortion law change in Michigan," by E. L. Hill, et al. J NATL MED ASSOC 64:52-58, January, 1972.

"Burger ruling delays court abortion decision," NAT CATH REP 8:3, July 21, 1972.

"Case for abortion on demand," by L. G. Forer. PENN BA Q 43: 203, January, 1972.

"Catholic left torn on abortion," by J. Castelli. NAT CATH REP 8:6, July 21, 1972.

"Civil conflicts," LANCET 2:335, August 12, 1972.

"Clarification of the so-called clouded figures on abortion," by H. J. Prill. MED KLIN 67:619-622, April 28, 1972.

"Commission backs abortion," NAT CATH REP 8:5, March 24, 1972.

"Connecticut abortion laws ruled unconstitutional," CHR CENT 89:539, May 10, 1972.

"Conscientious objection to abortion," by R. L. Walley. BR MED J 4:234, October 28, 1972.

"Constitutinoal law-abortion-lack of compelling state interests-California's American law institute-type therapeutic abortion statute substantially voided because interests in the woman's health and in the fetus dictate that abortions prior to twenty weeks of pregnancy may be restricted only for medical reasons," U CLIN L REV 41:235, 1972.

"Constitutional law-abortion statute as invasion of a woman's right of privacy," ST LOUIS U L J 15:642, Summer, 1971.

"Constitutinoal law-denial of medicaid reimbursement for elective abortions-City of New York v. Wyman," ALBANY L REV 36:794, 1972.

"Constitutional law-expanding the grounds for abortion," WAKE

FOREST L REV 7:651, October, 1971.

"Constitutional law--'liberalized' abortion statute held constitutional," FORDHAM L REV 41:439, December, 1972.

"Constitutional right to life from the moment of conception," SOC JUST 64:408-418, March, 1972.

"Court bars fetal death notices identifying aborting patients: New York," HOSP WOLRD 1:11, October, 1972.

"Court-ordered sterilization performed at St. Vincent's Hospital, Billings," by L. Cory. HOSP PROG 53:22 plus, December, 1972.

"Criminal abortion as dominant etiological factor in ectopic pregnancy," by V. Masic. MED ARH 26:41-44, January-February, 1972.

"The death peddlers. N. Y. appeals court rules against fetus," by P. Marx. NAT CATH REP 8:21, March 10, 1972.

"Deformed infants' suits for failure to recommend abortions," J KANS MED SOC 73:80 passim, February, 1972.

"The demand for abortion," by G. Deshaies. REV INFIRM 22:130-132, February, 1972.

"Development of the population growth question and the abortion law," by L. Gronsky. CESK GYNEKOL 37:584, October, 1972.

"Discussion about Article 218 of the Penal Code. Position of the Federal Ministry of Justice," by A. Bayerl. DTSCH KRANKENPFLEGEZ 25:241-242, May, 1972.

"Drop in maternal deaths follows liberal abortion law enactment," US MED 8:4 plus, December 15, 1972.

"Easy abortion loses in two states," NAT CATH REP 9:4, November 24, 1972.

"The effect of legislation for interruption of pregnancy on the level of birth rate," by G. Stoimenov, et al. AKUSH GINEKOL (Sofiia) 11:1-7, 1972.

"Effects of legal abortion on gynaecology," by A. H. John, et al. BRIT MED J 3:99-102, July 8, 1972.

"Effects of a liberalized abortion law in New York City," by J. Pakter, et al. MT SINAI J MED NY 39:535-543, November-December, 1972.

"18 month experience in New York City with a liberalized abortion law," by J. Pakter. N Y MED 28:333 plus, September, 1972.

"The embattled minority: out of sight, out of mind," by L. J. Hogan. MARYLAND LAW FORUM 2:50-54, Winter, 1972.

"The ethics of abortion," by J. Monagle. SOC JUST 65:112-119, July-August, 1972.

"Federal court in New York invalidates order banning abortions for indigents under Medicaid," HOSPITALS 46:25, September 16, 1972.

"Federal judges rule abortion ads mailable," ED & PUB 105:12, October 7, 1972.

"The fertility response to abortion reform in eastern Europe: demographic and economic implications," by R. J. McIntyre. AM ECONOMIST 16:45-65, Fall, 1972.

"Fight for Life: Missouri, March 8, 1972," SOCIAL JUSTICE REVIEW 65:89-94, June, 1972.

"Findings of the Committee on Legal Abortion," by L. Pekhlivanov. AKUSH GINEKOL (Sofiia) 10:279-283, 1971.

"Florida abortion law--reform or regression in 1972," U FLA L REV 24:346, Winter, 1972.

"Florida's century-old antiabortion law declared unconstitutional," HOSPITALS 46:43, March 1, 1972.

"The freedom and the responsibility," by D. E. Gray. J KANS MED SOC 73:32-34, January, 1972.

"Freeing the prisoners: campaign for legal abortion goes on," TIME 99:89-90, March 20, 1972.

"The future of the abortion act," by M. Simms. MIDWIVES CHRON 85:6-10, January, 1972.

"The future of therapeutic abortions in the United States," by R. E. Hall. CLIN OBSTET GYNECOL 14:1149-1153, December, 1971.

"The general practitioner and the Abortion Act," J R COLL GEN PRACT 22:543-546, August, 1972.

"Georgia board rules Medicaid will cover abortion fees," RN 35:19, March, 1972.

"Governor signs Connecticut's new abortion law," HOSPITALS 46:25, June 16, 1972.

"Gynaecological aftermaths of the 1967 Abortion Act," by M. Brudenell. PROC R SOC MED 65:155-158, February, 1972.

"Has legal abortion contributed to U.S. 'birth dearth'?" FAM PLANN PERSPECT 4:7-8, April, 1972.

"High court hears cases on abortion," NAT CATH REP 8:18, October 20, 1972.

"The impact of the Abortion Act: a psychiatrist's observations," by R. G. Priest. BR J PSYCHIATRY 121:293-299, September, 1972.

"Impact of legalized abortion laws on private practice," by W. O. Duck. J FLORIDA MED ASS 59:41-43, November, 1972.

"The impact of recent changes in therapeutic abortion laws," by J. B. Kahn, et al. CLIN OBSTET GYNECOL 14:1130-1148, December, 1971.

"Implementation of the Abortion Act: report on a year's working of abortion clinics and operating sessions," by A. E. R. Buckle, et al. BRIT MED J 3:381-384, August 12, 1972.

"Implementation of legal abortion: a national problem. Epilogue," by J. R.Marshall. CLIN OBSTET GYNECOL 14:1336-1338, December, 1971.

"In center of latest disputs on abortion: Nixon, Rockefellers," US NEWS 72:50, May 22, 1972.

"Indiana Supreme Court upholds state abortion law," SOC JUST 65: 197-199, October, 1972.

"Introduction of a bill for new regulations for pregnancy interruption," TIJDSCHR ZIEKENVERPL 25:784-785, July 25, 1972.

"Judge backs defender of fetus," NAT CATH REP 8:4, January 14, 1972.

"Kansas opponents fail to modify abortion law," HOSPITALS 46: 182, March 1, 1972.

"A key battle: outcome of next Tuesday (November 7, 1972)'s abortion referendum in Michigan will likely have national implications," by W. Mossberg. WALL ST J 180:30, November 3, 1972.

"Large majority of public supports liberalization of abortion laws," GALLUP OPINION INDEX 13-15, September, 1972.

"L'avortement sur demande: des chiffres et des faits," by M. Marcotte. RELATIONS 374:242-247, September, 1972.

"Law on abortion," by M. A. Duffy. PENN BA Q 43:212, January, 1972.

"Le droit a la vie . . . doit etre laisse a chacun," by L. Fortier. J CAN BA 3:23, October, 1972.

"Le droit de naitre; document du Conseil permanent de la Conference episcopale italienne sur l'avortement," DOC CATH 69:312-314, April 2, 1972.

"Legal abortion," by J. Lavoie. CAN MED ASSOC J 106:855 passim, April 22, 1972.

"Legal abortion," by J. D. Williamson. BR MED J 3:349-350, August 5, 1972.

"Legal abortion--The act and its effects, Part 1," by A. Hordern. MIDWIFE HEALTH VISIT 8:121-124, April, 1972.

"Legal abortion--The act and its effects, Part 2," by A. Hordern. MIDWIFE HEALTH VISIT 8:169-173, May, 1972.

"Legal abortion and the hospital's role," by E. B. Connell. HOSP PRACT 7:143-150, February, 1972.

"Legal abortion: a critical assessment of its risks," by J. A. Stallworthy. LANCET 2:1245-1249, December 4, 1971.

"Legal abortion effect seen long-term," AMER MED NEWS 15:12, January 17, 1972.

"Legal abortion: how safe? How available? How costly?" CONSUMER REP 37:466-470, July, 1972.

"Legal abortions: early medical complications. An interim report of the joint program for the study of abortion," by C. Tietze, et al. J REPROD MED 8:193-204, April, 1972.

"Legal induced abortion," by K. Kristoffersen. UGESKR LAEGER 134:403-404, February 21, 1972.

"Legal induced abortion. The first year under the new abortion law," by J. G. Lauritsen, et al. UGESKR LAEGER 134:405-410, February 21, 1972.

"Legal rights of the unborn," by W. W. McWhirter. ARIZ MED 29: 926-929, December, 1972.

"Legalized abortion; reprint from The Missoulian, January 31, 1971," by C. Brooke. C MIND 70:24-34, May, 1972.

"Life and death of the law," by D. J. Keefe. HOSP PROGRESS 53:64-74, March, 1972.

"Life in the dark age; Governor Rockefeller's veto," CHR CENT 89:624, May 31, 1972.

"Living with the Therapeutic Abortion Act of 1967," by Z. Leavy. CLIN OBSTET GYNECOL 14:1154-1164, December, 1971.

"Maryland ruling permits abortion referral ads," ADV AGE 43:21, January 3, 1972.

"Memorandum on working of the Abortion Act," OR 6(202)12, February 10, 1972.

"Minors, ObGyn practice and the law," by D. R. Jasinski. HAWAII MED J 31:116, March-April, 1972.

"Missouri court upholds state's abortion law," HOSPITALS 46:125, November 1, 1972.

"New abortion laws and help for nurses," by M. Heiman. AM J PSYCHIATRY 129:360, September, 1972.

"New abortion laws won't change old attitudes," by R. Shafer. MOD HOSP 118:96-98, February, 1972.

"New Jersey's Abortion Law: An establishment of religion?" RUTGERS L REV 25:452-475, Spring, 1972.

"New laws bring new approaches. Method for the evaluation of therapeutic abortion candidates meets the requirements of California state law and the needs of patients, while conserving the time of the medical staff," by S. Loos, et al. HOSPITALS 46:76-79, July, 1972.

"New perspectives on abortion reform," by R. B. Benjamin. WIS MED J 71:10-11, June, 1972.

"New standards for legal abortion in DDR," MED WELT 23:Suppl:37, January 29, 1972.

"New trends in legal abortion," by P. Kestelman. LANCET 2:1307-1308, December 16, 1972.

"New study reveals who gets legal abortions and how it's done: New York," MOD HOSP 118:47, February, 1972.

"New York State obstetricians and the new abortion law: physician experience with abortion techniques," by S. M. Wassertheil-Smoller, et al. AM J OBSTET GYNECOL 113:979-986, August 1, 1972.

"New York's abortion law upheld by appeals court," HOSPITALS 46: 214, April 1, 1972.

"New York's abortion reform law: unanswered questions," by V.N. Duin. ALBANY L REV 37:22, 1972.

"Newspeak wins in abortion; one-issue talk may self-defeat," AMERICA 127:305, October 21, 1972.

"Nixon vs. Rockeferler: the politics of abortion," by P. Hoffman. NATION 214:712-713, June 5, 1972.

"Non-consentual destruction of the fetus: abortion or homicide?" by R. L. Shencopp. UCLA-ALASKA LAW REVIEW 1:80-101, Fall, 1971.

"Nurses talk about abortion," by H. Branson. AM J NURS 72:106-109, January, 1972.

"On the subject of abortion: Massachusetts," by C. Moynahan. SOC JUST 65:49-53, May, 1972.

"Open legal abortion 'on request' is working in New York City, but is it the answer?" by A. I. Weisman. AM J OBSTET GYNECOL 112:138-143, January, 1972.

"Outpatient abortions," by L. Rauramo. ANN CHIR GYNAECOL FENN 61:45-46, 1972.

"Parts of Kansas abortion statute held unconstitutional," NEWS-

LETTER (Amer Soc Hosp Attorneys) 5:3-4, May, 1972.

"Politics of abortion," by S. Alexander. NEWSWEEK 80:29, October 2, 1972.

"The politics of abortion (United States)," by W.M. Hern. PROGRESSIVE 36:26-29, November, 1972.

"Pregnancy termination: the impact of new laws. An invitational symposium," J REPROD MED 6:274-301, June, 1971.

"Prevention of unwanted pregnancies," by E. F. Daily. AM J OBSTET GYNECOL 113:1148, August 15, 1972.

"Problems of our population trends and the abortion law in practice," by R. Houdek. CESK GYNEKOL 37:582-583, October, 1972.

"Problems of our population trends and the abortion law in practice," by K. Schmidt, et al. CESK GYNEKOL 37:583-584, October, 1972.

"Procedural due process limitations on state abortion statutes," MARQ L REV 55:137, Winter, 1972.

"Psychiatric aftermaths of the 1967 Abortion Act," by A. Hordern. PROC R SOC MED 65:158-160, February, 1972.

"The psychological reaction of patients to legalized abortion," by J. D. Osofsky, et al. AM J ORTHOPSYCHIATRY 42:48-60, January, 1972.

"Psychosomatic aspects of the reform of the abortion law (218)," by H. Poettgen. GEBURTSHILFE FRAUENHEILKD 32:493-500, June, 1972.

"Public health and the law. Presidential morality, abortion, and federal-state law," by W. J. Curran. AM J PUBLIC HEALTH 61:1042-1043, May, 1971.

"The putting into effect of the artificial abortion act in Warasw in the years 1957-1968: an analysis," by K. Waszynski. GINEKOL POL 43:371-376, 1972.

"Rcn Congress report. First session: the abortion act. Part 1," NURS MIRROR 134:9, March 31, 1972.

"Reflections on legalized abortion," by P. Piraux. INFIRMIERE 49:24-25, December, 1971.

"Reforming the abortion law," TABLET 226:119-122, February 5, 1972.

"Der Regierungsentwurf zur Reform des Art. 218," HERDER KORRESPONDENZ 110-111, 1972.

"Right to life has a message for New York state legislators," by F. C. Shapiro. N Y TIMES MAG 10-11 plus, August 20, 1972; Discussion 23 plus, September 10, 1972.

"Right to life: new strategy needed," TRIUMPH 7:46, April, 1972.

"Risks of legal abortion," by R. Goodlin. LANCET 1:97, January 8, 1972.

"Rockefeller vetoes abortion repeal," NAT CATH REP 8:21, May 26, 1972.

"The role of the federal government," by B. Packwood. CLIN OBSTET GYNECOL 14:1212-1224, December, 1971.

"Role of local government in therapeutic abortions," by C. F. Coffelt. CLIN OBSTET GYNECOL 14:1197-1203, December, 1971.

"The Royal College of Psychiatrists' memorandum on the Abortion Act in practice," BR J PSYCHIATRY 120:449-451, April, 1972.

"SA abortion law: its implications on our society," by E. G. Cleary. AUSTRALAS NURSES J 1:12, July, 1972.

"Scores abortion code," NAT CATH REP 8:13, August 18, 1972.

"A secular case against abortion on demand," by R. Stith. COMM 95: 151-154, November 12, 1971; Reply by J. Ducore 95:468-469, February 18, 1972; Rejoinder 95:469-470, February 18, 1972.

"The social effects of legal abortion," by R. A. Schwartz. AM J PUBLIC HEALTH 62:1331-1335, October, 1972.

"Sudden death of feticide," NAT R 24:1407, December 22, 1972.

"Supreme Court resumes abortion hearings." HOSP PROGRESS 53: 22-23, November, 1972.

"Supreme Court to consider woman's right to abortion," HOSP PROG 53:10-11 plus, March, 1972.

"Surveillance of legal abortions in the United States, 1970," by J. P. Bourne, et al. JOGN NURS 1:11-22, June, 1972.

"Survey of the present statutory and case law on abortion: the contradictions and the problems," U ILL L F 1972:177, 1972.

"Symposium: Abortion and the Law," CASE W RES L REV 23:705-895, Summer, 1972.

"Syndrome of multiple osseous defects," by J. Kucera. LANCET 1: 260-261, January 29, 1972.

"Therapeutic abortion: the role of state government. I.," by R. D. Lamm. CLIN OBSTET GYNECOL 14:1204-1207, December, 1971.

"Therapeutic abortion: the role of the state government. II.," by A. L. Seltzer, et al. CLIN OBSTET GYNECOL 14:1208-1211, December, 1971.

"Therapeutic abortion: two important judicial pronouncements," by S. A. Strauss. S AFR MED J 46:275-279, March 11, 1972.

"Three years' experience of the abortion act," by A. G. W. Weir. NURS J INDIA 62:395-396, December, 1971.

"Three years' experience of the working of the Abortion Act in Britain," by C. Pannell. NZ MED J 76:117-119, August, 1972.

"Three years of the Abortion Act: gynecological and psychiatric aftermaths," by D. Baird. PROC R SOC MED 65:160-162,

February, 1972.

"Torts--the Illinois wrongful death act held inapplicable to a viable fetus," LOYOLA U L J 3:402, Summer, 1972.

"Twisted logic; proposals to legalize abortion," CHR TODAY 17: 24-25, December 22, 1972.

"U. S. courts strike down restrictive abortion laws. British nurses ask special hospital abortion units," AMER J NURSING 72:867, May, 1972.

"Vesical sclerosis with reflux due to caustic injection treated by uretero-ceco-cytoplasty," by J. Auvert, et al. J UROL NEPHROL 73:476-482, June, 1967.

"Washington: first in the performance of illegal (?) abortions," by D. C. Crain. MED ANN DIST COLUMBIA 41:1-2, August, 1971.

"What happens when abortion is available on demand," MED WORLD NEWS 13:57-58, November 3, 1972.

"What will abortion regulations be if law is reformed? Here are clues," by J. W. Eliot. MICH MED 71:959-962, November, 1972.

"Who wants abortion reform?" TRANS-ACTION 8:14, May, 1971.

"Women obstetricians in New York and the state abortion law," by S. Wassertheil-Smoller, et al. HSMHA HEALTH REP 87:328-334, April, 1972.

"Y.W.C.A. v. Kugler, 342 F Supp 1048," MISS L J 43:728, November, 1972.

LEGAL COUNSELLING AND ABORTION
see: Sociology, Behavior and Abortion

MALE ATTITUDES
see: Sociology, Behavior and Abortion

MARRIAGE COUNSELLING AND ABORTION
see: Sociology, Behavior and Abortion

MENSTRUATION
see: Complications
Induced Abortion

MICROBIOLOGY
see also: Research and Abortion

"Anaerobic sepsis following abortion," by I. R. Zak. AKUSH GINEKOL 47:11-13, November, 1971.

"Microbiological findings in cervical and vaginal secretions in threatened pregnancies," by E. Linder, et al. ZENTRALBL GYNAEKOL 94:449-452, April 8, 1972.

"The renal lesions of toxaemia and abruptio placentae studied by light and electron microscopy," by D. Thomson, et al. J OBSTET GYNAECOL BR COMMNW 79:311-320, April, 1972.

MISCARRIAGES
"Abortion and miscarriage," by R. F. Gardner. BR MED J 3:51, July 1, 1972.

"Miscarriage and abortion. Statistical studies on miscarriage in relation to family development and soicoeconomic factors," by H. J. Staemmler, et al. DTSCH MED WOCHENSCHR 97:885-892, June 9, 1972.

"Miscarriage a hazard for OR nurses? research reports say it is!" RN 35:OR/ER 13-14, February, 1972.

"Treatment of habitual miscarriages with long-acting steroid hormones," by M. D. Moiseenko, et al. VOPR OKHR MATERIN DET 17:60-62, June, 1972.

"What causes miscarriages?" GOOD H 174:171, June, 1972.

MORBIDITY
see: Complications

MORTALITY

see also: Complications
Sepsis
Septic Abortion and Septic Scock

"Abortion deaths," BR MED J 4:176-177, October 21, 1972.

"Abortion deaths," BR MED J 4:295, November 4, 1972.

"Abortion deaths," by G. E. Godber. BR MED J 4:424, November 18, 1972.

"Abortion deaths," by H. C. McLaren. BR MED J 3:826, September 30, 1972.

"Drop in maternal deaths follows liberal abortion law enactment," US MED 8:4 plus, December 15, 1972.

"The impact of abortion on maternal and perinatal mortality rates," by J. R. Evrard. AM J OBSTET GYNECOL 113:415-418, June 1, 1972.

"Liberalization of abortions and female sterilizations," by D. M. Potts. CAN MED ASSOC J 105:901, November, 1971.

"Liberalized abortion: devastation--preservation," by R. Zahourck. AORN J 15:91-106, April, 1972.

"On the uterine etiology of suspicious deaths in young women," by J. Caroff, et al. MED LEG DOMM CORPOR 4:267-272, July-September, 1971.

"A statement on abortion in Victoria," by B. A. Smithurst, et al. MED J AUST 1:240-241, January 29, 1972.

"Study of maternal mortality," J KY MED ASSOC 70:168, March, 1972.

"Use of sigetin for the prevention of perinatal mortality and morbidity after the 1st half of complicated pregnancy (experimental and clinical data)," by N. G. Kosheleva. AKUSH GINEKOL 47:40-43, March, 1971.

MULTIPLE SCLEROSIS
see: Complications

MYASTHENIA
see: Complications

NAACOG
"NAACOG statement on abortion," SUPERV NURSE 3:14, September, 1972.

"NAACOG statement on abortions and sterilizations," JOGN NURS 1:57, June, 1972.

NACPA
"NACPA on abortion," SOC JUST 65:167-168, September, 1972.

NURSES AND ABORTION
"Abortion: do attitudes of nursing personnel affect the patient's perception of care," by M. W. Harper, et al. NURS RES 21:327-331, July-August, 1972.

"Abortion yes or no; nurses organize both ways: New York," AMER J NURSING 72:416 plus, March, 1972.

"Abortions and acute identity crisis in nurses," by W. F. Char, et al. AM J PSYCHIATRY 128:952-957, February, 1972.

"Alberta nurses discuss abortion care," CAN HOSP 49:12, March, 1972.

"Developing professional parameters: nursing and social work roles in the care of the induced abortion patient," by L. M. Tanner. CLIN OBSTET GYNECOL 14:1271-1272, December, 1971.

"In-hospital care and post-hospital followup," by L. M. Tanner, et al. CLIN OBSTET GYNECOL 14:1278-1288, December, 1971.

"Miscarriage a hazard for OR nurses? research reports say its is!" RN 35:94/ER 13-14, February, 1972.

"N.E. area. . .the abortion patient and the nurse," CHRIST NURSE

39-40, April, 1972.

"New abortion laws and help for nurses," by M. Heiman. AM J PSYCHIATRY 129:360, September, 1972.

"Nurses and lawyer fight end of abortion restrictions: Santa Barbara, California," HOSP PROGRESS 53:19, February, 1972.

"Nurses Association of the American College of Obstetricians and Gynecologists takes stand on abortion," AMER J NURSING 72: 1311, July, 1972.

"Nurses talk about abortion," by H. Branson. AM J NURS 72:106-109, January, 1972.

"Obstetrical nurses propose abortion policy," AMER MED NEWS 15: 15, June 19, 1972.

"Pregnancy interruption. What is my function as a nurse?" by C. Guller. Z KRANKENPFL 65:173-174, May, 1972.

"Statement on abortions and sterilizations: Nurses Association of the American College of Obstetricians and Gynecologists," JOGN NURSING 1:57, June, 1972.

OBSTETRICS

"Advances in obstetrics and gynaecology," by V. R. Tindall. PRACTITIONER 209:437-443, October, 1972.

"Developing applications of prostaglandins in obstetrics and gynecology," by J. W. Hinman. AM J OBSTET GYNECOL 113:130-138, May 1, 1972.

"Experience in the treatment of septic shock in obstetric practice," by R. Schwarz, et al. AKUSH GINEKOL 47:8-11, November, 1971.

"Newer possibilities of tocolytic treatment in obstetrics," by K. H. Mosler, et al. Z GEBURTSHILFE PERINATOL 176:85-96, April, 1972.

"A statement on abortion by one hundred professors of obstetrics,"

OBSTETRICS

AM J OBSTET GYNECOL 112:992-993, April 1, 1972.

OUTPATIENT ABORTION
see: Hospitals and Abortion

OXYTOCIN
"Oxytocics used by practitioners--with special reference to induced abortions," by K. Sato. SANFUJINKA JISSAI 21:203-208, March, 1972.

"Oxytocin, 'salting out,' and water intoxication," by D. R. Gupta, et al. JAMA 220:681-683, May 1, 1972.

"Prostaglandin-oxytocin enhancement," by M. Seppala, et al. BR MED J 1:747, March 18, 1972.

"Prostaglandin-oxytocin enhancement and potentiation and their clinical applications," by A. Gillespie. BR MED J 1:150-152, January 15, 1972.

PARAMEDICS AND ABORTION
"The paramedic abortionist," by H. Karman. CLIN OBSTET GYNECOL 15:379-387, June, 1972.

PARAPLEGICS
see: Complications

PATIENT COUNSELLING
see: Sociology, Behavior and Abortion

PHYSICIANS AND ABORTION
see also: Psychology
Sociology, Behavior and Abortion

"Abortion and the general practitioner," MED J AUST 2:513-514, August 26, 1972.

"Abortion: defining G P's attitudes," NEW HUMANIST 88:74-76, June, 1972.

"Abortion in a general practice. The fourth baby syndrome," by E.

J. Hopkins, et al. PRACTITIONER 208:528-533, April, 1972.

"Abortion on request: the physician's view," by A. F. Guttmacher. AM BIOL TEACH 34:514-517, December, 1972.

"Abortion, the patient, the physician and the law: the first year's experience," by E. S. Gendel. J KANS MED SOC 73:18-19, January, 1972.

"Attitude of the woman to artificial interruption of pregnancy and the gynecologist's tasks," by J. Kveton, et al. CESK GYNEKOL 37: 533-534, September, 1972.

"Black physicians' experience with abortion requests and opinion about abortion law change in Michigan," by E. L. Hill, et al. J NATL MED ASSOC 64:52-58, January, 1972.

"Comment and controversy. . .should abortions be performed in doctors' offices," by S. Neubardt, et al. FAMILY PLANN PERSPECT 4:4-7, July, 1972.

"Doctor, what does the aborted baby feel while it's dying?" TRIUMPH 7:20-23 plus, March, 1972.

"The general practitioner and the Abortion Act," J R COLL GEN PRACT 22:543-546, August, 1972.

"Gynecologist: abortion--a decision between the woman and her physician," by N. G. Holmberg. LAKARTIDNINGEN 68:5845-5848, December 8, 1971.

"The gynecologist and the problem of therapeutic abortion," by J. P. Pundel. GYNECOL PRAT 23:9-16, 1972.

"Impact of legalized abortion laws on private practice," by W. O. Duck. J FLORDIA MED ASS 59:41-43, November, 1972.

"Is the individual life still the highest value? (A gynecologist's thoughts on abortion and sterilization)," by H. Wagner. MED MONATSSCHR 26:303-307, July, 1972.

"Medical ethics--malpractice and the conscience of the practitioner," by W. J. Curran. NEW ENGL J MED 285:1306-1307, December 2, 1971.

"New Jersey physicians back abortion change," AMER MED NEWS 15:10, July 24, 1972.

"New York State obstetricians and the new abortion law: physician experience with abortion techniques," by S. M. Wassertheil-Smoller, et al. AM J OBSTET GYNECOL 113:979-986, August 1, 1972.

"New York's obstetricians surveyed on abortion," by R. C. Lerner, et al. FAM PLANN PERSPECT 3:56, January, 1971.

"Newfoundland doctors concerned over abortion curb at Grace Hospital, St. John's," CAN HOSP 49:17, May, 1972.

"Obstetricians and legal abortions in San Francisco," by B. Behrstock, et al. CALIF MED 117:29-31, September, 1972.

"Of doctors, deterrence, and the dark figure of crime--a note on abortion in Hawaii," by F. E. Zimring. J CHI L REV 39:699, Summer, 1972.

"Oxytocics used by practitioners--with special reference to induced abortions," by K. Sato. SANFUJINKA JISSAI 21:203-208, March, 1972.

"Physicians' attitudes toward abortion," by L. A. LoSciuto, et al. J REPROD MED 9:70-74, August, 1972.

"The problem of abortion from the medical viewpoint," by H. Husslein. WIEN MED WOCHENSCHR 2:Suppl:3-7, November, 1971.

"Q: What, doctor is the difference between you and Adolph Hitler...," TRIUMPH 7:18-20, February, 1972.

"Should abortions be performed in doctors' offices?" by S. Neubardt, et al. FAM PLANN PERSPECT 4:4-7, July, 1972.

PHYSICIANS AND ABORTION

"A survey of Milwaukee obstetricians and gynecologists attitudes toward abortion," by P. Halverson, et al. WIS MED J 71:134-139, April, 1972.

"When your patient is pregnant," EMERGENCY MED 4:99-101 plus, April, 1972.

"Women obstetricians in New York and the state abortion law," by S. Wassertheil-Smoller, et al. HEALTH SERV REP 87:328-335, April, 1972.

POPULATION
see also: Demography

"Continuing thoughts on abortion and population control," by W. M. Dabney. J MISS STATE MED ASS 13:211, May, 1972.

"Development of the population growth questions and the abortion law," by L. Gronsky. CESK GYNEKOL 37:584, October, 1972.

"Ethics and population limitation," by D. Callahan. SCIENCE 175: 487-494, February 4, 1972.

"Problems of our population trends and the abortion law in practice," by R. Houdek. CESK GYNEKOL 37:582-583, October, 1972.

"Problems of our population trends and the abortion law in practice," by K. Schmidt, et al. CESK GYNEKOL 37:583-584, October, 1972.

"Problems of our population trend and the artificial interruption of pregnancy in practice," by A. Kotasek. CESK GYNEKOL 37:565-568, October, 1972.

"Rh-immune globulin in induced abortion: utilization in a high-risk population," by R. G. Judelsohn, et al. AM J OBSTET GYNECOL 114:1031-1034, December 15, 1972.

"The role of Planned Parenthood-World Population in abortion," by G. Langmyhr. CLIN OBSTET GYNECOL 14:1190-1196, December, 1971.

PROGESTERONE

"Action of a natural progesterone associated with a synthetic progestogen and vitamin E in the treatment of threatened abortion and premature labor," by S. Panariello. ARCH OSTET GINECOL 75:492-506, December, 1970.

"Retarded embryonic development and pregnancy termination in ovariectomized guinea-pigs: progesterone deficiency and decidual collapse," by R. Deanesly. J REPROD FERTIL 28:241-247, February, 1972.

"Serum human chorionic gonadotropin, human chorionic somatomammotropin, and progesterone following intra-amniotic injection of hypertonic urea," by H. R. Raud, et al. AM J OBSTET GYNECOL 113:887-894, August 1, 1972.

PROMEDAL

"Experience with the use of promedol in anesthesia for artificial abortion," by Z. P. Drozdovskaia, et al. AKUSH GINEKOL 47:61-62, December, 1971.

PROSTAGLANDINS

"Abortion: use of prostaglandins and epidural analgesia," by I. Craft. LANCET 2:41, July 1, 1972.

"Abortion with extra-amniotic prostaglandins," by J. E. Bruce. LANCET 2:380, August 19, 1972.

"Abortion with extra-amniotic prostaglandins," by M. P. Embrey, et al. LANCET 2:654-655, September 23, 1972.

"Abortion with prostaglandins," by B. Alderman. LANCET 2:279, August 5, 1972.

"Abortion with prostaglandins," by R. C. Strickler. LANCET 2:539, September 9, 1972.

"The action of PGF 2 prostaglandin on the pregnant uterus," by F. Szontagh, et al. ORV HETIL 113:919-922, April,16, 1972.

"Analysis of prostaglandin F 2 and metabolites in blood during constant intravenous infusion of progestaglandin F 2 on the human female," by F. Beguin, et al. ACTA PHYSIOL SCAND 86:430-432, November, 1972.

"Bronchospasm complicating intravenous prostaglandin F 2a for therapeutic abortion," by J. I. Fishburne, Jr., et al. OBSTET GYNECOL 39:892-896, June, 1972.

"Contraception, abortion, prostaglandins and sterilization," by J. H. Ravina. NOUV PRESSE MED 1:1989-1990, August 26, 1972.

"Cyanosis due to intravenous prostaglandin F," by G. Roberts, et al. LANCET 2:425-426, August 26, 1972.

"Developing applications of prostaglandins in obstetrics and gynecology," by J. W. Hinman. AM J OBSTET GYNECOL 113:130-138, May 1, 1972.

"High-dose intravenous administration of prostaglandin E 2 and F 2 for the termination of midtrimester pregnancies," by K. Hillier, et al. J OBSTET GYNAECOL BR COMMONW 79:14-22, January, 1972.

"Hormone levels during prostaglandin F 2 infusions for therapeutic abortion," by L. Speroff, et al. J CLIN ENDOCRINOL METAB 34:531-536, March, 1972.

"Induction of abortion by extra-amniotic administration of prostaglandins E2 and F2-alpha," by M. P. Embrey, et al. BR MED J 3:146-149, July 15, 1972.

"Induction of abortion using prostaglandin F 2," by F. F. Lehmann, et al. GEBURTSHILFE FRAUENHEILKD 32:477-483, June, 1972.

"Interruption of pregnancy using F2 alpha prostaglandins," by T. Brat, et al. J GYNECOL OBSTET BIOL REPROD 1:385-387, June, 1972.

"Intra-amniotic administration of prostaglandin F2 for abortion," by A. C. Wentz, et al. AM J OBSTET GYNECOL 113:793-803, July 15, 1972.

"Intrauterine administration of (S)-15-methyl-prostaglandin F 2 for induction of abortion," by M. Bygdeman, et al. LANCET 1:1336-1337, June 17, 1972.

"Intravenous prostaglandin F 2 for therapeutic abortion," by E. J. Kirshen, et al. AM J OBSTET GYNECOL 113:340-344, June 1, 1972.

"Intravenous prostaglandin F2 for therapeutic abortion: the efficacy and tolerance of three dosage schedules," by W. E. Brenner. AM J OBSTET GYNECOL 113:1037-1045, August 15, 1972.

"Lactation following therapeutic abortion with prostaglandin F 2," by I. D. Smith, et al. NATURE (London) 240:411-412, December 15, 1972.

"New antifertility agent--an orally active prostaglandin..ICI 74,205," by A. P. Labhsetwar. NATURE (London) 238:400-401, August 18, 1972.

"Prostaglandin E 2: anaylsis of effects on pregnancy and corpus luteum in hamsters and rats," by A. P. Labhsetwar. ACTA ENDOCRINOL 170:Suppl:3-32, 1972.

"Prostaglandin-oxytocin enhancement and potentiation and their clinical applications," by A. Gillespie. BR MED J 1:150-152, January 15, 1972.

"Prostaglandins and abortion," by M. Seppala. DUODECIM 88:1029-1031, 1972.

"Prostaglandins and therapeutic abortion," by P. G. Gillett. J REPROD MED 8:329-334, June, 1972.

"Prostaglandins in fertility control," by J. S. Carrel. SCIENCE 175: 1279, March 17, 1972.

"Prostaglandins in human reproduction," by V. Vakhariya, et al. MICH MED 71:777-784, September, 1972.

"Prostaglandins in inducing labour and abortion," by Z. Polishuk.

HAREFUAH 80:332-333, March 15, 1971.

"Release of prostaglandin F 2 following injection of hypertonic saline saline for therapeutic abortion: a preliminary study," by B. Gustavil, et al. AM J OBSTET GYNECOL 114:1099-1100, December 15, 1972.

"Termination of pregnancy by continuous intrauterine infusion of prostaglandins," by A. W. Miller, et al. LANCET 2:5-7, July 1, 1972.

"Termination of second trimester pregnancy with 15 methylanalogues of prostaglandins E2 and F2," by S. M. Karim, et al. J OBSTET GYNAECOL BR COMMONW 79:737-743, August, 1972.

"Therapeutic abortion by intra-amniotic injection of prostaglandins," by G. Roberts, et al. BR MED J 4:12-14, October 7, 1972.

"Therapeutic abortion with the use of prostaglandin F 2. A study of efficacy, tolerance, and plasma levels with intravenous administration," by P. G. Gillett, et al. AM J OBSTET GYNECOL 112: 330-338, February 1, 1972.

"The use of prostaglandin E 2 for therapeutic abortion," by S. M. Karim, et al. J OBSTET GYNAECOL BR COMMONW 79:1-13, January, 1972.

"Uterine stimulation. Prostaglandins," by M. P. Embrey. PROC R SOC MED 64:1018-1020, October, 1971.

PSYCHOLOGY

see also: Sociology, Behavior and Abortion

"Abortion: Changing attitudes of psychiatrists," by J. C. Little. LANCET 1:97, January 8, 1972.

"Abortion in psychological perspective," by H. P. David. AMER J ORTHOPSYCHIAT 42:61-68, January, 1972.

"Abortion, psychiatry, and the quality of life," by Z. M. Lebensohn. AMER J PSYCHIAT 128:946-951, February, 1972.

PSYCHOLOGY

"Abortion: what are the psychiatric indications?" by H. G. DeCherney. DEL MED J 44:230-231, August, 1972.

"Ban upheld on abortions for psychiatric reasons," AMER MED NEWS 15:10, December 25, 1972.

"Characterization of 100 women psychiatrically evaluated for therapeutic abortion," by K. H. Talan, et al. ARCH GEN PSYCHIATRY 26:571-577, June, 1972.

"Contemporary psychiatric consultation: evaluation or rehabilitation," by R. O. Pasnua. CLIN OBSTET GYNECOL 14:1258-1262, December, 1971.

"Harmfulness of the interruption of pregnancy in primigravidae," by K. Balak. CESK GYNEKOL 37:585, October, 1972.

"The impact of the Abortion Act: a psychiatrist's observations," by R. G. Priest. BR J PSYCHIATRY 121:293-299, September, 1972.

"Maternal trauma during pregnancy," by A. T. Fort. MED TRIAL TECH Q 233-242, 1972.

"Mental aspects of abortion," by L. Florean, et al. CESK GYNECOL 37:530-531, September, 1972.

"Preabortion evaluation: selection of patients for psyhciatric referral," by J. R. Bragonier, et al. CLIN OBSTET GYNECOL 14:1263-1270, December, 1971.

"Psychiatric aftermaths of the 1967 Abortion Act," by A. Hordern. PROC R SOC MED 65:158-160, February, 1972.

"Psychiatric aspects of abortion," by A. C. Gullattee. J NAT MED ASS 64:308-311, July, 1972.

"Psychiatric complications of therapeutic abortion," by R. O. Pasnau. OBSTET GYNECOL 40:252-256, August, 1972.

"Psychiatrists and abortion," by H. P. Dunn, et al. NZ MED J 74: 411-412, December, 1971.

PSYCHOLOGY

"Psychiatrists' attitudes to abortion," by J. C. Little. BR MED J 1:110, January 8, 1972.

"Psychologic issues in therapeutic abortion," by C. Nadelson. WOMAN PHYSICIAN 27:12-15, January, 1972.

"Psychological reaction to therapeutic abortion. II. Objective response," by K. R. Niswander, et al. AM J OBSTET GYNECOL 114:29-33, September 1, 1972.

"The psychological antecedent and consequences of abortion," by J. L. Maes. J REPROD MED 8:341-344, June, 1972.

"Psychological reaction of patients to legalized abortion," by J. D. Osofsky, et al. AMER J ORTHOPSYCHIAT 42:46-60, January, 1972.

"Psychosocial aspects of selective abortion," by E. J. Lieberman. BIRTH DEFECTS 7:20-21, April, 1971.

"Psychosomatic aspects of the reform of the abortion law (218)," by H. Poettgen. GEBURTSHILFE FRAUENHEILKD 32:493-500, June, 1972.

"The right to abortion: a psychiatric view," GROUP ADV PSYCHIATRY 7:203-227, October, 1969.

"Social work service to abortion patients," by A. Ullmann. SOC CASEWORK 53:481-487, October, 1972.

"Some problems in the evaluation of women for therapeutic abortion," by D. S. Werman, et al. CAN PSYCHIATR ASSOC J 17: 249-251, June, 1972.

"Staff reactions to abortion. A psychiatrist's view," by H. D. Kibel. OBSTET GYNECOL 39:128-133, January, 1972.

"Therapeutic abortion in the Maori in psychiatric perspective," by L. K. Gluckman. NZ MED J 75:22-24, January, 1972.

"Three phases of the abortion process and its influence on women's mental health," by N. Kapor-Stanulovic. AM J PUBLIC HEALTH 62:906-907, July, 1972.

"Three years of the Abortion Act: gynecological and psychiatric aftermaths," by D. Baird. PROC R SOC MED 65:160-162, February, 1972.

"Toward a family planning program in psychiatric hospitals," by V. D. Abernethy, et al. AMER J PUBLIC HEALTH 62:1638-1646, December, 1972.

"Voluntary interruption of pregnancy: its psychiatric and contraceptive correlates," by S. L. Corson, et al. J REPROD MED 8: 151-154, March, 1972.

RADIOLOGISTS AND ABORTION

"Pregnancy interruption from the radiologist's viewpoint," by V. Bohringer. RADIOBIOL RADIOTHER 13:187-191, 1972.

"Problems of abortion from the radiobiological indication viewpoint," by K. Neumeister, et al. DTSCH GESUNDHEITSW 27: 549-553, March 23, 1972.

REFERRAL AGENCIES

see: Sociology, Behavior and Abortion

RELIGION, ETHICS AND ABORTION

see also: Sociology, Behavior and Abortion

"Abortion and Christian compassion," by T. Glenister. TABLET 226:518, June 3, 1972.

"Abortion and Islam," by H. Hathout. J MED LIBAN 25:237-239, 1972.

"Abortion and morality," by P. R. Ehrlich, et al. CAN NURSE 68: 37, June, 1972.

"Abortion and the value of life," by T. Cooke. OR 6(202)7, February 10, 1972.

"Abortion: assault on human life," by P. Gastonguay. LIGUORIAN 60:27-30, December, 1972.

"Abortion debate is revealing our values," by G. L. Chamberlain. NEW CATH WORLD 215:206-208, September, 1972.

"Abortion, coercion and anti-Catholicism," AMERICA 126:502, May 13, 1972.

"Abortion is not the answer," by M. J. Bulfin. J FLORIDA MED ASS 59:40-42, October, 1972.

"Abortion: a metaphysical approach," by T. L. Johnson. FREEMAN 22:498-505, August, 1972.

"Abortion? No!" by E. F. Diamond. MED INSIGHT 4:36-41, February, 1972.

"Abortion: parameters for decision," by R. J. Gerber. INT PHILOS Q 11:561-584, December, 1971; also in ETHICS 82:137-154, January, 1972.

"Abortion: the uptake argument," by D. Gerber. ETHICS 83:80-83, October, 1972.

"Abtreibung: Moraltheologisch gesehen," by G. Ermecke. THEOLOGIE UND GLAUBE 23-33, 1972.

"Abtreibung - ja oder nein; ein synoptischer Beitrag zur Diskussion der Reformvorschlage im Strafrecht," by K.H. Wrage. Z EV ETHIK 15:239-251, July, 1971.

"Acute identity crisis' hits hospital abortion staff--morality the issue: North Carolina Memorial Hospital, Chapel Hill," US MED 8:8-9, May 15, 1972.

"The bishops' strange love," by W. Marshner. TRIUMPH 7:11-14, June, 1972.

"Cet enfant que sa mere refuse -- a propos de l'avortement sur demande," by M. Marcotte. RELATIONS 375:276-279, October, 1972.

"Colorado parish survey reveals laity's opinions," NAT CATH REP 8:7, May 12, 1972.

"Conscience and responsible parenthood," by F. M. Pinon. S TOMAS NURS J 11:24-33, April-May, 1972.

"Continuing thoughts on abortion and population control," edited by W. W. M. Dabney. J MISS STATE MED ASS 13:211, May, 1972.

"Crushing the life of a child in the womb," by H. McCabe. NEW BLCKFRS 53:146-147, April, 1972.

"Death by abortion absolutely unacceptable," by P. O'Boyle. SOC JUST 65:234-237, November, 1972.

"Zur Diskussion um den Art. 218," by A. Leenen. MANN IN DER KIRCHE 21-27, January-February, 1972.

"The emotional conflicts behind an abortion," by R. E. Hall. MED INSIGHT 4:22-25 plus, July, 1972.

"Ethics and population limitation," by D. Callahan. SCIENCE 175: 487-494, February 4, 1972.

"The ethics of abortion," by J. Fletcher. CLIN OBSTET GYNECOL 14:1124-1129, December, 1971.

"The ethics of abortion," by J. Monagle. SOC JUST 65:112-119, July-August, 1972.

"Experiments and the unborn child," by N. St. John-Stevas. TABLET 226:514, June 3, 1972.

"For defence of life in the mother's womb," OR 8(204)9-10, February 24, 1972.

"Freedom of choice concerning abortion (pronouncement, United Church of Christ, 8th General Synod)," SOC ACT 38:9-12, September, 1971.

"Geburtenregelung und Abtreibung," by H. Modesto-Niederhuber.

ENTSCHLUSS 168-173, January, 1972.

"Greatness of the unborn child," by M. Gervais. CATH HOSP 2:7, September, 1971.

"Has life ceased to be precious," by E. Job. RANF REV 4:5, January, 1972.

"Il diritto a nascere," by D. Tettamanzi. PRESENZA PASTORALE 207-241, 1972.

"Il diritto a nascere," REGNO 128-129, March 1, 1972.

"Innocent human life must be protected," by J. J. Brennan. WIS MED J 71:20, August, 1972.

"Is abortion murder?" by R. E. Groves. NURS TIMES 68:624-625, May 18, 1972.

"Is there any justification for abortion?" by F. P. Doyle. CATH HOSP 3:8-11, September, 1972.

"Issues of conscience," by T. M. Schorr. AM J NURS 72:61, January, 1972.

"L'aborto come ideologia," by G. Campanini. PRESENZA PASTORALE 243-253, 1972.

"La disumanita dell'aborto e il diritto," by S. Lener, S.J. CIVILTA CATTOLICA 128-144, January 15, 1972.

"Let the day perish. . .," by M. J. Frazer. CATHOL NURSE 2-5, Autumn, 1972.

"Letter to Cardinal Cooke: President Nixon condemns abortion," by R. Nixon. OR 20(216)3, May 18, 1972.

"Liberalized abortion: devastion--preservation," by R. Zahourek, et al. AORN J 15:91-106, April, 1972.

"Life; the other choice," by E. Shriver. OSV 61:6, July 16, 1972.

"Lifeline--can I help you?" by E. Anstice. NURS TIMES 68:1222-1223, September 28, 1972.

"Moral problems in genetic counseling," by J. C. Fletcher. PAST PSYCH 23:47-60, April, 1972.

"Moralists confronting abortion," by A. J. Schaller. VIE MED CAN FR 1:175-181, February, 1972.

"Moraltheologische Uberlegungen zur Abtreibung," by H. Rotter. DIAKONIA 180-185, 1972.

"No 'unwanted child,' but 'unloving parent'," by Cardinal J. F. Dearden. CATH HOSP 3:8, March, 1972.

"Notes on moral theology; September 1970-March, 1971; abortion," by R.H. Springer. TH ST 32:483-487, September, 1971.

"Nos ventres sont a nous -- avortement sur demande et feminisme de choc," by M. Marcotte. RELATIONS 376:299-303, November, 1972.

"A pastoral approach to abortion," by J. F. Hickey. J REPROD MED 8:355-358, June, 1972.

"Pastoral letter on abortion; July 26, 1972," by J. Garner. OR 48 (244)3, November 30, 1972.

"Problemi attuali dell'aborto," by D. Tettamanzi. RIVISTA DEL CLERO ITALIANO 312-324, 1972.

"Pro-life activities committee set up," NAT CATH REP 9:15, November 24, 1972.

"A Protestant minister's view of abortion," by W. E. Wygant, Jr. JOURNAL OF RELIGION AND HEALTH 269-277, 1972.

"The quality of life as opposed to the right to life," by H. I. Posin, et al. AM J PSYCHIATRY 129:358-360, September, 1972.

"Recht auf Leben: Moraltheologische Erwagungen zur Diskussion um Art. 218 StGB," by K. Demmer. THEOLOGIE UND GLAUBE 1-22, 1972.

"Resolving ethical conflicts in a surgical suite in which abortions are performed," AORN J 16:15, September, 1972.

"Right not to be born," J TENN MED ASS 65:250, March, 1972.

"The rising tide of abortion," by N. St. John-Stevas. TABLET 226: 98, February 5, 1972.

"Some Catholics on abortion," by E. Miller. LIGUORIAN 60:8, October, 1972.

"S.P.U.C.: its people and their sayings," NEW HUMANIST 15-17, May, 1972.

"Stellungnahme Munsteraner Theologen zu 218," Z EV ETHIK 15: 380-381, November, 1971.

"Straflose Schwangerschaftsunterbrechung?" by P. Kaufmann. REF 21:155-162, March, 1972.

"Therapeutic abortion conflict and resolution," by R. Zahourek. AORN J 16:114-119, October, 1972.

"Thesen zur Schwangerschaftsunterbrechung?" by M. Stahli. REF 21:162-169, March, 1972.

"The tragic results of abortion in England," by N. St. John-Stevas. LINACRE 39:30-38, February, 1972.

"Tu ne tueras pas! L'interruption de grossesse selon l'Eglise catholique," by Ch. Robert. ESPRIT ET VIE 33-48, 1972.

"Tubingen theologian condemned by bishop; interview by Konkret (periodical)," by N. Greinacher. OR 22(218)4, June 1, 1972.

"UK 'Conscience Clause' examined," AUSTRALAS NURSES J 1:15, August, 1972.

"Unborn child," by N. Jeffcoate. NURSING MIRROR 134:10-14, April 28, 1972.

"Unwanted by whom; reprint from Catholic Currents, February 1, 1972," by W. Sayers. FAM DGST 27:2-5, August, 1972.

"U. S. bishops clash with national commission on abortion proposal," HOSP PROGRESS 53:23.24, May, 1972.

"What is LIFE?" NEW HUMANIST 88:192-194, September, 1972.

"What sisters should know about abortion; interview by D. Durken," by P. Marx. SISTERS 43:519-531, May, 1972.

"When does human life start?" by H. Berger. OSTERR SCHWESTERNZTG 25:143-146, June, 1972.

"Wirksamer Schutz fur das ungeborene Leben - Aufgabe von Recht und Gesellschaft," by F. G. von Westphalen. DIAKONIA 27-37, 1972.

"Youth--and the VAD," by L. Porritt. NZ NURS J 65:4, August, 1972.

RESEARCH AND ABORTION

"Abnormalities of intrauterine development in non-human primates," by J. G. Wilson. ACTA ENDOCRINOL 166:Suppl:261-292, 1972.

"Abortion in mouse," by H. Heinecke, et al. Z VERSUCHSTIERKD 13:320-326, 1971.

"Action of a serotonin antagonist, methysergide, on the abortive or lethal effect of bacterial endotoxins in mice," by F. Darrieulat, et al. ANN INST PASTEUR 121:665-673, November, 1971.

"Bacteriological, biochemical and virulence studies on Salmonella dublin from abortion and enteric disease in cattle and sheep," by J. R. Walton. VET REC 90:236-240, February 26, 1972.

"Blockage of pregnancy in mice by the odor of male litter mates," by S. Bloch, et al. EXPERIENTIA 28:703, June 15, 1972.

"Bovine abortion associated with Aeromonas hydrophila," by K. Wohlgemuth, et al. J AM VET MED ASSOC 160:1001-1002, April 1, 1972.

"Bovine abortion associated with Nocardia asteroides," by K. Wohlgemuth, et al. J AM VET MED ASSOC 161:273-274, August 1, 1972.

"Bovine abortion associated with Torulopsis glabrata," by C. A. Kirkbride, et al. J AM VET MED ASSOC 161:390-391, August 15, 1972.

"Chromosome aberrations in oogenesis and embryogenesis of mammals and man," by G. Rohrborn. ARCH TOXIKOL 28:115-119, 1971.

"Clinical aspects, pathogenesis and prevention of animal toxoplasmosis (with special reference to toxoplasmosis abortion in sheep)," by J. K. Beverley. MONATSH VET MED 26:893-900, December 1, 1971.

"A comparison between the contribution of increasing and decreasing liveweight to ovulation and embryonic survival in the Border Leicester Merino ewe," by I. A. Cumming. J REPROD FERTIL 28:148, January, 1972.

"Comparison of methods for diagnosing equine rhinopneumonitis rivus abortion," by A. L. Trapp, et al. VET MED SMALL ANIM CLIN 67:895 passim, August, 1972.

"Diagnosis of bovine abortion," by E. A. Woelffer. J AM VET MED ASSOC 161:1284-1287, December 1, 1972.

"Effect of levorin on the course of pregnancy and on the fetus of rabbits," by N. N. Sionitskaia, et al. ANTIBIOTIKI 17:742-745, August, 1972.

"The effects of high altitude on the reproductive cycle and pregnancy in the hamster," by R. H. Printz. ANAT REC 173:157-171, June, 1972.

"Epidemiologic investigation of an outbreak of fatal enteritis and abortion associated with dietary change and Salmonella typhimurium infection in a dairy herd. A case report," by R. F. Kahrs, et al. CORNELL VET 62:175-191, April, 1972.

"Equine abortion (herpes) virus: purification and concentration of enveloped and deenveloped virus and envelope material by density gradient centrifugation in colloidal silica," by B. Klingeborn, et al. VIROLOGY 48:618-623, May, 1972.

"Experimental Brucella ovis infection in ewes. 1. Breeding performance of infected ewes," by K. L. Hughes. AUST VET J 48: 12-17, January, 1972.

"Experimental vibrio infections in sheep," by M. A. Luchko, et al. VETERINARIIA 48:72-73, June, 1972.

"Failure of dietary supplementation to prevent the abortions and congenital malformations of lathyrism and locoism in sheep," by R. F. Keeler, et al. CAN J COMP MED 35:342-345, October, 1971.

"The fluorescent antibody technique in the diagnosis of equine rhinopneumonitis virus abortion," by I. M. Smith, et al. CAN J COMP MED 36:303-308, July, 1972.

"The identification of Mortierella wolfii isolated from cases of abortion and pneumonia in cattle and a search for its infection source," by M. E. Di Menna, et al. RES VET SCI 13:439-442, September, 1972.

"Infectious abortions of Leptospira origin in cattle," by J. Vosta, et al. VET MED 16:683-688, December, 1971.

"Infectious bovine rhinotracheitis virus-induced abortion: rapid diagnosis by fluorescent antibody technique," by D. E. Reed, et al. AM J VET RES 32:1423-1426, September, 1971.

"Interim report on the joint program for the study of abortion," by C. Tietze, et al. CLIN OBSTET GYNECOL 14:1317-1335, December, 1971.

"Isolation of an OLT group virus from sheep with enzootic abortions," by Kh. Z. Gaffarov, et al. VETERINARIIA 7:109-111, 1971.

"Isolation of a strain of infectious bovine rhinotracheitis virus from aborted fetuses," by Y. Shimizu, et al. NATL INST ANIM HEALTH Q 12:110-111, Summer, 1972.

"Listeic abortion studies in sheep. I. Maternofetal changes," by C. O. Njoku, et al. CORNELL VET 62:608-627, October, 1972.

"Listeria induced abortion in pigs," by A. Weber, et al. BERL MUNCH TIERAERZTL WOCHENSCHR 85:105-107, March 15, 1972.

"Mycotic abortions in cows," by E. P. Kremlev. VETERINARIIA 4:89-91, April, 1971.

"Mycotic abortion in ewes produced by Aspergillus fumigatus: intravascular and intrauterine inoculation," by A. C. Pier, et al. AM J VET RES 33:349-356, February, 1972.

"Nocardia asteroides associated with swine abortion," by J. R. Cole, Jr., et al. VET MED SMALL ANIM CLIN 67:496 passim, May, 1972.

"Observations on Leptospira hardjo infection in New South Wales," by R. J. Hoare, et al. AUST VET J 48:228-232, May, 1972.

"Pathomorphology and pathogenesis of streptococcal abortion in cows," by V. Jelev, et al. ZENTRALBL VETERINAERMED 18: 610-616, October, 1971.

"Pine-needle (Pinus ponderosa)-induced abortion in range cattle," by A. H. Stevenson, et al. CORNELL VET 62:519-524, October, 1972.

"Prenatal losses in border Leicester-Merino cross ewes in Victoria," by D. J. Cannon, et al. AUST VET J 47:323-325, July, 1971.

"Prostaglandin E 2: analysis of effects on pregnancy and corpus luteum in hamsters and rats," by A. P. Labhsetwar. ACTA ENDOCRINOL 170:Suppl:3-32, 1972.

"Restoration of nidation in aureomycin-treated mice," by D. Boucher. C R SOC BIOL 163:1131-1134, 1969.

"Retarded embryonic development and pregnancy termination in ovariectomized guinea-pigs: progesterone deficiency and decidual collapse," by R. Deanesly. J REPROD FERTIL 28:241-247, February, 1972.

"Significance of aerobic vibrios in the etiology of abortions and sterility in cows," by V. F. Shatalov. VETERINARIIA 9:97-99, August, 1971.

"Spontaneous abortion in wild-caught rhesus monkeys, Macaca mulatta," by A. T. Hertig, et al. LAB ANIM SCI 21:510-519, August, 1971.

"Susceptibility of Alveonasus lahorensis neumann ticks to the agent of enzootic abortion of sheep," by I. I. Tershikh, et al. VOPR VIRUSOL 17:430-432, July-August, 1972.

"Virological studies of the central nervous system of horse fetuses and findings in mares suffering from central nervous system disease following abortion caused by equine herpesvirus 1," by K. Petzoldt, et al. SCHWEIZ ARCH TIERHEILKD 114:129-139, February, 1972.

RHEUMATIC CARDIOPATHY
see: Complications

RUBELLA
see: Complications

SACRAILIAC ARTHRITIS
see: Complications

SEPSIS
"Adrenocorticotropic function of the hypophisis in postabortive sepsis," by A. D. Makatsariia, et al. VOPR OKHR MATERIN DET 17:94, May, 1972.

"Anaerobic sepsis following abortion," by I. R. Zak. AKUSH GINE-

GINEKOL 47:11-13, November, 1971.

"Immunologic indices and serum protein fractions in patients with peritonitis and sepsis following non-hospital abortions," by N. N. Kulikova, et al. AKUSH GINEKOL 47:14-18, November, 1971.

SEPTIC ABORTION AND SEPTIC SHOCK

see also: Complications
Sepsis

"Bacterial endocarditis with 'associated bacteria'," by E. Bergogne-Berezin, et al. NOUV PRESSE MED 1:271-272, January 22, 1972.

"Effects of exchange transfusion on hemostatic disorders during septic shock after abortion," by C. Gibert, et al. REV MED SUISSE ROMANDE 91:689-696, October, 1971.

"Effects of haemodialysis on dynamics of some antibiotics in blood of patients with kidney insufficiency complicated by purulent infection," by M. Kuzin, et al. BULL SOC INT CHIR 31:298-303, July-August, 1972.

"Experience in the treatment of septic shock in obstetric practice," by R. Schwarz, et al. AKUSH GINEKOL 47:8-11, November, 1971.

"Participation of biogenic amines in the pathogenesis of bacterial shock," by L. S. Persianinov, et al. AKUSH GINEKOL 47:3-7, November, 1971.

"Proteins of the blood serum in patients with pyoseptic diseases following infected abortion (electrophoresis on polyacrylamide gel)," by M. I. Kotliar, et al. AKUSH GINEKOL 48:73-74, March, 1972.

"Septic abortion masquerading as thrombotic thrombocytopenic purpura," by M. Yudis, et al. AM J OBSTET GYNECOL 111:350-352, October 1, 1971.

"Septic abortions," by A. Marzuki, et al. MED J MALAYA 26:77-83, December, 1971.

SEPTIC ABORTION AND SEPTIC SHOCK

"Study of maternal mortality," J KY MED ASSOC 70:168, March, 1972.

"Treatment of septic soap abortion," by G. Gerisch, et al. ZENTRALBL GYNAEKOL 94:520-523, April 22, 1972.

SEXUAL DISORDERS AND ABORTION

see: Complications
Induced Abortion

SIGETIN

"Use of sigetin for the prevention of perinatal mortality and morbidity after the 1st half of complicated pregnancy (experimental and clinical data)," by N. G. Kosheleva. AKUSH GINEKOL 47:40-43, March, 1972.

SKIN DISEASES AND ABORTION

see: Complications

SOCIOLOGY, BEHAVIOR AND ABORTION

see also: Family Planning
Religion, Ethics and Abortion

"Abortion and slavery arguments same, ad says," NAT CATH REP 8:4, March 31, 1972.

"Abortion counseling," by A. D. Asher. AM J PUBLIC HEALTH 62:686-688, May, 1972.

"Abortion counseling and behavioral change," by B. Dauber, et al. FAM PLANN PERSPECT 4:23-27, April, 1972.

"Abortion. . .human aspects," by D. Goyette. INFIRM CAN 14:30-34, June, 1972.

"Abortion: influences on health professionals' attitudes," by J. P. Bourne. HOSPITALS 46:80-83, July 16, 1972.

"Abortion questionnaire and RCOG," by B. Corkill. NZ MED J 74: 410-411, December, 1971.

"Abortion referral agencies," by N. L. Bosworth, et al. J KY MED ASSOC 70:795-796, October, 1972.

"Abortion referral in a large college health service," by M. W. Bridwell, et al. J AM MED WOM ASSOC 27:420-421, August, 1972.

"Abortion: work of Clergy counseling service for problem pregnancies, Los Angeles and Birthright of Chicago," by C. Remsberg, et al. SEVENTEEN 31:140-141 plus, September, 1972.

"Abortions regaining objectivity or rationalization?" by E. F. Kal, et al. AM J PSYCHIATRY 129:484-485, October, 1972.

"Administrative guidelines for an abortion service," by G. Felton, et al. AM J NURS 72:108-109, January, 1972.

"Advising about pregnancy termination," by J. D. Bottomley. BR MED MED J 1:54, January 1, 1972.

"Alternatives to abortion for the unwed mother," by J. S. Morris, Jr. VA MED MON 99:844-847, August, 1972.

"Anaesthetic practice and pregnancy. Controlled survey of women anaesthetists in the United Kingdom," by R. P. Knill-Jones, et al. LANCET 1:1326-1328, June 17, 1972.

"Comparative studies on effects of previous pregnancy interruption, spontaneous abortion and term labor on the incidence of immature and premature labors," by S. Rozewicki, et al. WIAD LEK 25:31-38, January 1, 1972.

"A comparison between unmarried women seeking therapeutic abortion and unmarried mothers," by J. Naiman. LAVAL MED 42:1086-1088, December, 1971.

"Counseling the abortion patient is more than talk," by C. Keller, et al. AM J NURS 72:102-106, January, 1972.

"Counseling for women who seek abortion," by E. M. Smith. SOC WORK 17:62-68, March, 1972.

"Developing professional parameters: nursing and social work roles in the care of the induced abortion patient," by L. M. Tanner. CLIN OBSTET GYNECOL 14:1271-1272, December, 1971.

"Figures and fetuses; findings of New York TV surveys," by R. J. Neuthaus. COMMONWEAL 97:175-178, November 24, 1972.

"Half favor easier abortion, poll says," NAT CATH REP 8:24, March 17, 1972.

"Health visitors and birth control advice 1970-1971," by M. Waite. NURSING TIMES 68:Suppl:157-159, October 12, 1972; Suppl:161-164, October, 1972.

"Induced abortion and marriage counseling in epilepsy," by F. Rabe. MED WELT 23:330-331, March 4, 1972.

"Induced abortion and marriage counseling in multiple sclerosis," by R. C. Behrend. MED WELT 23:326-330, March 4, 1972.

"Induced abortion and marriage counseling in myasthenia," by H. G. Mertens. MED WELT 23:332-335, March 4, 1972.

"Influences on health professionals' attitudes," by J. P. Bourne. HOSPITALS 46:80-83, July 16, 1972.

"Is abortion black genocide?" by M. Treadwell. FAM PLANN PERSPECT 4:4-5, January, 1972.

"Konflikt zwischen Katholiken und Sozialisten? Auseinandersetzung um das Abtreibungsstrafrecht in Osterreich," HERDER KORRESPONDENZ 278-281, 1972.

"Large majority of public supports liberalization of abortion laws," GALLUP OPINION INDEX 13-15, September, 1972.

"Male view in abortion surveyed," US MED 8:19, December 15, 1972.

"Maryland ruling permits abortion referral ads," ADV AGE 43:21, January 3, 1972.

"Mass-produced, assembly-line abortion. A prime example of unethical, unscientific medicine," by J. H. Ford. CALIF MED 117:80-84,

November, 1972.

"McHugh: valley of death," NAT CATH REP 8:5, March 24, 1972.

"Movement for L.I.F.E. -- a revolution in embryo," by M. C. Shumiatcher. CAN MONTH 12,5:13-14, 1972.

"Mr. Abortion," by H. D. Dublin. NEWSWEEK 80:70, November 13, 1972.

"The muddled issue of abortion; interview by H. Cargas," by N. St. John-Stevas. NAT CATH REP 9:7, November 3, 1972.

"Need for counseling follows abortions," by J. Wykert. PSYCHIAT NEWS 8:29 plus, February 16, 1972.

"New anti-abortion campaigns launched," HOSP PROGRESS 53:21, January, 1972.

"Nigerian bishops condemn abortion," OR 20(216)3-4, May 18, 1972; also in SOC JUST 65:85-86, June, 1972.

"Nixon on abortion," NAT R 24:570, May 26, 1972.

"N.O.P.: abortion survey," NEW HUMANIST 88:30-33, May, 1972.

"Now I understand abortion," by R. Scheiber. OSV 61:5, July 16, 1972.

"Observations on health care instructions given to pregnant women. Survey of women with past history of abortion," by M. Nohara. JAP J PUBLIC HEALTH NURSE 28:48-54, January, 1972.

"Oklahoma abortion survey tabulation completed," J OKLA STATE MED ASS 65:465-466, November, 1972.

"On going to jail," by L. Bozell. TRIUMPH 7:31, January, 1972; 21, February, 1972; 19, March, 1972.

"On responsibility for children not yet born," OR 12(208)8, March 23, 1972.

"Options of the single pregnant woman," by D. D. Wachtel. R RADICAL POL ECON 4:86-106, July, 1972.

"Personal business (abortion)," edited by W. Flanagan. BUS W 65-66, July 22, 1972.

"Personal experience at a legal abortion center," AM J NURS 72: 110-112, January, 1972.

"Perplexities for the would-be liberal in abortion," by A. J. Dyck. J REPROD MED 8:351-354, June, 1972.

"Poll says Catholics back abortion," NAT CATH REP 8:6, September 15, 1972.

"Possible guidelines for problem pregnancy counseling," by L. Scott. PAST PSYCH 23:41-49, May, 1972.

"Post abortion group therapy," by G. M. Burnell, et al. AM J PSYCHIATRY 129:220-223, August, 1972.

"Preabortion evaluation: decision-making, preparation and referral," by L. M. Tanner, et al. CLIN OBSTET GYNECOL 14:1273-1277, December, 1971.

"Preabortion evaluation: selection of patients for psychiatric referral," by J. R. Bragonier, et al. CLIN OBSTET GYNECOL 14: 1263-1270, December, 1971.

"President Nixon condemns abortion," by R. Nixon. SOC JUST 65:88, June, 1972.

"The problem of abortion," by J. Williamson. R SOC HEALTH J 92: 85-87 passim, April, 1972.

"Problem pregnancy. A perspective on abortion and the quality of human life," by S. A. Plummer. ROCKY MT MED J 69:64-66, November, 1972.

"Problems of abortion patients after one-day stay studied at Vancouver General Hospital," CAN NURSE 68:16, April, 1972.

"Psychosocial aspects of induced abortion. Its implications for the woman, her family and her doctor. 1.," by B. Raphael. MED J AUST 2:35-40, July 1, 1972.

"Psychosocial aspects of induced abortion. Its implications for the woman, her family and her doctor. 2.," by B. Raphael. MED J AUST 2:98-101, July 8, 1972.

"Psychosocial sequelae of therapeutic abortion in young unmarried women," by J. S. Wallerstein, et al. ARCH GEN PSYCHIAT 27: 828-832, December, 1972.

"Public health perspective on the limitation of births," by W. B. Jones, Jr., et al. N C MED J 33:688-691, August, 1972.

"Public opinion trends: Elective abortion and birth control services to teenagers," by R. Pomeroy, et al. FAMILY PLANN PERSPECT 4:44-55, October, 1972.

"Punishment: the hidden issue in abortion," by F. H. Hoffman. CONSULTANT 12:65-67, July, 1972.

"Q: What, doctor is the difference between you and Adolph Hitler. . .," TRIUMPH 8:18-20 plus, February, 1972.

"Recommended program guide for abortion services: American Public Health Association," AMER J PUBLIC HEALTH 62:1669-1671, December, 1972.

"Reflections on abortion. Research and new solutions," by F. Hanon. REV INFIRM 22:139-145, Februray, 1972.

"Reflexiones sobre el aborto," by A. Lopez. RAZON Y FE 143-154, February, 1972.

"Release of prostaglandin F 2 following injection of hypertonic saline for therapeutic abortion: a preliminary study," by B. Gustavii, et al. AM J OBSTET GYNECOL 114:1099-1100, December 15, 1972.

"Respect Life Week in U.S.A.," OR 37(233)4, September 14, 1972.

"Respectable killing. A review by K. D. Whitehead," by D. W. Cooper. NAT R 24:1415-1416, December 22, 1972.

"Revised standards on abortion issued by American Public Health Association task force," NATIONS HEALTH 2:1 plus, December, 1972.

"Right to abortion," TIDSKR SVER SJUKSKOT 39:6-7, February 24, 1972.

"The right to be born," by E. Shriver. MARRIAGE 54:8-12, June, 1972.

"Right to life," by L. Adams. CATH HOSP 3:2, July, 1972.

"The right to life: the Harvard statement; continued from the Boston Globe, October 29, 1971," by A. Dyck, et al. C DGST 36:29-32, March, 1972.

"Right to life has a message for New York state legislators," by F. C. Shapiro. N Y TIMES MAG 10-11 plus, August 20, 1972; Discussion 23 plus, September 10, 1972.

"Right to life: new strategy needed," TRIUMPH 7:46, April, 1972.

"Rights of the unborn -- a CAS looks at abortion," by T. T. Daley. CAN WEL 48:19-21, May-June, 1972.

"The role of private counseling for problem pregnancies," by J. H. Anwyl. CLIN OBSTET GYNECOL 14:1225-1229, December, 1971.

"Seesaw response of a young unmarried couple to therapeutic abortion," by J. Wallerstein, et al. ARCH GEN PSYCHIATRY 27:251-254, August, 1972.

"Slavery and abortion; continued from a press release distributed by Minesota Citizens Concerned for Life, August 18, 1972," by W. Schaller. C DGST 37:24-26, December, 1972.

"The social effects of legal abortion," by R. A. Schwartz. AM J PUBLIC HEALTH 62:1331-1335, October, 1972.

"Social indication in pregnancy interruption," by W. Becker. THER GGW 111:587-588 passim, April, 1972.

"Social perspectives: abortion and female behavior," by W. P. Nagan. VALPARAISO UNIV LAW R 6:286-314, Spring, 1972.

"Social work service to abortion patients," by A. Ullmann. SOC CASEWORK 53:481-487, October, 1972.

"Society for Developmental Biology backs 'right to abortion'," J AMER MED ASS 221:646, August 14, 1972.

"Some thoughts on the illegitimate child," by J. M. Lomax-Simpson. HEALTH VISIT 45:66-68, March, 1972.

"Some thoughts on medical evaluation and counseling of applicants for abortion," by A. J. Margolis. CLIN OBSTET GYNECOL 14: 1255-1257, December, 1971.

"Stop the death merchants," by L. Bozell. TRIUMPH 7:19, October, 1972; 31, November, 1972; 18-19, December, 1972.

"Suicide American style: the danger of birth rate decline," by J. Diamond. LIGUORIAN 60:45-49, April, 1972.

"Surveillance of legal abortions in the United States, 1970," by J. P. Bourne, et al. JOGN NURS 1:11-22, June, 1972.

"A survey of Milwaukee obstetricians and gynecologists attitudes toward abortion," by P. Halverson, et al. WIS MED J 71:134-139, April, 1972.

"Survey of the present statutory and case law on abortion: the contradictions and the problems," U ILL L F 1972:177, 1972.

"Survey on the incidence of criminal abortion in Sofia," by D. Vasilev. AKUSH GINEKOL (Sofija) 10:271-278, 1971.

"Teaching social conscience," by D. Rottenberg. TODAYS HEALTH 50:40-43 plus, September, 1972.

"Therapeutic abortion: middle-class privilege or curse?" by F. G.

Surawicz. J AM MED WOM ASSOC 27:590-597, November, 1972.

"Thomson on abortion," by B. A. Brody. PHIL PUB AFFAIRS 1: 335-340, Spring, 1972.

"Those against legal abortion," by E. Hackett. AUSTRALAS NURSES J 1:15, August, 1972.

"Thoughts after viewing an abortion; continued from National Observer, December 18, 1971," by E. Roberts, Jr. C DGST 36:6-8, April, 1972.

"Thoughts for the New Year," by L. Valvanne. KATILOLEHTI 77: 52, February, 1972.

"A time for dialogue on abortion," by A. Swidler. NAT CATH REP 9:7, December 1, 1972.

"Two-minute abortion is here--are we ready?" MED WORLD NEWS 13:15-17, May 12, 1972.

"Ways to cut U.S. birth rate--findings of an official study," US NEWS NEWS WORLD REP 72:64, March 27, 1972.

"Women who seek therapeutic abortion: a comparison with women who complete their pregnancies," by C. V. Ford, et al. AM J PSYCHIATRY 129:546-552, November, 1972.

"Why I favour abortion," by H. Calderot. AUSTRALAS NURSES J 1:9, July, 1972.

SODIUM CHLORIDE

"Interruption of late term pregnancy by intra-amnion transcervical administration of a hypertonic solution of sodium chloride," by G. A. Palladi, et al. AKUSH GINEKOL 48:58-61, May, 1972.

"Transcervical intra-amnionic administration of a 20 per cent sodium chloride solution for artificial interruption of late term pregnancy," by A. A. Lebedev, et al. AKUSH GINEKOL 48:55-58, May, 1972.

SODIUM-CITRATE

"Excellent effect of sodium-citrate-EDTA combination therapy in severe lead poisoning during pregnancy," by K. Abendroth. DTSCH GESUNDHEITSW 26:2130-2131, November 4, 1971.

S.P.U.C.

see: Religion, Ethics and Abortion

SPONTANEOUS ABORTION

see also: Threatened Abortion

"ABO incompatibility as a cause of spontaneous abortion: evidence from abortuses," by K. Takano, et al. J MED GENET 9:144-150, June, 1972.

"Arias-Stella phenomenon in spontaneous and therapeutic abortion," by S. G. Silverberg. AM J OBSTET GYNECOL 112:777-780, March 15, 1972.

"Chromosome aberrations and spontaneous abortions," by A. M. Kuliev. AKUSH GINEKOL 47:38-40, April, 1971.

"Chromosome studies in selected spontaneous abortions. IV. Unusual cytogenetic disorders," by D. H. Carr, et al. TERATOLOGY 5:49-56, February, 1972.

"Chromosome studies on spontaneous and threatened abortions," by T. Ikeuchi, et al. JAP J HUN GENET 16:191-197, March, 1972.

"A clinical and pathologic survey of 91 csaes of spontaneous abortion," by J. Brotherton, et al. FERTIL STERIL 23:289-294, April, 1972.

"Comparative studies on effects of previous pregnancy interruption, spontaneous abortion and term labor on the incidence of immature and premature labors," by S. Rozewicki, et al. WIAD LEK 25:31-38, January, 1972.

"Cytogenetic aspects of induced and spontaneous abortions," by D. H. Carr. CLIN OBSTET GYNECOL 15:203-219, March, 1972.

"Do Rh-negative women with an early spontaneous abortion need Rh immune prophylaxis?" by R. D. Visscher, et al. AM J OBSTET GYNECOL 113:158-165, May 15, 1972.

"Experiences in the therapy of spontaneous and habitual abortions with the oral administration of Gestanon A," by B. Beric, et al. MED PREGL 24:505-507, 1971.

"Incidence of chromosome abnormalities in spontaneous abortion and study of the risk in subsequent pregnancies," by J. G. Boue. REV FR GYNECOL OBSTET 67:183-187, February-March, 1972.

"Monosomy 21 in spontaneous abortus," by K. Ohoma, et al. HUMANGENETIK 16:267-270, 1972.

"Morphological study of the placenta in spontaneously interrupted pregnancies," by B. Kiutukchiev, et al. AKUSH GINEKOL (Sofiia) 10:435-439, 1971.

"The morphology and histochemistry of the fetal liver in spontaneous abortion," by G. I. Sibiriakova, et al. VOPR OKHR MATERIN DET 17:62-65, June, 1972.

"Preventive treatment of spontaneous abortion, such as it results from the study of mechanism of contraction and relaxation of uterine muscle," by K. Kato, et al. GYNECOL PRAT 23:89-94, 1972.

"Prospective study of fertility in the District of Sao Paulo. I. Comparison of retrospective and prospective methods to estimate the rates of spontaneous and induced abortions," by M. L. Milanesi, et al. BOL OF SANIT PANAM 72:234-243, March, 1972.

"Relationship between placental aklaline phosphatase phenotypes and the frequency of spotnaneous abortion in previous pregnancies," by L. Beckman, et al. HUM HERED 22:15-17, 1972.

"Spontaneous abortions in women-carriers of the phenylketonuria gene," by M. G. Bliumina. AKUSH GINEKOL 48:52-55, May, 1972.

"Trisomy 14 in spontaneous abortus," by T. Kajii, et al. HUMAN-

GENETIK 15:265-267, 1972.

"Value of placenta examination in spontaneous abortions of the 1st trimester," by J. Cohen. REV FR GYNECOL OBSTET 67:123-126, February-March, 1972.

STATISTICS

"Abortion (occurrence of abortion in a catchment area)," by H. Krabisch. ZENTRALBL GYNAEKOL 94:1127-1133, August 26, 1972.

"Ambulatory abortion: experience with 26,000 cases (July 1, 1970, to August 1, 1971)," by B. N. Nathanson. NEW ENGL J MED 286:403-407, February 24, 1972.

"Attitudes toward abortion among young black (based on a study of 300 young Negro women in Baltimore, Md.)," by F. F. Furstenburg, Jr. STUDIES IN FAMILY PLANNING 3:66-69, April, 1972.

"California abortion statistics for 1971," by W. M. Ballard. CALIF MED 116:55, April, 1972.

"Clarification of the so-called clouded figures on abortion," by R. J. Prill. MED KLIN 67:619-622, April 28, 1972.

"A clinical and pathologic survey of 91 cases of spontaneous abortion," by J. Brotherton, et al. FERTIL STERIL 23:289-294, April, 1972.

"Current opinion on abortion," by P. Worden. PTA MAG 66:12-14, May, 1972.

"Histopathology of abortion. Study of 256 cases," by E. A. Ceron. GINECOL OBSTET MEX 31:617-623, June, 1972.

"Miscarriage and abortion. Statistical studies on miscarriage in relation to family development and socioeconomic factors," by H. J. Staemmler, et al. DTSCH MED WOCHENSCHR 97:885-892, June, 1972.

"Report on therapeutic abortions for fiscal 1971," by J. K. Seegar, Jr.

MD STATE MED J 21:32-35, February, 1972.

"Results of a year's liberal regulation of abortion in the State of New York," by F. K. Beller. MED WELT 23:471-472, March 25, 1972.

"Scottish abortion statistics--1970," HEALTH BULL 30:27-35, January, 1972.

"Temporary submucosal cerclage for cervical incompetecne: report of forty-eight cases," by C. L. Jennings, Jr. AM J OBSTET GYNECOL 113:1097-1102, August 15, 1972.

"Therapeutic abortion: government figures show big increase in 1971," CAN MED ASS J 106:1131, May 20, 1972.

"Therapeutic abortion without inpatient hospitalization: an early experience with 325 cases," by I. M. Golditch, et al. CALIF MED 116:1-3, March, 1972.

"3 cases of defibrination in the course of retro-placental hematomas," by M. Samama, et al. BULL FED SOC GYNECOL OBSTET LANG FR 23:368-378, September-October, 1971.

"2,000 Catholic abortions," NAT CATH REP 8:12, August 18, 1972.

STERILITY

"A case of fecundity disorders: chromosomal discussion," by H. Dar, et al. REV FR GYNECOL OBSTET 67:193-194, February-March, 1972.

"Causes of infertility," by R. Gergova, et al. CESK GYNEKOL 37:529-530, September, 1972.

"The course and outcome of pregnancy for women treated for infertility," by M. S. Biriukova, et al. PEDIATR AKUSH GINEKOL 71:46-48, September-October, 1971.

"Fecundity and high risk pregnancy," by D. S. F. Garnot. REV FR GYNECOL OBSTET 67:235-238, April, 1972.

STERILITY

"Fertility control through abortion: an assessment of the period 1950-1980," by C. Dierass. BULLETIN OF THE ATOMIC SCIENTISTS 28,1:9-14, 41-45, January, 1972.

"Fertility effects of the abolition of legal abortion in Romania," by M. S. Teitelbaum. POPULATION STUDIES 26:405-417, November, 1972.

"The fertility response to abortion reform in eastern Europe: demographic and economic implications," by R. J. McIntyre. AM ECONOMIST 16:45-65, Fall, 1972.

"New antifertility agent--an orally active prostaglandin..ICI 74,205," by A. P. Lebhsetwar. NATURE (London) 238:400-401, August 18, 1972.

"Prospective study of fertility in the District of Sao Paulo. I. Compairson of retrospective and prospective methods to estimate the rates of spontaneous and induced abortions," by M. L. Milanesi, et al. BOL OF SANIT PANAM 72:234-243, March, 1972.

"Prostaglandins in fertility control," by J. S. Carrel. SCIENCE 175: 1279, March 17, 1972.

"Reduction in fertility due to induced abortions: a simulation model (India)," by K. Venkatacharya. DEMOGRAPHY 9:339-352, August, 1972.

STERILIZATION

"Abortion and sterilization. Comment on the outline of a fifth law for the reform of the criminal law 5th StRG from 14 February 1972 (BR-print. 58-72) prepared by the Commission on Questions of Rights," by H. Ehrhardt. NERVENARZT 43:338-340, June, 1972.

"Contraception, abortion, prostaglandins and sterilization," by J. H. Ravina. NOUV PRESSE MED 1:1989-1990, August 26, 1972.

"Court-ordered sterilization performed at St. Vincent's Hospital, Billings," by L. Cory. HOSP PROG 53:22 plus, December, 1972.

"Hysterectomy for therapeutic abortion with sterilization," by C.

Grumbrecht, et al. GEBURTSHILFE FRAUENHELIKD 32:205-208, March, 1972.

"Is the individual life still the highest value? (A gynecologist's thoughts on abortion and sterilization)," by H. Wagner. MED MONATSSCHR 26:303-307, July, 1972.

"Liberation of abortions and female sterilizations," by D. M. Potts. CAN MED ASSOC J 105:901, November, 1971.

"Major surgery for abortion and sterilization," by H. Schulman. OBSTET GYNECOL 40:738-739, November, 1972.

"NAACOG statement on abortions and sterilizations," JOGN NURS 1:57, June, 1972.

"'Pill,' IUD, sterilization reduce unwanted births," AMER MED NEWS 15:10-11, August 14, 1972.

"Relationship between prevalence of sterilization surgery and pregnancy, parity and induced abortion," JAP J PUBLIC HEALTH NURSE, 27:50-56, December, 1971.

"Statement on abortions and sterilizations: Nurses Association of the American College of Obstetricians and Gynecologists," JOGN NURSING 1:57, June, 1972.

"Surgical sterilization and interruption of pregnancy as means of fertility regulation," by W. Dalicho. BEITR GERICHTL MED 29:344-350, 1972.

"Tiny gold valves to control fertility in men and laparoscopies for women," LIFE 73:54-56, July 28, 1972.

STREPTIDIN

"The relaxant and antispasmotic effects of streptidin on smooth muscles," by O. Altinkurt. TURK HIJ TECR BIYOL DERG 30:242-244, 1970.

STUDENTS

see: Youth

SURGICAL TREATMENT AND MANAGEMENT
see also: Techniques of Abortion

"Hysterectomy for therapeutic abortion with sterilization," by C. Grumbrecht, et al. GEBURTSHILFE FRAUENHEILKD 32:205-208, March, 1972.

"Isthmico-cervical insufficiency as a factor in prematurity (late abortions and premature labor) and its surgical treatment," by R. Tokin. AKUSH GINEKOL (Sofiia) 8:169-177, 1969.

"Major surgery for abortion and sterilization," by H. Schulman. OBSTET GYNECOL 40:738-739, November, 1972.

"Management of recurring abortion," by H. C. McLaren. PRACTITIONER 209:661-664, November, 1972.

"Management of uterine perforations suffered at elective abortion," by B. N. Nathanson. AM J OBSTET GYNECOL 114:1054-1059, December 15, 1972.

"Results of surgical treatment of cervical incompetence in pregnancy," by F. Glenc, et al. POL TYG LEK 27:834-836, May 29, 1972.

"Surgical management of abortion," by J. F. Palmoaki, et al. N ENGL J MED 287:752-754, October 12, 1972.

"Surgical sterilization and interruption of pregnancy as means of fertility regulation," by W. Dalicho. BEITR GERICHTL MED 29: 344-350, 1972.

"Surgical treatment of abruptio placentae," by I. Kosowsky, et al. ZENTRALBL GYNAEKOL 94:754-756, June 10, 1972.

"Surgical treatment of pregnant women with habitual abortion caused by cervix insufficiency," by J. Bocev. AKUSH GINEKOL 47:69-70, April, 1971.

"Temporary submucosal cerclage for cervical incompetence: report of forty-eight cases," by C. L. Jennings, Jr. AM J OBSTET

GYNECOL 113:1097-1102, August 15, 1972.

"Transabdominal cervico-uterine suture," by R. A. Watkins. AUST NZ J OBSTET GYNAECOL 12:62-64, February, 1972.

SURVEYS

see: Sociology, Behavior and Abortion

SYMPOSIA

"Pregnancy termination: the impact of new laws. An invitational symposium," J REPROD MED 6:274-301, June, 1971.

"Symposium: abortion and the law," CASE W RES L REV 23:705, Summer, 1972.

TECHNIQUES OF ABORTION

see also: Induced Abortion
Surgical Treatment and Management

"Abortion by aspiration technic," by T. B. Cheikh, et al. TUNIS MED 2:119-120, March-April, 1971.

"Abortion during the 1st trimester by means of polyclinical vacuum apsiration without anesthesia," NED TIJDSCHR GENEESKD 116:165, January 22, 1972.

"Abortion experiment in the polyclinic," by E. Vartiainen. SAIRAANH VUOSIK 48:341-343, April 25, 1972.

"Clinical experiences in induced abortion using vacuum extraction and the metranoikter," by J. Hoffman, et al. ZENTRALBL GYNAEKOL 94:913-917, July 22, 1972.

"Early abortion without cervical dilation: pump or syringe aspiration," by A. J. Margolis, et al. J REPROD MED 9:237-240, November, 1972.

"Early abortions. Surgical technics and patient care," LAKARTIDNINGEN 69:4490-4495, September 27, 1972.

"Effect of the method of induced abortion (currettage v. aspiration) on feto-maternal isoimmunization," by M. Asztalos, et al. ZENTRALBL GNYAEKOL 94:926-930, July 22, 1972.

"Evacuation of the uterine cavity by vacuum aspiration," by L. V. Castro. REV CHIL OBSTET GINECOL 34:23-32, 1969.

"Forane increases bleeding in therapeutic suction abortion," by W. M. Dolan, et al. ANESTHESIOLOGY 36:96-97, January, 1972.

"Interruption of pregnancy in the 1st trimester under neurolepto-analgesia," by R. Muzelak, et al. CESK GYNEKOL 37:79-80, March, 1972.

"The Karman catheter: a preliminary evaluation as an instrument for termination of pregnancies up to twelve weeks of gestation," by B. Beric, et al. AM J OBSTET GYNECOL 114:273-275, September 15, 1972.

"Ketamine for dilatation and currettage procedures: patient acceptance," by W.H. Hervey, et al. ANESTH ANALG 51:647-655, July-August, 1972.

"Laminaria-metreurynter method of midterm abortion in Japan," by Y. Manabe, et al. OBSTET GYNECOL 40:612-615, October, 1972.

"Laminaria tent as a cervical dilator prior to aspiration-type therapeutic abortion," by C. J. Eaton, et al. OBSTET GYNECOL 39: 535-537, April, 1972.

"Laminaria tent: relic of the past or modern medical device?" by B. W. Newton. AM J OBSTET GYNECOL 113:442-448, June 15, 1972.

"New abortion method," NAT CATH REP 8:17, August 4, 1972.

"Pregnancy and labor after cerclage," by M. Vitse, et al. BULL FED SOC GYNECOL OBSTET LANG FR 23:425-426, September-October, 1971.

"Suction curettage," by A. Sikkel. NED TIJDSCHR GENEESKD 116: 1757-1758, September 23, 1972.

"Termination of second trimester pregnancy with 15 methylanalogues of prostaglandins E2 and F2," by S. M. Karim, et al. J OBSTET GYNAECOL BR COMMONW 79:737-743, August, 1972.

"Treatment of habitual abortion by the Mitchell-Bardavil method," by V. I. Finik. AKUSH GINEKOL 48:61-63, February, 1972.

"Unofficial abortion; menstrual extraction," TIME 100:47, September 11, 1972.

"Unusual complication during pregnancy interruption by vacuum extraction," by K. Mirkov, et al. AKUSH GINEKOL (Sofiia) 11: 85-86, 1972.

"Use of maninaria tents with saline abortion," by J. H. Lischke, et al. LANCET 1:49, January 1, 1972.

"Vacuum aspiration in the management of abortions," by V. E. Aimakhu. INT SURG 57:13-16, January, 1972.

"Vacuum aspirations at a hospital outpatient clinic," by R. Fahraeus. LAKARTIDNINGEN 69:4665-4670, October 4, 1972.

"Very early abortion using syringe as vacuum source," by H. Karman, et al. LANCET 1:1051-1052, May 13, 1972.

THERAPEUTIC ABORTION

"Abortion...medical aspects," by G. Pepin. INFIRM CAN 14:24-26, June, 1972.

"Abortion--the role of private foundations," by D. H. Minkler. CLIN OBSTET GYNECOL 14:1181-1189, December, 1971.

"Abortion: a special demand," JAMA 221:400, July 24, 1972.

"An abuse of prenatal diagnosis," by M. A. Stenchever. JAMA 221: 408, July 24, 1972.

"Advising about pregnancy termination," by J. D. Bottomley. BR MED J 1:54, January 1, 1972.

"Air embolism and maternal death from therapeutic abortion," by R. A. Munsick. OBSTET GYNECOL 39:688-690, May, 1972.

"Arias-Stella phenomenon in spontaneous and therapeutic abortion," by S. G. Silverberg. AM J OBSTET GYNECOL 112:777-780, March 15, 1972.

"Bronchospasm complicating intravenous prostaglandin F 2a for therapeutic abortion," by J. I. Fishburne, Jr., et al. OBSTET GYNECOL 39:892-896, June, 1972.

"Care and treatment of therapeutic abortion patients in Canadian hospitals: January 1 to September 30, 1971," HOSP ADMIN CAN 14:25-31, March, 1972.

"Characterization of 100 women psychiatrically evaluated for therapeutic abortion," by K. H. Talan, et al. ARCH GEN PSYCHIATRY 26:571-577, June, 1972.

"A comparison between unmarried women seeking therapeutic abortion and unmarried mothers," by J. Naiman. LAVAL MED 42: 1086-1088, December, 1971.

"Contraceptive antecedents to early and late therapeutic abortions," by W. Oppel. AM J PUBLIC HEALTH 62:824-827, June, 1972.

"Cyanosis due to intravenous prostaglandin F," by G. Roberts, et al. LANCET 2:425-426, August 26, 1972.

"Declaration of Oslo: statement on therapeutic abortion--World Medical Assembly," WORLD MED J 19:30, March-April, 1972.

"Deformed infants' suits for failure to recommend abortions," J KANS MED SOC 73:80 passim, February, 1972.

"Discussion about Article 218 of the Penal Code. Position of the Federal Ministry of Justice," by A. Bayerl. DTSCH KRANKENPFLEGEZ 25:241-242, May, 1972.

"Effect of aminocentesis, selective abortion, and reproductive compensation on the incidence of autosomal recessive diseases," by G. W. Hagy, et al. J HERED 63:185-188, July-August, 1972.

"Effects of termination of pregnancy and general anesthesia on acid-base equilibrium in blood," by J. Denk, et al. WIAD LEK 25:500-503, March 15, 1972.

"8 cases of therapeutic abortion in advanced pregnancy by injections of hypertonic saline serum," by T. B. Cheikh, et al. TUNIS MED 2:117-118, March-April, 1971.

"The experience of two county hospitals in implementation of therapeutic abortion," by J. R. Bragonier, et al. CLIN OBSTET GYNECOL 14:1237-1242, December, 1971.

"Experience with therapeutic abortion clinic: methods and complications," by R. Egdell. DEL MED J 44:207-212, August, 1972.

"Factors affecting gestational age at therapeutic abortion," by I. Chaimers, et al. LANCET 1:1324-1326, June 17, 1972.

"Fetal indications for therapeutic abortion," by A. C. Christakos. N. C. MED J 33:115-119, February, 1972.

"Follow-up of patients recommended for therapeutic abortion," by N. A. Todd. BR J PSYCHIATRY 120:645-646, June, 1972.

"Forane increases bleeding in therapeutic suction abortion," by W. M. Dolan, et al. ANESTHESIOLOGY 36:96-97, January, 1972.

"Four years' experience with mid-trimester abortion by amnio-infusion," by C. A. Ballard, et al. AM J OBSTET GYNECOL 114:575-581, November 1, 1972.

"The future of therapeutic abortions in the United States," by R. E. Hall. CLIN OBSTET GYNECOL 14:1149-1153, December, 1971. 1971.

"The gynecologist and the problem of therapeutic abortion," by J. P. Pudnel. GYNECOL PRAT 23:9-16, 1972.

"High-dose intravenous administration of prostaglandin E 2 and F 2 for the termination of midtrimester pregnancies," by K. Hillier, et al. J OBSTET GYNAECOL BR COMMONW 79:14-22, January, 1972.

"A histological study of the effect on the placenta of intra-amniotically and extra-amniotically injected hypertonic saline in therapeutic abortion," by B. Gustavii, et al. ACTA OBSTET GYNECOL SCAND 51:121-125, 1972.

"Hormone levels during prostaglandin F 2 infusions for therapeutic abortion," by L. Speroff, et al. J CLIN ENDOCRINOL METAB 34:531-536, March, 1972.

"How safe is abortion?" by J. S. Metters, et al. LANCET 1:197-198, January 22, 1972.

"How safe is abortion?" by A. S.Moolgaoker. LANCET 1:264, January 29, 1972.

"How safe is abortion?" by C. Tietze, et al. LANCET 1:198, January 22, 1972.

"Hysterectomy for therapeutic abortion with sterilization," by C. Grumbrecht, et al. GEBURTSHILFE FRAUENHEILKD 32:205-208, March, 1972.

"I.M.A. and A.I.M.L.A.," by S. Raichaudhury. J INDIAN MED ASSOC 57:467, December 16, 1971.

"The impact of recent changes in therapeutic abortion laws," by J. B. Kahn, et al. CLIN OBSTET GYNECOL 14:1130-1148, December, 1971.

"Implementation of therapeutic abortion in the Kaiser Hospital-Southern California Premanente medical group," by A. Saltz. CLIN OBSTET GYNECOL 14:1230-1236, December, 1971.

"Increasing consumer participation in professional goal setting: contraception and therapeutic abortion," by R. W. Tichauer, et al. J AM MED WOMENS ASSOC 27:365 passim, July, 1972.

"Indication and contraindication for interruption of pregnancy in skin diseases," by H. Schleicher, et al. DERMATOL MONATSSCHR 157:599-607, August, 1971.

"Induced abortion and marriage counseling in epilepsy," by F. Rabe. MED WELT 23:330-331, March 4, 1972.

"Induction of abortion using prostaglandin F 2," by F. F. Lehmann, et al. GEBURTSHILFE FRAUENHEILKD 32:477-483, June, 1972.

"Interruption of pregnancy for urological indications," by K. Geza. ORV HETIL 113:2045-2050, August 20, 1972.

"Intravenous prostaglandin F 2 for therapeutic abortion," by E. J. Kirshen, et al. AM J OBSTET GYNECOL 113:340-344, June 1, 1972.

"Intravenous prostaglandin F2 for therapeutic abortion: the efficacy and tolerance of three dosage schedules," by W. E. Brenner. AM J OBSTET GYNECOL 113:1037-1045, August 15, 1972.

"Introduction of a bill for new regulations for pregnancy interruption," TIJDSCHR ZIEKENVERPL 25:784-785, July 25, 1972.

"The Karman catheter: a preliminary evaluation as an instrument for termination of pregnancies up to twelve weeks of gestation," by B. Beric, et al. AM J OBSTET GYNECOL 114:273-275, September 15, 1972.

"Ketamine for dilatation and currettage procedures: patient acceptance," by W. H.Hervey, et al. ANESTH ANALG 51:647-655, July-August, 1972.

"Lactation following therapeutic abortion with prostaglandin F 2," by I. D. Smith, et al. NATURE (London) 240:411-412, December 15, 1972.

"Laminaria tent as a cervical dilator prior to aspiration-type therapeutic abortion," by C. J. Eaton, et al. OBSTET GYNECOL 39: 535-537, April, 1972.

"Major surgery for abortion and sterilization," by H. Schulman.

OBSTET GYNECOL 40:738-739, November, 1972.

"Medical and surgical complications of therapeutic abortions," by G. K. Stewart, et al. OBSTET GYNECOL 40:539-550, October, 1972.

"Methods of therapeutic abortion," by H. Stamm. GEBURTSHILFE FRAUENHEILKD 32:541-547, July, 1972.

"Myometrial necrosis after therapeutic abortion," by A. C. Wentz, et al. OBSTET GYNECOL 40:315-320, September, 1972.

"New case reporting system for therapeutic abortions introduced," by J. S. Bennett. CAN MED ASS J 106:196-198, January 22, 1972.

"New laws bring new approaches. Method for the evaluation of therapeutic abortion candidates meets the requirements of California state law and the needs of patients, while conserving the time of the medical staff," by S. Loos, et al. HOSPITALS 46:76-79, July, 1972.

"New trends in therapeutic abortion," by S. L. Barron. LANCET 2: 1193, December 2, 1972.

"New trends in therapeutic abortion," by R. G. Priest. LANCET 2: 1085, November 18, 1972.

"Outpatient management of first trimester therapeutic abortions with and without tubal ligation," by J. A. Colins, et al. CAN MED ASS J 106:1077-1080, May 20, 1972.

"Ovulation following threapeutic abortion," by E. F. Boyd, Jr., et al. AM J OBSTET GYNECOL 113:469-473, June 15, 1972.

"Plasms volume, electrolyte, and coagulation factor changes following intra-amniotic hypertonic saline infusion," by W. E. Easterling, Jr., et al. AM J OBSTET GYNECOL 113:1065-1071, August 15, 1972.

"Post-abortion group therapy," by G. M. Burnell, et al. AMER J PSYCHIAT 129:220-223, August, 1972.

"Pregnancy, abortion, and the developmental takss of adolescence," by C. Schaffer, et al. J AM ACAD CHILD PSYCHIATRY 11:511-536, July, 1972.

"Pregnancy interruption due to polyneuritis," by G. K. Kohler, et al. MED WELT 23:1726-1766, November 18, 1972.

"Premature placental detachment: physiopathology and therapeutic management," by B. Neme. MATERN INFANC 30:127-134, April-June, 1971.

"Prevention of Rh immunization after abortion with Anti-Rh (D)-immunoglobulin," by J. A. Goldman, et al. OBSTET GYNECOL 40:366-370, September, 1972.

"Preventive control of the Lesch-Nyhan syndrome," by P. J. Van Heeswijk, et al. OBSTET GYNECOL 40:109-113, July, 1972.

"Problems of abortion from the radiobiological indication view-point," by K. Neumeister, et al. DTSCH GESUNDHEITSW 27: 549-553, March 23, 1972.

"Prostaglandins and therapeutic abortion," by P. G. Gillett. J RE-PROD MED 8:329-334, June, 1972.

"Psychiatric complications of therapeutic abortion," by R. O. Pasnau. OBSTET GYNECOL 40:252-256, August, 1972.

"Psychologic issues in therapeutic abortion," by C. Nadelson. WOMAN PHYSICIAN 27:12-15, January, 1972.

"Psychological reaction to therapeutic abortion. II. Objective re-sponse," by K. R. Niswander, et al. AM J OBSTET GYNECOL 114:29-33, September 1, 1972.

"Psychosocial sequelae of therapeutic abortion in young unmarried women," by J. S. Wallerstein, et al. ARCH GEN PSYCHIATRY 27:828-832, December, 1972.

"Release of prostaglandin F 2 follwoing injection of hypertonic saline for therapeutic abortion: a preliminary study," by B. Gustavii, et al. AM J OBSTET GYNECOL 114:1099-1100,

December 15, 1972.

"Report on therapeutic abortions for fiscal 1971," by J. K. B. E. Seegar. MARYLAND STATE MED J 21:32-35, February, 1972.

"Rhesus sensitization in abortion," by P. S. Gavin. OBSTET GYNECOL 39:37-40, January, 1972.

"The risks of abortion," CAN MED ASSOC J 106:295-298, February 19, 1972.

"Role of local government in therapeutic abortions," by C. F. Coffeit. CLIN OBSTET GYNECOL 14:1197-1203, December, 1971.

"The role of private counseling for problem pregnancies," by J. H. Anwyl. CLIN OBSTET GYNECOL 14:1225-1229, December, 1971.

"Rubella and medical abortion," by E. Hervet, et al. NOUV PRESSE MED 1:379-380, February 5, 1972.

"Rubella reinfection during early pregnancy: a case report," by R. L. Northrop, et al. OBSTET GYNECOL 39:524-526, April, 1972.

"Rubella vaccination and termination of pregnancy," by H. J. Mair, et al. BR MED J 4:271-273, November 4, 1972.

"Second-trimester abortion after vaginal termination," by D. M. Potts. LANCET 2:133, July 15, 1972.

"Seesaw response of a young unmarried couple to therapeutic abortion," by J. Wallerstein, et al. ARCH GEN PSYCHIATRY 27:251-254, August, 1972.

"Selective abortion, gametic selection, and the X chromosome," by G. R. Fraser. AM J HUM GENET 24:359-370, July, 1972.

"Some problems in the evaluation of women for therapeutic abortion," by D. S. Werman, et al. CAN PSYCHIATR ASSOC J 17:249-251, June, 1972.

"A statement on abortion by one hundred professors of obstetrics," AM J OBSTET GYNECOL 112:992-993, April 1, 1972.

"A statement on abortion in Victoria," MED J AUST 1:443, February 26, 1972.

"A statement on abortion in Victoria," by J. R. Coulter. MED J AUST 1:32-33, January 1, 1972.

"A statement on abortion in Victoria," by J. R. Coulter. MED J AUST 1:550, March 11, 1972.

"A statement on abortion in Victoria," by I. Hemingway, et al. MED J AUST 1:608, March 18, 1972.

"A statement on abortion in Victoria," by B. A. Smithurst, et al. MED J AUST 1:240-241, January 29, 1972.

"Teenage mothers," by J. E. Hodgson. MINN MED 55:49, January, 1972.

"Termination of a mid-trimester pregnancy," by J. O. Greenhalf. NURS MIRROR 134:34-36, June 2, 1972.

"Termination of pregnancy," by E. J. Hill. NZ MED J 74:412, December, 1971.

"The termination of pregnancy in adolescent women," by R. U. Hausknecht. PEDIATR CLIN NORTH AM 19:803-810, August, 1972.

"Termination of pregnancy in the unmarried," by E. M. Briggs, et al. SCOTT MED J 17:399-400, December, 1972.

"Termination of pregnancy in the unmarried," by M. C. Macnaughton. SCOTT MED J 17:381-382, December, 1972.

"Therapeutic abortion and ultrasound," by K. E. Hodge. CAN MED ASSOC J 105:1021, November 20, 1971.

"Therapeutic abortion by intra-amniotic injection of prostaglandins," by G. Roberts, et al. BR MED J 4:12-14, October 7, 1972.

"The Therapeutic Abortion Committee," by I. M. Cushner. CLIN OBSTET GYNECOL 14:1248-1254, December, 1971.

"Therapeutic abortion conflict and resolution," by R. Zahourek. AORN J 16:114-119, October, 1972.

"Therapeutic abortion: government figures show big increases in 1971," CAN MED ASS J 106:1131, May 20, 1972.

"Therapeutic abortion in the Maori," by V. G. Deobhakta. NZ MED J 75:174, March, 1972.

"Therapeutic abortion in Maryland, 1968-1970," by R. J. Melton, et al. OBSTET GYNECOL 39:923-930, June, 1972.

"Therapeutic abortion is more than an operation," by L. J. Dunn. AORN J 16:120-123, October, 1972.

"Therapeutic abortion practices in Chicago hospitals--vagueness, variation, and violation of the law," by P. Broeman, et al. L & SOC ORDER 1971:757, 1971.

"Therapeutic abortion: the role of state government. II.," by A. L. Seltzer, et al. CLIN OBSTET GYNECOL 14:1208-1211, December, 1971.

"Therapeutic abortion: the role of state government. I.," by R.D. Lamm. CLIN OBSTET GYNECOL 14:1204-1207, December, 1971.

"Therapeutic abortion trends in the United States," by A. Heller. CURR PSYCHIATR THER 12:171-184, 1972.

"Therapeutic abortion: two important judicial pronouncements," by S. A. Strauss. S AFR MED J 46:275-279, March 11, 1972.

"Therapeutic abortion with the use of prostaglandin F 2. A study of efficacy, tolerance, and plasma levels with intravenous administration," by P. G. Gillett, et al. AM J OBSTET GYNECOL 112:330-338, February 1, 1972.

"Therapeutic abortion without inpatient hospitalization. An early experience with 325 cases," by I. M. Golditch, et al. CALIF MED 116:1-3, March, 1972.

"Therapeutic abortions in Virginia," by M. I. Shanholtz. VIRGINIA MED MON 99:876-878, August, 1972.

"Trends in therapeutic abortion in San Francisco," by P. Goldstein. AM J PUBLIC HEALTH 62:695-699, May, 1972.

"Women who seek therapeutic abortion: a comparison with women who complete their pregnancies," by C. V. Ford, et al. AMER J PSYCHIAT 129:546-552, November, 1972.

"The use of prostaglandin E 2 for therapeutic abortion," by S. M. Karim, et al. J OBSTET GYNAECOL BR COMMONW 79:1-13, January, 1972.

THREATENED ABORTION

"Action of a natural progesterone associated with a synthetic progestogen and vitamin E in the treatment of threatened abortion and premature labor," by S. Panariello. ARCH OSTET GINECOL 75:492-506, December, 1970.

"Alylestenol (Gestanone) in the treatment of threatened abortion," by D. Vasilev. AKUSH GINEKOL (Sofiia) 10:413-419, 1971.

"Changes in chorionic gonadotropins time as a test for the prognosis of threatened abortion in the 1st trimester," by P. De Patre. MINERVA MED 63:549-553, February 7, 1972.

"Changes in the concentration of copper and ceruloplasmin, and cholinesterase activity in the blood in threatened abortion," by L. I. Priakhina. AKUSH GINEKOL 47:61-63, April, 1971.

"Chromosome studies on spontaneous and threatened abortions," by T. Ikeuchi, et al. JAP J HUM GENET 16:191-197, March, 1972.

"A clinical study on prognosticating threatened abortions by vaginal cytogram in the first trimester of pregnancy," by J. Aoki. ACTUAL PHARMACOL 23:257-266, 1970; also in J JAP OBSTET GYNECOL SOC 24:257-266, April, 1972.

"Colpocytogram and some indices of hormone levels in women with threatened abortion," by O. S. Badiva. PEDIATR AKUSH

GINEKOL 4:38-41, July-August, 1971.

"Complications of cervical suture," by A. Adoni, et al. HAREFUAH 83:146-147, August 12, 1972.

"Electromyographic method of examining neuromuscular excitability in threatened abortion," by D. Dylewska, et al. POL TYG LEK 27:1036-1039, July 3, 1972.

"Evaluation of the immunologic method of determining chorionic gonadotropin in the diagnosis of threatened abortion in its early stages," by V. M. Savitskii, et al. PEDIATR AKUSH GINEKOL 71:38-40, September-October, 1971.

"Fractionated analysis of human chorionic gonadotropins and ultrasonic studies. Supplementary methods for the diagnosis and differential diagnosis of abortions," by H. Wallner, et al. Z ALLGEMEINMED 48:75-79, January 20, 1972.

"Hormone therapy of threatened abortion," by S. Stojanov. ZENTRALBL GYNAEKOL 94:1323-1326, October 7, 1972.

"Management of threatened abortion and premature delivery with Duvadilan and Dilatol," by P. Hengst, et al. Z AERZTL FORTBILD 65:850-854, August 15, 1971.

"Must the fruit of love always be saved?" by L. Kuthy. KRANKENPFLEGE 26:55, February, 1972.

"Placental lactogen levels as guide to outcome of threatened abortion," by P. A. Niven, et al. BR MED J 3:799-801, September 30, 1972.

"Pregnancy and labor in women with ABO incompatibility," by A. B. Saturskaia. AKUSH GINEKOL 47:51-53, August, 1971.

"Preventive treatment of spontaneous abortion, such as it results from the study of mechanism of contraction and relaxation of uterine muscle," by K. Kato, et al. GYNECOL PRAT 23:89-94, 1972.

"Serotonin content and excretion of 5-hydroxyindoleacetic acid during threatened abortion at early and late stages," by Z. V. Urazaeva, et al. AKUSH GINEKOL 48:65-66, May, 1972.

"Serum levels of oestradiol-17 dehydrogenase in normal and abnormal pregnancies," by G. Plotti, et al. J OBSTET GYNAECOL BR COMMONW 79:603-611, July, 1972.

"Significance of cervical cerclage for the child," by G. Mau. Z GEBURTSHILFE PERINATOL 176:331-342, August, 1972.

"Silicone-plastic cuff for the treatment of the incompetent cervix in pregnancy," by E. E. Yosowitz, et al. AM J OBSTET GYNECOL 113:233-238, May 12, 1972.

"Threatened abortion," by E. Pirvulescu. MUNCA SANIT 20:133-135, March, 1972.

"Threatened abortions, immature and premature birth in women infected with Toxoplasma gondii," by K. Nowosad, et al. WIAD PARAZYTOL 18:265-267, 1972.

"Treatment of threatened abortion and premature labor with isoxsuprine hydrochloride," by P. Scillieri, et al. ARCH OSTET GINECOL 76:129-137, 1971.

"Use of choriogonin in threatened abortion," by Ia. M. Gel'man, et al. PEDIATR AKUSH GINEKOL 71:40-42, September-October, 1971.

"The use of human chorionic gonadotropin levels in assessing the prognosis of threatened abortion," by P. R. Grob, et al. PRACTITIONER 209:79-81, July, 1972.

"Value of pregnanetriol determination in threatened abortion," by S. Sonnino, et al. RASS INST CLIN TER 52:191-196, February 29, 1972.

"The value of studying acidophilic and kariopicnotic indices in abnormal pregnancies," by H. Venegas, et al. REV CHIL OBSTET GINECOL 34:14-16, 1969.

TOXOPLASMAS
see: Complications

TRANSPLACENTAL HEMORRHAGE
see: Complications

TRICHLOROETHYLENE
"Anesthesia in minor gynecologic surgery with trichloroethylene," by V. S. Lesiuk. AKUSH GINEKOL 48:70-71, April, 1972.

VETERINARY ABORTIONS
see: Research and Abortion

VITAMIN E
"Action of a natural progesterone associated with a synthetic progestogen and vitamin E in the treatment of threatened abortion and premature labor," by S. Panariello. ARCH OSTET GINECOL 75:492-506, December, 1970.

WOMEN'S LIBERATION
see also: Laws and Legislation
Sociology, Behavior and Abortion

"Abortion and women's lib," by M. K. Williams. HOSP PROGRESS 53:17-18, February, 1972.

"The battle of women. Discussion of Paragraph 218," by M. I. Kischke. KRANKENPFLEGE 26:54-55, February, 1972.

"The liberation of women from unwanted pregnancy," by S. L. Israel. CLIN OBSTET GYNECOL 14:1113-1123, December, 1971.

"Women's lib pill," by D. Gould. NEW STATESM 84:542, October 20, 1972.

YOUTH
"American Academy of Pediatrics. Committee on Youth. Teen-age pregnancy and the problem of abortion," PEDIATRICS 49:303-304, February, 1972.

"Attitudes toward abortion among young black (based on a study of

300 young Negro women in Baltimore, Md.)," by F. F. Furstenburg, Jr. STUDIES IN FAMILY PLANNING 3:66-69, April, 1972.

"Birth control for teen-agers--is it legal?" by C. A. Gravenor, Jr. CAN DOCTOR 38:103-104, October, 1972.

"Incidence of abortion in a group of young patients with rheumatic cardiopathy," by R. M. Del Bosque, et al. GINECOL OBSTET MEX 32:167-171, August, 1972.

"Medical problems of abortion among adolescents," by N. Bregun-Dragic. MED PREGL 25:55-56, 1972.

"Minors, ObGyn practice and the law," by D. R. Jasinski. HAWAII MED J 31:116, March-April, 1972.

"Pregnancy, abortion, and the developmental tasks of adolescence," by C. Schaffer, et al. J AM ACAD CHILD PSYCHIATRY 11:511-536, July, 1972.

"Preparing students for abortion care," by D. Malo-Juvera. NURS J INDIA 63:223-224 plus, July, 1972.

"Public opinion trends: Elective abortion and birth control services to teenagers," by R. Pomeroy, et al. FAMILY PLANN PERSPECT 4:44-55, October, 1972.

"Teenage mothers," by J. E. Hodgson. MINN MED 55:49, January, 1972.

"The teenage sexual revolution and the myth of an abstinent past," by P. Cutright. FAMILY PLANN PERSPECT 4:24-31, January, 1972.

"Teen birth control information requested," US MED 8:3 plus, November 15, 1972.

"The termination of pregnancy in adolescent women," by R. U. Hausknecht. PEDIATR CLIN NORTH AM 19:803-810, August, 1972.

"Youth--and the VAD," by L. Porritt. NZ NURS J 65:4, August, 1972.

AUTHOR INDEX